SECRECY

AND THE

ARMS RACE

A THEORY OF THE ACCUMULATION
OF STRATEGIC WEAPONS
AND HOW SECRECY AFFECTS IT

Martin C. McGuire

HARVARD UNIVERSITY PRESS

CAMBRIDGE, MASSACHUSETTS

1965

PREFACE

This book is a revision of a dissertation submitted in December 1963 to the Department of Economics, Harvard University, and entitled *Information and Arms Races*. Professor Wassily Leontief first suggested the topic to me, and Professor Thomas Schelling supervised the thesis. Without Professor Schelling's repeated encouragement and criticism, the study would not have materialized. My intellectual debt to him is great. I also wish to thank Professor Donald Farrar, Dr. Martin Bailey, Professor Clopper Almon, and Professor F. M. Scherer for helpful comments on various aspects of my work. The simulation reported in Appendix A was programmed by Mr. John Perry of Cambridge, Mass. In the early stages of the study I profited from discussions with Professors Hendrik S. Houthakker, and Marshall Freimer, Dr. Donald Barrer, and Mr. Robert Madden. Financial assistance from Harvard, and later the Richard D. Irwin Foundation enabled me to proceed with the study.

The work was completed before I entered government service. The views expressed are my own personal views.

M.C.M.

Washington, D.C.
April 1965

CONTENTS

vii

SECRECY AND THE ARMS RACE

A THEORY OF THE ACCUMULATION
OF STRATEGIC WEAPONS
AND HOW SECRECY AFFECTS IT

NOTATION

X designates one country in a two-nation arms race

Y designates the other country in a two-nation arms race

x X's inventory of strategic missiles

y Y's inventory of strategic missiles

v_{xx} number of missiles X chooses to withhold from a counterforce attack against Y

v_{yy} number of missiles Y chooses to withhold from a counterforce attack against X

v_{xy} number of X's missiles to survive a counterforce attack by Y

v_{yx} number of Y's missiles to survive a counterforce attack by X

z_x minimum number of missiles X is sure (with some specified degree of confidence) will survive attack by Y

z_y minimum number of missiles Y is sure (with some specified degree of confidence) will survive attack by X

$\hat{x}$ national wealth of X

$\hat{y}$ national wealth of Y

I · INTRODUCTION

For the past two decades the major concern of our national security establishment has been to preclude the possibility of an atomic attack on the United States. This concern has become ever more immediate and demanding with the steady advance in the technology of weapons and delivery systems. Consequently, "those who have grappled with ideas like deterrence, being motivated largely by immediate problems, have not primarily been concerned with the cumulative process of developing a theoretical structure."[1] Moreover, as the immediate problems have taken precedence, the theoretical structure that has emerged is concentrated on how to preclude attack *today*. Most theories of deterrence suppose that in the international power confrontation both sides face three alternatives: to attack —to be attacked—to wait. Since the first two of these alternatives would end in disaster, a theory that satisfactorily explains what conditions—that is, what actions, promises, threats, understandings, communications, customs, and so on, will lead each side to choose to wait is enormously important.

However, what if the choice is "wait"—what then? What follows from the decision not to attack is the subject matter of the arms race. And while it is true that the problem of insuring immediate deterrence is logically prior to the problem of what follows from the choice to wait (obviously unless we solve the problem of immediate deterrence we need not bother to ponder the implications of a successful sequence of deterring postures

[1] Thomas C. Schelling, *The Strategy of Conflict* (Cambridge, Mass.: Harvard University Press, 1960), p. 7.

1

for tomorrow and the day after), the study of the arms race is immensely useful for several reasons.

First, at some point in the future the logic of our structure of deterrence (or of aggressive attack) may depend upon the course of the arms race to that point. That is, decisions on how to deter today will affect future possibilities for deterrence; and an understanding of the arms race may prove useful in preparing for deterrence and defense in the future.[2]

Second, the arms race is of interest in and of itself, on its own terms, if only because it is a time-consuming and expensive nuisance. Even disregarding the fact that the arms race may end in total thermonuclear catastrophe, or in stable mutual-deterrent security, the process of the arms competition itself is of scientific interest. Finally, an understanding of the arms race as a phenomenon to be studied in its own right—and an understanding of how its dynamics may influence the likelihood of war—may aid in efforts to control it, to reduce the burden of arms, and to reduce the risk of atomic war.

In this introduction the issues to which this book is addressed will be identified. The variables that combine to generate an arms race, the approaches developed to study the relations between these variables, and the conclusions reached in the body of the text will be summarized in a nontechnical fashion. The final section of the introduction is a review of the existing literature on the theory of arms races.

The Arms Race as Economic Theory

One main purpose of this study is to present a theory of the arms race. And the theory devised herein is essentially an eco-

---

[2] If, for example, a Polaris submarine was equipped with sixteen missiles to meet the requirements for deterrence in the early 1960's, and Soviets were to react to such lucrative concentrated targets with an expensive but successful Polaris detection-kill system, then fewer missiles per submarine might be more economical in the 1970's. Meeting requirements for deterrence in the sixties may complicate the problem in the seventies.

nomic theory, although many may wonder how it is possible to utilize theoretical economics for such a purpose. This can be done because abstract economics deals with the science of choice—choice between alternative ends (and how much of each) when the resources available for securing these ends are limited. The arms race can legitimately be viewed, also, as a sequence of choices made by antagonists, both of whom are seeking security and power. In this way, as a science of choice, economic theory is validly applied to more than the conventional problems of economics—to the arms race, for example.[3]

In addition the economist brings some useful concepts to a consideration of the arms race. He is accustomed to thinking in terms of costs, benefits, and prices. The division of arms-race phenomena into considerations of cost and benefit itself will result in valuable insights into the problem. Beyond that, the notion of price has particular utility as a result of its role in summarizing the great and complex varieties of information that are required for the making of rational, best choices—of incurring costs so as to achieve benefits. The information summarized is essentially of two sorts: that which describes the preferences of the decision-maker, and that which describes the technology available for attaining a desired result. To know the price that some element in a nation's military force structure commands is to have a rule for accepting or rejecting proposed alternatives in that military posture *without having to calculate out the total effects of a change.* Thus, the economist is inclined to seek out rules for facilitating choice and thereby for advancing the study of arms races.

Following through with this line of argument, our approach in this study is first to describe the choice to acquire arms—and to procure them in a specific quantity—as an economic, optimum

---

[3] Another good example is the economics of saving or prolonging human life with medical care or safety programs.

choice. Then we shall demonstrate how such a choice by one side depends upon (1) the character of its weapons technology; (2) its preferences for security, for power in the world, and for satisfying consumer wants; and (3) *the magnitude of the threat posed by the enemy.* Finally, we describe how arms competition is generated and propelled by the simultaneous choices made by both sides, and how the choices of one side depend upon the choices of the other and vice versa.

In our model we are forced to simplify to make the problem manageable. Theoretical advance often proceeds from propitious simplification. The first simplification in our model is to limit the variety of preparations for military conflict available to each side and the variety of actions open to each side at any point in the arms contest. Furthermore, we shall restrict our attention solely to the race to build strategic weapons and delivery systems. In particular, our model will deal with ballistic missiles carrying thermonuclear warheads, with the race to achieve "security" by improving the quality of or by building increasing numbers of such weapons, and with the dependence of each side's security on the others—and the interactions stemming therefrom. The rationale for restricting our model to missiles is first that such a model can be self-contained, and second that it allows us to specify precise, quantitative relations. "Self-contained" here means that all the repercussions from any changes in a side's armaments are assumed to affect only the variables in the model. For instance, an eventuality such as uncertainty over the number of one side's missiles causing the other to increase its ground forces is excluded. In other words, it is assumed that each side judges the other and, in its reaction, is confined to changing its missile force in one way or another. In addition, our model will allow for the effects upon both sides of various levels of, or changes in, armaments by one side or by the other to be specified with the precision of mathematical formulae.

4

Information as an Element in the Arms Race

The second main purpose of this book is to investigate the role that information—or its inverse, secrecy—plays in the arms race, and, in particular, to explore the question of how much secrecy is *worth*. Can information, or the lack of it, substitute for weapons—for missiles and megatons? How much does it profit a side to maintain secrecy, and how much should it pay to obtain its enemy's secrets? These questions are to be explored with the aid of our generalized economic theory of the arms race.

When two world powers face each other with massive allocations of resources to arms, when each regards the other as the major—if not the sole—threat to its own security, and when both recognize the situation to be such, the question of information about the adversary arises for each side in innumerable instances and in a variety of ways. This is the situation today. The United States and the Soviet Union expend vast sums of money to uncover information about the other, and each side holds its own secrets precious enough to order the execution of those who divulge them. An official U.S. government view on the role of intelligence in the currnet arms race is enlightening and deserves careful attention.

Disarmament in the real world would be far from easy, even without the problem of secrecy. With it the problems appear almost insurmountable. . . . at heart, there is no getting away from the fact that disarmament and secrecy are inconsistent goals . . .

I would also suggest that the passion for secrecy is far from an unqualified asset to Soviet security. To the extent that they agree with us that the national security of all countries is threatened by the danger of war, they should realize that secrecy has the unavoidable effect of increasing tensions and the arms race, and so adding to the risk of war.

To understand the impact of Soviet secrecy, one must understand the dynamic of the arms race between the great powers . . . Today the arms race is still quantitative in a sense, but to a large extent it is qualitative . . .

The Soviets can to a large extent react to what we are actually doing rather than to exaggerated fears of what we might be doing. But, unfortunately, so long as we have so little knowledge of what the Soviets are doing, we must base our preparations to a significant extent on what we think they are capable of doing. This is an important consideration in view of the relatively long lead times required for the development and production of weapon systems. Thus the Soviets are forced to work hard to match the efforts that they *know* we are making to match the efforts that we *think* they are making.[4]

Secretary Gilpatric's remarks bear the following interpretation. Hewing to traditional categories, we can say that each side seeks information about the other on two counts: (1) as to the other's intentions, and (2) as to his capabilities.[5] Reflection suggests that the capabilities-intention dichotomy bears a relation to the distinction made earlier between the question of how a war begins and the question of how "peaceful" preparations for war progress over time. If one is concerned with how a war starts, information about intentions would appear to be paramount (provided the capabilities of one's own country are not so superior to those of the enemy that one need not even consider preempting). The intelligence demanded of each party

[4] "Remarks by Deputy Secretary of Defense Roswell L. Gilpatric at the Aerospace Symposium, Air Force Academy, Colorado," *Department of Defense News Release No. 1308-62*, August 13, 1962.

[5] Some might say modern trends demand a third case, technological information, that is, information about the secret weapon that once possessed could change the balance of power qualitatively; but if we add a time subscript to the "capabilities" category, technological intelligence falls into this class as knowledge of capability at some future point in time.

in the reciprocal fear-of-surprise-attack game is knowledge of intentions. Intelligence about an adversary's capabilities is, on the other hand, of the greatest relevance, not when one is concerned with how wars start, but rather when one has time to react by altering one's own capabilities (and possibly intentions as well)—that is, when one is engaged in an arms race. Such lines cannot be drawn without reservation, however, since without some notion of intentions not only is it impossible to define enemy capabilities,[6] it is impossible to define the enemy. Nevertheless, in practice, knowledge of the size and composition of forces in being is important.

Mr. Gilpatric's remarks appear to be directed primarily toward operational intelligence, that is, information about current forces in being. Interposed between the true size and character of one side's forces and the reaction of the other to them must be intelligence. We react to the "threat" (as it is called) that we perceive. In large measure this study is an effort to approach analytically the question of the value of keeping secrets from or of the value of obtaining information about an enemy. Very broadly the questions to be asked are to find ways of measuring the value of information about one's adversary at any point in the arms confrontation, and to trace the effects of less-than-perfect information upon the interactions between adversaries. We shall be limited by a concern solely for operational intelligence, as previously defined.

In addition to the capabilities-versus-intentions distinction and the outbreak-of-war-versus-"peaceful"-arms-competition distinction, two other general considerations are relevant to a treatment of information in the arms competition. First, it should be recognized that the value and/or relevance of information varies with the national objective to which it relates.

---

[6] For example, does the Soviet commercial air fleet count in the military capability to which we react? Given sufficient time and malevolence of intent, almost anything is a military capability.

Within the context of a confrontation of two opposing strategic-missile forces, the information sought about an opponent, and its value, is different according as one is interested, for example, in deterrence or in threatening a first-strike. (There may be other national objectives in which one is interested, such as defense, or the consequences of actual attack; but for purposes of illustration, here we select only two.) Information about the adversary's strength may be necessary to or may allow us to build systems to attack his weapons directly. On the other hand, it may aid in determining the number of targets to provide the enemy, thereby forcing him to spread his attackers more thinly over our defending weapons. Since the relative importance of providing the enemy with targets and attacking his own forces is different in a first-strike than from what it is in a second-strike context, the usefulness of the two types of information varies from one context to the other. The prime concern when information is judged against a retaliation (or second-strike) criterion is its contribution to our ability to be assured of forces surviving an enemy first-strike—that is, to our ability persuasively to threaten punitive retaliation (not necessarily to actually retaliate)[7] and thereby to forestall attack.

Both types of information are of economic value. Insofar as we pursue a policy of deterrence, the value of intelligence about enemy capabilities is that it allows us to choose rationally, on the basis of economic cost-benefit considerations, among various deterrence weapons. Such, for example, must be the choice among building more Minutemen, building less vulnerable sites, and building Polaris submarines. How this choice should be made depends upon our knowledge of the threat. In particular, it depends upon our knowledge of the numbers and the characteristics of enemy missiles. Or to take another example, suppose our policy were to strike first, or to threaten to do so. The effectiveness

[7] See pp. 47–83 for a further discussion of this point.

of strategic forces as first-strike weapons depends upon a knowledge of enemy targets.[8] In particular, information as to location is required if one is to strike first or threaten to do so. Hence subsurface surveillance of the ocean is important if one side has Polaris-type missile carriers and the other desires to threaten a first-strike against enemy retaliation capabilities. How ignorant we are of these different characteristics of the enemy's (or our own) weapons systems influences our best choice among types of weapons and numbers of each type. It costs money to reduce such ignorance or uncertainty but it will save money elsewhere. The problem we address ourselves to in this study—namely to discover these relations so as to allow for a choice among weapons and information—therefore, is clearly economic. The factors influencing such a best choice, however, extend beyond a simple intelligence estimate of the threat. Specifically, the adequacy of our decision as to what weapons to build depends in turn upon the enemy's knowledge of us. For example, selection of ballistic-missile submarines places the enemy at an intelligence disadvantage. How will he react? How will this reaction change the threat to us and our knowledge of it? Without a grasp of the structure of such phenomena the relative merits of one weapon over another are only partially understood.

One possible objection to the entire direction of the argument presented above is that while the model may be consistent, it deals with a mere theoretical curiosity that is quantitatively of minor significance. To prove that this is not true the cost schedules for the potential attacker and the potential victim have been calculated. With the aid of a computer this has been done for a wide range of values of numbers, yields, and accuracies. Uncertainties in the form of probability distributions were next added, and cost schedules recomputed for various levels of uncertainty. As summarized in Appendix A, it turns out that

---

[8] Here again the example is illustrative; target-location intelligence may be useful for a second-strike, a point which is discussed further on pp. 112–113.

sometimes uncertainty can cause major shifts in the cost schedules (order of magnitude of 2). At other times the effect of uncertainty is negligible.

A grasp of the place of secrecy and information in the arms race, however, is of use not only for understanding the behavior of each side viewed as an independent security optimizer; it is useful, also, in efforts to understand, to contain, and to control the arms race itself. Ways of securing information about existing stocks of nuclear weapons, numbers of delivery vehicles, and the yields of warheads, account for a major part of the issues that impede arms-control agreements. The need for inspection with verification that agreements are being kept depends implicitly upon the notion that information about current forces in being has an objective, military value. Of course, information is also sought by arms-control schemes, which can verify the opponent's decisions, intentions, or actions already undertaken so as to give warning of attack (in time to threaten, preempt, rearm, and so on). Our study is designed to facilitate an approach to such questions as: What is the loss in being only 50-percent confident rather than certain that the adversary has not more than x missiles, or missiles of yield W megatons or of accuracy C thousand feet? Should one insist on being 95-percent sure when bargaining for arms control? Where can a side compensate for its uncertainty most efficiently? How are answers to such questions affected when both sides operate under uncertainty? When only one side does?

Thus far our context has been one in which one side or both try to keep secrets. It should be recognized that not only may a side profit from withholding information, it may require means for a convincing release of information. It may be imperative to prove to an adversary that one's intentions are not hostile, that one's bombs are not oversize, or one's missiles overaccurate. The information problem in the arms race, controlled or not, is not restricted to seeking enemy secrets or to withholding one's own; it also includes the very opposite problem, that is, to convince a rival that information released is true.

A SUMMARY OF THE ECONOMIC THEORY

We now turn to a summary of the economic theory set forth in the body of the text. Earlier it was stated in effect that an arms race may be viewed as an interacting sequence of decisions by two sides, in which each side in making any single decision makes the choice of employing given resources for the acquisition of arms, thereby exchanging for what those resources might have otherwise produced the contribution to national objectives that these arms may make. The problem is clearly within the realm of economics. Thus, in keeping with sound economic practice, we shall formulate and analyze the logic of a single choice by a single side—what we shall call the "one-sided" element in the problem—and only then proceed to the interactive sequence—the "two-sided" aspect, which is made up of a number of one-sided choices. Information also has been singled out as having a special relevance to the arms race. Accordingly, we further divide the problem into treatment with perfect versus imperfect information. This, therefore, gives us a four-part theory. Each part will be treated in turn, in order of its complexity with respect to the choice of armaments by (1) one side: perfect information; by (2) one side: imperfect information; by (3) two sides: perfect information; by (4) two sides: imperfect information.

The Prerequisites for an Economic Model

Why are weapons of war accumulated? A thorough-going answer to this would require extensive study of war itself, its initiation, and progress to conclusion. Our purpose here is less ambitious—namely, to fashion a set of plausible behavioral assumptions which, though not exhaustive, are sufficient to

11

generate an arms race thereby allowing us to proceed with the main study.

Suppose the two sides in an arms race are called side X and side Y, and that each possesses x and y missiles respectively. Either side can, potentially, strike the other first. Call the number of X's surviving missiles if Y were to strike first z_x, and the number of Y's if X were to strike first z_y. Our model of the arms race centers about these four variables, x, y, z_x, z_y. Side X has as its decision variable the value of x. Side Y has as its decision variable the value of y. Each combination (x, y) results in some potential outcome (z_x, z_y).[9] The numbers of surviving missiles on either side if the other attacks are of fundamental importance throughout our theoretical description. They hold a central place in our account, best likened to the position of a "good" in economic thought. The outcomes z_x and z_y are similar to economic goods in that they are sought as enhancing a side's utility—which is to say, as advancing that side's national purposes. But z_x and z_y are achieved only at a cost, the cost of other goods and other utilities foregone—which is to say, at the sacrifice of other national purposes.

Let it first be asked: How do z_x and z_y advance national objectives? In this study we make the assumption that the utility deriving from the allocation of resources to missiles is embodied entirely in the consequent potential increase in one's own surviving missiles if the enemy attacks, and potential *decrease* in the opponent's number of surviving weapons if one attacks first one's self. The rationalization for and the assumptions behind making utility a function solely of own and enemy surviving missiles are explored in Chapter II. In summary, what is said there is as follows: each side knows that if it attacks the other's

---

[9] In fact, there is no uniquely determinate number of missiles that will survive attack by an enemy. Rather, there is a probability (binomial) distribution of such numbers. In the light of this fact z_x and z_y will be reinterpreted in Ch. II. The reader is asked to ignore the difficulty, for pedagogical reasons, until then.

12

missiles there is some fixed (by assumption) probability that the victim will retaliate upon the attacker's cities, even though this would be an irrational decision for the victim to make. It would be irrational for the victim because, he would destroy most of the attacker's incentive to capitulate in the face of the *potential* destruction to his population from the *threat* of retaliation. But the initiation of a missile war puts such pressures on the victim that he knows and the attacker knows that rational control may be lost. Nevertheless, even knowing this, a side might begin the war with a counterforce strike. It might do so if it were provoked or challenged—short of being attacked—to the point that the loss consequent upon accepting the provocation or losing the challenge would exceed the uncertain destruction in the form of retaliation, following its first-strike. The attacker would in all probability not fire all his missiles in his first, counterforce blow; else he should encourage irrationality in the victim. (By firing all his missiles the attacker would also leave himself helpless in the face of the rational response—the *threat* of retaliation—by his victim.) According to our assumption the attacker therefore holds back a fraction of his arsenal of missiles, the percentage being fixed regardless of the size of the stock.

Such a view of the nature of international conflict and potential war supports the assumption that utility can be measured in terms of own and enemy potentially surviving missiles. For if I can reduce my enemy's potential residual, then he must be less provocative, since he will know that I am now more easily decided to attack. Having less to lose from his uncertain retaliation I will attack at a lower level of his provocation. At the same time if I can build up my own residual from a possible initial counterforce attack by the enemy, I then can be more provocative. *A fundamental axiom of this study is that the utility accruing to either partner in the arms race derives from these two sources.* An argument is offered in the text to show that the marginal utility to a side decreases as its own residual stock of missiles grows larger, and increases as its opponent's residual declines in size.[10]

The theory enunciated above is supposed to be factually descriptive and not in any way ethically prescriptive. I do not wish to recommend that any nation accumulate missiles so that it can be more provocative but I do think that *ceteris paribus* the more missiles a side has the better off it considers itself to be. The deterrent motive for possessing missiles can be explained in various ways, as can the diminishing marginal utility from increases in one's surviving force. But if one says an enemy is deterred from attacking one's own country, that must imply that he is deterred for some degree of one's provocation. I can always substitute surrender, retreat, or capitulation for deterrence. Since an enemy must have some reason for attacking me—something to gain from doing so—presumably I can bribe him not to attack. Conversely, the more deterrence I have the less conciliatory need I be to remain out of war. From this it follows that when one side increases its first-strike counterforce potential, the other must become less provocative or build up its own deterrence again.

"Provocation" here should be understood as any act which challenges an adversary's interests, other than the act of altering the balance of strategic weaponry. Hence, it is the desire to be able to confront an opponent with nonnuclear challenge and to be able to thwart his nonnuclear initiatives *with minor risk of nuclear war* that drives the accumulation of strategic nuclear weapons on both sides.

It is to be emphasized that this view is restricted in that it refers to a world with only two sides. No pretense is made to include third or Nth powers with independent interests, nor to analyze the place of allies or proxies in mutual deterrence. No

[10] See pp. 76–80. I am indebted to Professor F. M. Scherer for his helpful criticism on these aspects of the theory.

special attention is given to the deterrence of limited wars; but this is consistent with our theory, since a side's deterrence-potential only establishes the maximum in provocation it can undertake. Any level of provocation short of that maximum is open to either side—is not deterred. Hence the need for limited-war capabilities and so on.

The discussion to this point has proceeded on the assumption that the values z_x and z_y are uniquely determined by x and y. It is demonstrated in Chapter II that this is untrue in principle. The actual number of missiles that survive—say, v_x on side X from an attack by Y—follows a binomial distribution. It is possible that every one of Y's attacking missiles will kill its X target; it is possible that every one will miss; the exact number to survive can only be given with a probability appended. However, one can make such statements as "nine times out of ten no more than $v_x = z_x$ will survive," where z_x denotes one particular value of v_x; or "nine times out of ten no less than $v_x = z_x$ will survive." This is the interpretation we now wish to give to z_x and z_y. Let us assume both attacker and defender are "conservative" in this sense: when X considers attacking Y, he judges the disutility of Y's possible retaliation by asking himself, "What is the highest intensity of retaliation I could expect with 90-percent assurance (or some other high percentage)?"; but when X considers deterring Y from attack he asks himself, "What is the least number I can expect with high assurance (90 percent, 75 percent . . .) to have survive with which to retaliate against (or bargain with) Y after he has hit me?" A similar psychology is attributed to Y. Both X and Y, in other words, have high aversions to risk—that is, both prefer to avoid taking chances.

We have asked, "How do z_x and z_y contribute to or add to national objectives?" Now let it be asked, "How much do z_x and z_y cost? How much do they subtract from national objectives?" This is addressed in Chapter II. If it is assumed that the unit costs of fabricating missiles are constant, no matter what the total number built, then the cost-unit can be the missile itself, or the number of dollars required to build one missile. With this assumption, it turns out that for any fixed number of an opponent's missiles the marginal costs of increasing one's own potentially surviving missiles are falling, and the marginal costs of decreasing the adversary's potential residual are rising, where in both cases the z_x or z_y measured is the conservative, risk-averting minimum or maximum explained in the preceding paragraph. For whatever the number of the opponent's missiles there is a unique cost schedule that relates the numbers of one's own missiles to the numbers of own or enemy potential survivors. For any such cost schedule the marginal relations just enunciated hold true.

(1) One Side: Perfect Information

By relating losses and gains in national objectives to costs through the intermediaries z_x and z_y, we have now arrived at a position from which an explanation of one side's choice of weapons, their numbers, and characteristics, follows with little difficulty, *it being understood that the decision-maker regards his rival's weapons systems as constant.* Subject to some mathematical conditions[11] the decision-maker for X will continue to allocate money to increase numbers, yields, accuracies, and reliabilities, and to decrease vulnerabilities of his own missiles until the sum of the last additions to his utility that arise from higher z_x and lower z_y just equals the pain or disutility of parting with that last dollar. At this point he will refrain (1) from changing his total expenditure or armaments, and (2) from altering the particular number-yield-accuracy-reliability-vulnerability combination chosen, since to do so could only lower his over-all utility. The principle here can be illustrated very sim-

---

[11] Continuity plus second-order conditions may in practice be most important. They are assumed to hold throughout this study.

ply. In Fig. 1 side X is represented as having some total national wealth, measured in units of missiles, and shown as $\bar{x}$. Side X must decide how much of this wealth to allocate to arms. For ease of illustration, let us focus on X's concern with deterrence by measuring z_x along the ordinate, and by ignoring z_y. Then

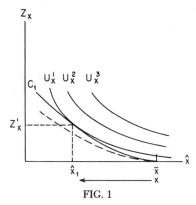

FIG. 1

the curves $U_x{}^1 < U_x{}^2 < U_x{}^3$ indicate indifference contours between wealth, $\hat{x}$, and the other national objectives embodied in z_x. Utility increases as one proceeds out from the origin. Next, for fixed yield, accuracy, and reliability, the curve C_1, illustrates X's technological constraint if Y has some given number of attackers—say, y_1. Clearly X should trade his national wealth for z_x up to $\hat{x}_1$, by spending $x - \hat{x}_1 = x_1$ on missiles, securing $z_x{}^1$ potential survivors, retaining $\hat{x}_1$ of his wealth for other expenditures, and achieving $U_x{}^1$, the highest U_x curve open to him.

(2) One Side: Imperfect Information

Imperfect information in this study is defined to include two sorts of uncertainty. In the body of the study partial uncertainty is analyzed as relevant to the parameters (1) numbers, (2) yield, (3) accuracy, and (4) vulnerability of own or enemy forces. In such cases the imperfection in information can be captured by

17

replacing sure knowledge of a true value with a probability distribution of values. The case of total uncertainty or ignorance about an enemy's system occurs in our analysis of the value of secrecy as to the locations of missiles. For some parameters it is seen that incomplete information affects the misinformed side primarily in its search for deterrent-originating utility. For other parameters the utility traceable to attack potential is primarily affected.

In both cases the effects of misinformation are characterized by a shift or rotation of the cost schedule of the ill-informed side. The shift is always toward the region of lower utility. For example, in Fig. 1, a probabilistic uncertainty in X's calculations over the numbers of Y's missiles will result in a new technological constraint that allows for invariably lower utilities. This is illustrated by the dotted line. What now can be said about the response of the uninformed side to this new factor? It would seem that the only universally true proposition to be stated is that this side will again seek an optimum by fulfilling the conditions set forth in the foregoing section.

Suppose as a beginning we assume that the side suffering from incomplete information can do nothing to improve its knowledge. In other words, consider uncertainty as a new parameter in the missile-duel equations. Then the following are true statements:

(1) At the new optimum choice, the uncertain side may spend more money or it may spend less on the arms race than it did when certain.

(2) At the new optimum the uncertain side will have a smaller z_{own} and/or a larger z_{enemy}.

(3) The entire sub-optimal allocation for any given budget, between numbers, accuracies, yields, and so on, will be altered.

(4) There will be a shift toward expenditures the efficacy of which is least reduced by uncertainty.

The last statement is particularly interesting; it suggests that the effects of incomplete information extend to changing the relative importance of deterring attack and threatening attack for a given side. If deterrent-originating utility is denied to a side by placing that side in an uncertainty context, one possible rational response, within the terms of our model, is to seek an optimum in utility via the reduction of its enemy's retaliatory potential. In short the character of the cold war may be altered by uncertainty; more interesting, it would appear that the degree of uncertainty can effect the intensity of prewar provocation.

Now suppose uncertainty is a variable instead of being a parameter.[12] Let us visualize that by dint of intelligence effort a side can reduce the magnitude of its partial uncertainty or the area of its total uncertainty at a cost. This simply introduces one more variable into the optimization process already described. The new variable may in practice be especially significant, because a moderate amount of secrecy, which can be overcome at a cost, can *reduce* the level of armaments by the following mechanism: if it is impossible to improve one's information, or possible only at exhorbitant cost, then one may resort to greater numbers of missiles, or greater yields, or accuracies, and so on, to compensate for one's ignorance. If, on the other hand, no uncertainty exists, then all defense resources can be spent on weapons in search of a high-utility level. If, however, a moderate amount of uncertainty exists, or uncertainty or ignorance that can be overcome at a high but not exhorbitant cost, then the side suffering from uncertainty may decide to *divert* resources away from arms toward intelligence. Thus secrecy so long as it is not too closely guarded may cause an increase in the total arms budget, but at the same time a de-

---

[12] A parameter and a variable are distinguished in that the value of a parameter can specified arbitrarily by the analyst while the allowable values of a variable are determined by the functional form of the relation assumed.

cline in the magnitude of armaments. If we regard spying as a relatively benign manifestation of international hostility compared to the brandishing of megatons, then we might welcome a modicum of secrecy—but not too much.[13]

(3) Two Sides: Perfect Information

From a strictly economic point of view, the interesting thing about our decision models when two, one for each side, are combined and examined simultaneously is that the analysis becomes an extension of the economic theory of duopoly into the region of consumer behavior, a region of economic theory generally regarded as the preserve of the perfectly competitive decision unit. The classical theory of consumer behavior assumes that the number of potential buyers in a market is so large that none can perceptibly influence the price at which he must exchange money for whatever goods he buys. Exactly the reverse is true of our decision model of the arms race. Here the cost schedules obtaining for each side are explicit functions of the decision variables of the other. For example, an increase in numbers of missiles by side Y will rotate or shift X's cost schedules toward lower regions of utility, both for deterrence and potential attack. The same assertion only with X and Y interchanged is equally true. Observe that we can now open the door for a virtually exhaustive translation of the techniques for describing economic duopoly into an arms-race context. This in turn supplies a logical structure for attributing meaning to and exploring instances of *interactions* between sides.

The basic conceptual tool in making such a translation is illustrated in Fig. 2, where total expenditures on armaments by

[13] If this argument is carried a step further, a less optimistic conclusion may result. If intelligence enhances one's subjective appreciation of one's position vis-a-vis an enemy then even with a lesser number of missiles one may be more confidently provocative—that is, one may brandish megatons all the more. See p. 109–110 for a discussion of objectively and subjectively rewarding information.

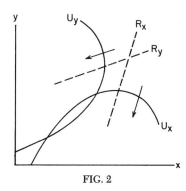

FIG. 2

X and Y are measured along the x and y axes respectively. Corresponding to each value of x and y, X attains some total utility; let it be denoted by U_x. Included in U_x is the utility accruing to X by virtue of his ability to provoke Y, to constrain Y in his provocation of X, and the disutility to X of spending money to buy x missiles (with optimum yield, accuracy, and so on). Some value of U_x attaches to every point (x, y). If all points of the same value are connected up, an indifference map for X will appear. Similarly an indifference map for Y can be put on the same diagram. In Fig. 2 one contour from the map of X and one from the map of Y are drawn in. For a verification that such shapes are indeed plausible, and in fact follow from our earlier constructions and that the utility maps will show higher contours as one proceeds in the direction of the arrows in Fig. 2 the reader is referred to Chapter V. We will now simply state—leaving argument and proof to the body of the text—some defensible duopolistic interpretations of arms-race phenomena.

(1) Reaction curves: as in the classical theory of duopoly, the locus of utility-maximizing responses by one side to fixed (parametrically-varied) initiatives by the other has been called the "reaction curve." In Fig. 2 the two reaction curves are drawn as broken lines and labeled R_x and R_y. This allows for

21

investigation of stability and instability in arms races as in economic theory, and serves as a paradigm illustration of interaction.

(2) Solutions: Professor Shubik's work summarizes proposed solutions to the formal problem of economic duopoly.[14] The arms race in its theoretical aspect would seem to allow for an equal variety. Corresponding to most duopoly solutions a translation into an arms-race context is possible. Each of the following four cases is discussed in the text:

a. The Cournot, or naïve duopolist solution: this corresponds to an unrelenting race to the intersection of reaction curves.

b. The Pareto contract curve or Von Neumann and Morgenstern solution: an analogy is drawn to the possibilities for mutual improvement through reciprocal, partial disarmament, or other variations on arms control.

c. The optimal threat or maximin curve: in the theory of economic duopoly, this describes a predatory attack by one firm on another, by means of flooding the market, or as in a price war. In the context of international conflict it corresponds to an effort by one side to drive its rival into economic bankruptcy or a political *cul-de-sac* by massively outspending him.

d. The leader-follower solution: this solution is associated with the same of Stackelberg[15] in discussions of the theory of duopoly; it describes the outcome when one side obliviously follows its own reaction curve while the second recognizes that he can therefore select which point on that reaction curve the first side will choose. An analogy is drawn between this behavior and proposals for unilateral disarmament.

(3) The bargaining problem: while no effort has been made in this study to analyze the fashion in which total increases in

[14] Martin Shubik, *Strategy and Market Structure* (New York: John Wiley, 1959).

[15] Heinrich von Stackelberg, *The Theory of the Market Economy* (New York: Oxford University Press, 1952).

utility—resulting from formal or tacit agreement between two adversaries in an arms race—may be distributed between the two, the study does indicate that negotiation on disarmament is formally very closely akin to negotiation over prices and outputs.

(4) Time paths: no explicit effort is made in this direction, but the model allows for study of the rate and direction of approach toward equilibria.[16]

(5) Non-economic constraints: because of the vagaries of decision by committee, certain constraints external to our formal, utility maximizing decision model may be imposed on the process of an arms build-up. Such factors are likely to be of greater significance for decisions by government on how many missiles to build than for decision by firms on what price to charge or quantity to offer. Thus some absolute ceiling or floor[17] may be imposed on the total expenditure for arms, or some minimum number of potentially surviving missiles may be demanded regardless of the cost. Such additional constraints will influence and perhaps dominate possible solutions, bargaining outcomes, stability conditions, or time paths.

(4) Two Sides: Imperfect Information

The increase in the number of trade-offs occasioned by the introduction of uncertainty or ignorance, has made an exhaustive account of the effects of secrecy on the arms race as a phenomenon of interaction impossible. The body of our study and, in particular, Chapter VI nevertheless covers a wide enough range of the effects to allow us to claim some generality for the findings. The reader must remember that, as in the "one-sided, imperfect-information" case, misinformation may be introduced as a param-

---

[16] Kenneth E. Boulding, A *Reconstruction of Economics* (New York: John Wiley, 1950), explains a graphical approach on pp. 9ff.

[17] A ceiling or floor in expenditures may be reached as a matter of course if the interactive sequence of rational, utility-optimizing decisions leads to a Cournot solution. The ceiling or floor referred to above is of a different kind; it is imposed externally and supersedes the economic optimizing decision process. See pp. 178–182.

eter, or as a variable that can be altered by the expenditure of resources on intelligence. If it appears that no unambiguous tendencies in the arms race arise from the introduction of uncertainty, this can be explained by the fact that in our theory no specific designations of the parameters in the utility functions have been made nor of relative costs of the various components in those strategic weapons systems considered.

The text supports the following generalizations:

(1) Solutions at junctures of reaction curves: whether we regard secrecy as a variable or a parameter, its introduction can radically alter the existence and/or nature of such solutions. Some intersections may disappear, other new solutions may appear. Where new points are stable, old points may have been unstable and vice versa. As a lesser included class, it may turn out that the nature of such a solution remains unchanged while the equilibrium point itself moves in or out toward higher or lower arms levels. Misinformation may cause such a point to shift from higher to lower or from lower to higher arms levels. Misinformation is more likely to lower the level of total arms if it is a variable, and therefore draws resources off for intelligence acquisition.[18]

(2) Levels of utility: uncertainty primarily tends to reduce the levels of utility for both sides at all combinations of x and y. The model in Chapter II suggests that this should dampen the extent of mutual provocation in the cold war, since the degree of provocation varies directly with the difference between peacetime and wartime utility. If, in addition, the Cournot duopoly solution moves toward greater (but stable) arms levels when

[18] Experienced people may question this on the grounds that (1) moneys devoted to intelligence are but a negligible fraction of expenditures on hardware, or that (2) the decision-making process does not allow for the trade-off between hardware and information. The first objection concerns facts and, if true, it reduces the point made to an academic curiosity. The second objection is a matter of logic and, if true, reflects irrationality in the decision process.

imperfect information is introduced, we might expect an arms race in missiles to end in great weapons inventories on both sides, low utilities on both sides, and, therefore, relatively minor mutual provocation.

(3) Optimal threat solutions: by lowering utilities throughout $x-y$ space, secrecy should tend to reduce arms levels when one side has initiated an effort to force the other into bankruptcy or political ruin by a massive outspending maneuver. This effect is more pronounced when secrecy is considered to be a variable. Moreover, the introduction of secrecy—especially if one side holds an advantage in this regard—may reverse the roles between the side attempting to enforce ruin and the one striving to forestall such ruin.

(4) Mutual disarmament: whether secrecy is understood to be a parameter or a variable the general tendency appears to be to shift the Pareto contract curve toward the origin such that at a joint-utility maximum both sides will possess fewer armaments than in the case of perfect information.

(5) Unilateral partial disarmament, and time paths to equilibria; no specific conclusions have been reached. It appears clear that the degree of information obtaining must be an integral part of an analysis of such questions.

CONTROL OF THE ARMS RACE

For those with a special interest in arms control, and the hope of finding new avenues toward the relaxation of tensions and serenity in an ordered world, the final chapter of this book studies the prospects for information exchange explicitly. In broad generalizations essentially three points result from that chapter.

The first is that there is a marked similarity in the inconvenience one suffers from (1) being uncertain about the capabilities of an enemy and (2) being uncertain about one's own capabilities. In both instances the costs of achieving a degree of security are greater than they otherwise would be. In principle, therefore, in so far as a side willingly diverts funds to refine its knowledge of its own weapons—their yields, accuracies, reliabilities, vulnerabilities to surprise or destruction, and so forth—that side should countenance spending money to reduce ignorance of the enemy either by supporting an intelligence apparatus or by overtly bribing secrets out of him or both.

The second point is that the amount and quality of information either side has are variables in the arms race just as are all the other features of the opposing arsenals—determined by and determining all the other variables in the armaments contest. The state of information influences the rate and direction of the arms competition, equilibria, and the opportunities for mutually profitable arms agreements. Secrecy can be an objectively desirable military weapon. (Under some circumstances it can have a negative value.) Therefore arms negotiations that would effect an exchange of information for money, information for weapons, or information for information, are founded on the same principles, promise the same gains, and deserve the same consideration as proposals to exchange weapons reduction for weapons reduction (or limitation).

Third, unless one believes that an automatic effect of disarmament would be to establish fraternity among nations, and eliminate fears, hostilities, and suspicions, we must argue emphatically that not all arms-control schemes merit approval. It is easy to imagine disarmament arrangements from which *both sides* could suffer. One example would be an agreement to limit numbers of missiles with no limitations on warhead technology. This could allow both sides to achieve a disarming capability. Some mutual exchanges of information could also result in a loss for both sides.

These three major points are fully discussed in Chapter VII; beyond these the reader may want to examine the entire structure of the arms race as recounted in Chapters II through VI with a view toward its implications for arms-control arrangements. It is only prudent, therefore, to point out in advance that this study is limited as a basis for normative assertions about arms control. Rehearsing a few of the well-known features of conflict among nations and the dilemmas central thereto will serve to caution the reader.

To be successful arms-control negotiations must proceed from an understanding of a variety of problems. All have been featured in the arms-control and disarmament efforts since the end of World War II, undertaken in the hope of forestalling war, of finding political settlements to preclude it, and of limiting the evil if it comes. The first problem to be understood is what causes war to break out. A second problem is to understand the process of weapons development and build-up that precedes war. A third problem is to understand the relations between the first two phenomena—how the course of preparation for war influences the probability, the nature, the timing, and the results of war once it comes. A fourth problem is what political arrangements, what division of territories, of spheres of influence, and so on, effect the arms race and the nature of future war. *This study is directed primarily toward the second of these problems, with some attention to the third.*

One legitimate aim of arms negotiation may be simply to limit the arms race because it is so costly. But in attempting to assess arms-control schemes and to judge which controls may be beneficial and which detrimental the third of these problems may assume critical significance. For this reason it will pay to dwell upon the connection between the arms race and strategic war at some length before launching into the body of our study.

A central criterion by which an arms-control proposal should be judged is by its influence on the probability of war. Another possible objective of arms control is to stabilize the arms race. Our theory has something to say about this although the reader

27

should keep in mind that stability in the arms race itself and stability in the decision-making processes leading to war though related are not identical. An arms race with stable equilibrium may settle upon a point at which the psychology of mutual fear, distrust and preemption causes the state of no-attack to be unstable. An unstable arms race in principle can yield a stable no-attack environment. The analysis in the chapters to follow allows of the possibility that as the arms competition itself progresses, the likelihood of an attack by either side may diminish. If an arms race were to take this course, then in one respect the continuance of the arms competition would be positively beneficial.

Correspondingly the informational environment obtaining at some point during the competition is of significance in two respects: first, as to its influence upon the arms contest itself; second, as to its influence on the risk and nature of war. Release of information on weapons locations could allow both sides to cutback defense budgets while making each more trigger happy. An agreement to limit numbers without limiting yields could in the course of time have a like effect.

The relevance of the control of armaments to the risks of war is itself complex and replete with dilemmas. One particular complexity arises from the duality in motivation behind the arms race, namely, first-strike and deterrent-oriented potentials. As another example, attention must be given to the differences between limiting the chances of attack by mistake or inadvertence, and limiting the incentive for deliberate or premeditated attack.[19] The methods of our study of information and arms races can be applied here only with caution. The paradigm case for war by mistake occurs when one side preempts out of a misfounded fear that the other will attack or will preempt. War can explode when neither side truly intends it, because technology

[19] These may not be all equally undesirable risks.

allows incredibly swift and catastrophic surprise in the attack. In order to reduce the probability of surprise attack, one price to be paid—in the short run when capital is fixed—is an increase in the probability of a misinterpretation of the signals of attack, and the consequent compounding of fears and incentives for pre-emption which can lead to war by mistake.[20] Information and its availability impinge upon this problem in a variety of ways. Obviously information as to intentions has a large role. If each side can convince the other its intentions are peaceful, the chance of a misinterpretation of signals declines. On the other hand, each side may lower the risk of finding itself in an unintended war by informing the adversary not only of its intentions but of its weapon characteristics, so as to allow him to know for sure when an attack is coming.

Another way of limiting the probabilities of mutually unintended war is to reduce the *possibilities* of surprise attack—to reduce the underlying, fundamental plausibility that any attack at all will take place. For if the character of the arsenals on either side is such that any one side considers it inherently implausible that the other would attack, then false signals of such attack are less likely to be misinterpreted. If the arms race can be redirected toward a competition in arms suitable for deterrence but ill-suited for attack and if there is a mutual recognition of this on the part of both sides, then each side will be inherently suspicious of signals of attack, inclined to hesitate, to delay or postpone its decision to preempt, and in so doing to reassure its attacker that false signals have in fact been interpreted as false. The ultimate in such insurance against war by mistake is reached when both sides positively prefer being attacked by the opponent to attacking the opponent first. One way of directing the arms race toward a no-attack, or deterrence-oriented equilibrium is through the manipulation of information. But suppose this is accom-

---

[20] Schelling, *Strategy of Conflict,* p. 220.

plished. The risk of surprise attack has been reduced but at what cost?

The cost is a loss of the capability for threatening a first strike. To what extent is it in the interest of both sides to limit their ability to attack deliberately? A good first-strike capability —by virtue of the potential for intimidation that it allows—may more than compensate for the undesired risk of unintended war that it can create. Unpleasant as this possibility is, it can not be overlooked. Competitive or zero-sum elements in relations between states dictate that we attend to the implications of possible arms-control schemes for the capacity for making threats. What responses to extremely provocative acts on the part of one's adversary are to be allowed in the arms-controlled or partially disarmed world? (Is there to be a place for type-II deterrence?) Today the threat of deliberate nuclear attack doubtless does limit provocations by either side in the cold war. How are grave provocations to be handled in a disarmed world? Chapter II suggests that the greater a side's secure retaliatory capacity the less has it to fear from and therefore the more does it undertake provocative adventures in search of cold-war gains. For an arms-control agreement to prove feasible, some substitute—other than the threat of response with a deliberate first-strike should have to be found to dissuade an opponent from provocations. Otherwise an agreement to create and enhance stability in deterrence might have the perverse effect of raising the level of cold-war challenge and counter-challenge. Our study of the arms race has rather little to offer in solution of this problem.

Another possibility, albeit pessimistic, is to imagine that arms agreements will not for the present be reached because one or both parties are unwilling to surrender the potential for threatening to strike first—or for other reasons. If this proves to be an impasse, an alternative is to alter armaments in such a way that while the option of intentionally striking first is not lost, the devastation of war is limited.

James E. King, Jr. defines "arms control" as including agreements to limit destruction from war.

The term "arms control" will be interpreted to mean explicit international agreements based upon a recognized common interest in two purposes: (1) to reduce the likelihood of war, and (2) if that fails, to diminish the violence of war.[21]

In direct contrast to the supposition that excellence in counterforce weapons is bad, it is interesting to reflect that improvements in weapons technology may serve to reduce the annihilation and catastrophe of war if it comes. For example, improvements in the accuracy of missiles may persuade the potential user of such missiles to change his targets from enemy cities to enemy missiles. Or again, improvement in the warheads themselves—such as reductions in fallout-producing components— may allow counterforce exchanges to occur with a minimum loss in assets of basic national value. In short, one avenue open to arms-control negotiators leads toward improvements in weapons so as to make war less catastrophic for most people. Observe that if the way to minimizing damage from potential future wars lies in the direction of technological improvements, there may be a direct inconsistency between attempting both to minimize the chances of war and to minimize the potential damage once such a war arises. Such paradoxes are common enough in the analysis of conflict between nations. Information exchange and arms agreements aimed at mutual *defense* against war, one should expect, would differ from those directed toward prevention of war. Agreements to declare war, to forego surprise, or to cooperate in mutual civil-defense programs come to mind. Limiting the yields and fallout-producing components of weapons, raising the vulnerabilities of missile sites, and exchanging reassurances that *countervalue* attacks are not programmed,

---

[21] James E. King, Jr., "Arms Control and United States Security," in *Arms Control: Issues for the Public*, ed. Louis Henkin (New York: Prentice Hall, 1961), p. 96.

are other examples. The value of information in the context of defense obviously differs from what it is in schemes to stabilize deterrence. The latter calls for protecting weapons, while the former dictates protecting people.[22]

The suggestion that arms negotiations be directed toward limiting the pain of war and therefore the efficacy of deterrence is susceptible to a standard objection. Deterrence proceeds from an assumption of rational behavior on the part of both sides. As mutual deterrence increases it becomes ever more the place of rationality to avoid striking first. Among the roles of the arms negotiator is that of persuading both sides to recognize their own rational self-interest. Efforts to limit the perils of war are therefore to be discouraged. A persuasive threat to be irrational is in some circumstances, however, a very profitable posture. Arms-control schemes tending toward increased stabilized mutual deterrence do not automatically reduce the payoff from being "irrational." With a more formidable deterrence posture on both sides, it is likely to be more difficult for one side to persuade the other that it is truly reckless, but the payoffs from so persuading the second side may be all the greater. Arms control may put a premium on this special variety of deceit.

Another aspect of possible arms-control agreements illustrated by our theory is the effect such agreements could have upon a strategy aimed at deliberately lowering an adversary's utility in the course of the cold war. An overwhelming capacity for outspending an adversary in national defense can be a useful capability to be held in reserve. Not that the capability for massive defense spending must actually be realized; the potential threat may be sufficient. However, one consequence, it would seem, of almost any negotiated arms agreement would have to be that both sides forego this strategy. Here the loss of options open to the United States deserves particular attention since a cold-war strategy of massively outspending one's opponent is

[22] Schelling, *Strategy of Conflict*, p. 233.

really available only to this country. To give up this option may involve considerable loss, and some compensation for such a loss might reasonably be expected by U.S. arms negotiators.

In summary, this study shows that the underlying structure of the arms competition is an intricate economic balance among a variety of motives for accumulating arms and a technology of production, of protection, and of detection of armaments. In view of the great intricacy and diversity of the military balance, simplistic or one-dimensional approaches to the control of armaments are automatically suspect. Unless we assume outright that basic hostilities will abate with such an agreement, a partial, one-dimensional restraint on the arms race will probably simply send it off in a new direction. This study provides a structure for analyzing how such partial restraints may alter certain critical relative advantages on either side. But as for evaluating one advantage over another and coming to a universal understanding of alternative arms control approaches the reader must turn to the wider literature, which we now survey.

ARMS RACE THEORIES: A SURVEY OF THE LITERATURE

One legitimate way to introduce and define a concept is to offer an example. It happens that the inventory of models presuming to capture the essential features of arms races is quite small. For this reason it is practicable to expound the notion of an arms race by surveying virtually all the models. That is the first intent of this section. The second is to assist the reader in relating the constructs of this book to the body of literature outstanding on the subject.

Richardson's Model

First in point of time and originality, Lewis F. Richardson's thought is remarkable as an effort to account for the essential structure of the arms race in mathematical terms. Richardson supposes that there are two nations; call them X and Y. "A rule of the theoretical game is that a nation is to be represented by a single variable," say, x and y. Now, "the various motives which lead a nation in time of peace to increase or decrease its preparations for war may be classified according to the manner of its dependence on its own existing preparations and on those of other nations."[23]

First nation X considers nation Y's level of armaments to be a menace to its own security; the menace X perceives in Y's arms level can be measured by the product ky, where y is Y's arms level and k, a constant term, a "defense coefficient," denoting X's perception of the menace. Similarly Y believes itself to be threatened by X in the amount lx, where l is Y's "defense coefficient."

Secondly, both X and Y are pained by the expense and effort of preparations for war, the greater the preparation the greater the pain. This is expressed by αx for X and βy for Y, where α and β are "fatigue-and-expense-of-keeping-up-defenses" coefficients.

Lastly, both X and Y harbor, on balance, some independent friendship or enmity for each other, to be denoted by g (X's independent attitude toward Y, or X's grievances) and h (Y's independent attitude toward X, or Y's grievances).

In a bold generalization Richardson then proposes to explain the structure of the arms race by the hypothesis that each of the above three motives determines the *rate* at which X and Y accumulate arms. This is expressed by:

$$\frac{dx}{dt} = ky - \alpha x + g,$$
$$\frac{dy}{dt} = lx - \beta y + h.$$

(1)

[23] Lewis F. Richardson, *Arms and Insecurity*, ed. Nicholas Rashevsky and Ernesto Trucco (Pittsburgh, Pa.: Boxwood Press, 1960).

Only if a side's fears, friendships and enmities, expenses and fatigues, balance out to zero will that side remain at its current arms level. Whether or not such a balance exists, itself depends on the level of arms on both sides.

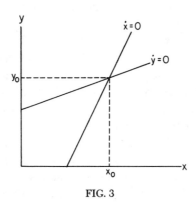

FIG. 3

Suppose, as shown in Fig. 3, that the level of arms accumulation is measured off on the axes x and y. The line

$$ky - \alpha x + g = 0 = \dot{x} \tag{2}$$

then indicates all combinations of x and y which will allow X to rest unchanged. The line

$$lx - \beta y + h = 0 = \dot{y} \tag{3}$$

shows a similar set of points for Y. If the coefficients k, l, α, β, g, and h are such that $\dot{x} = 0$ and $\dot{y} = 0$ intersect, then at that point (x_0, y_0), or level of arms on each side, each side has simultaneously found a combination of threat and response from which it has no incentive to change.

So truncated an account of so rich a theory as Richardson's cannot fail to do the theory some injustice. But enough has been said to give the reader an example of what an "arms race" can mean.[24]

The virtue of Richardson's approach consists not so much in the strength of mathematics—which is to say its deductive rigor —as in what mathematics in his hands suggests. The most pregnant suggestion and one which must be incorporated in *all* models of arms races is that the level of arms prevailing on one side is a function of, or depends on, the level prevailing on the other, in short the suggestion that the actual levels of armaments are mutually interdependent. A mathematical formulation allows this relation to be expressed explicitly. It should serve as a warning to the policy-maker to ask not, "How much do we need to counter what the enemy has got?" but rather, "How much do we need to counter what the enemy will choose to counter what we need?" The answers to these two questions may differ not only in amount, but also in sign (+ or −). The second major virtue in Richardson's model is his explicit introduction of time. The model is, therefore, inherently dynamic; it allows for explicit consideration of questions of stability and instability, and creates a context in which these terms—today in such common use—have empirically specifiable and unambiguous meanings; it allows for treatment of paths toward or away from equilibrium points over time. Lastly, being mathematical, his model directs our attention to measurable, quantifiable elements in the arms race.

The weaknesses of the Richardson model are, in the main, two. The first is that no formal connection is asserted between the course which preparations for warfare take, and the risk, likelihood, or likely outcome of hostilities themselves. We know not, in this regard, whether the arms race is to be applauded or

---

[24] Anatol Rapoport, *Fights, Games, and Debates* (Ann Arbor: The University of Michigan Press, 1960); and Kenneth Boulding, *Conflict and Defense* (New York: Harper, 1962) will serve the interested reader well who wishes to pursue Richardson's theory further.

condemned; in this respect the model is neither optimistic nor pessimistic, it is vacant. Richardson in this connection remarks:

> A failure of equations to describe both small and very large disturbances is familiar in many departments of applied mathematics and need not unduly dispirit us: for example, Hooke's law is important in connection with the strength of materials although it does not describe fracture.[25]

But, of course, Hooke's law is of use *in practice* precisely because we also have knowledge of breaking strengths.

Secondly, Richardson's model does not describe a sequence of choices by both sides in an arms race; it is not policy-choice oriented. Rapoport offers a reasoned defense of this statistically determinate approach and Richardson himself avows: "The process described by the ensuing equations is not to be thought of as inevitable. It is what *would occur if instinct* and tradition were allowed to act uncontrolled."[26] It will be shown in our study in the chapters to follow that an arms race can be described as a sequence of rational choices in which fears, expenses and fatigue, fundamental grievances, and so forth do play a role. While the basic idea of independence and interaction between the levels of armament on each of two sides in an arms race can be illustrated neatly with an instinctive or deterministic model of Richardson's type, such determinism is not required. It may be that a "controlled" series of moves can lead to war—or peace—via an interactive process not drastically dissimilar. The introduction of plausible motives for arming, with no structure for explaining how such motives plus the levels of armaments

[25] Richardson, *Arms and Insecurity*, p. 15. Hooke's Law states that stress is proportional to strain.

[26] Richardson, *Arms and Insecurity*, p. 12. It should be pointed out, though not in fair criticism of Richardson, that his model does not allow for many important contemporary distinctions, such as first vs. second strike, retaliation vs. bargaining, or quantities of armaments vs. ratios, in the psychology of the two antagonists. See also Rapoport, *Fights, Games, and Debates*, chaps. i, ii, v.

on both sides, converge on the decision maker, opens the way for richer and more useful developments of Richardson's pioneering technique.

Huntington's Model

In an article published in 1958, Professor Huntington, attempts to generalize about arms races from an historical study. In doing so he admits to his consideration many of the significant aspects omitted in Richardson's treatment.

He defines an arms race as "a progressive competitive peacetime increase in armaments by two states or coalitions of states resulting from conflicting purposes or mutual fears. An arms race is thus a form of reciprocal interaction between two states or coalitions."[27] Or equally, "An arms race is a series of interrelated increases in armaments which if continued over a period of time produces a dynamic equilibrium of power between two states."[28] It seems quite clear that Huntington has the ideas central to Richardson's model, that the arms levels on either side depend, among other things, on the level of arms of the other. Huntington then proceeds to define certain preconditions of an arms race. These may be enumerated as follows:

(1) Arms races only occur in an international balance-of-power context. They are an integral part of the balance, and proceed only between states in the same balance of power system.

(2) Armed forces in being must be of prime importance to the power of a state.

(3) Sustained arms races require the economic power and governmental-social organization characteristic of the nineteenth and twentieth centuries.

[27] Samuel P. Huntington, "Arms Races: Prerequisites and Results," *Public Policy* 8:41 (1958).
[28] *Ibid.*, p. 55.

(4) Both states must recognize and react in accordance with a functional interdependence. This in turn entails two conditions: (a) armaments available to each state must be designed for combat with the other; (b) both governments must be well informed of the rival's military capabilities.[29]

For the remainder of the essay Huntington is concerned less with the actual course of an arms build-up, with examining possible points of mutual equilibrium or with the stability of instability of such points, as was Richardson. Rather he addresses himself to the question of the effect of an arms race on the risk of war. Huntington is concerned more with the conditions of fracture than with a "Hooke's Law" of an arms race itself.

On the risks and likelihood of war Huntington has this to say:

The likelihood of war arising from an arms race depends in the first instance upon the relation between the power and grievances of one state to the power and grievances of the other. War is least likely when grievances are low or if grievances are high, the sum of the grievances and power of one state approximates the sum of the grievances and power of the other . . . Assuming a fairly equal distribution of grievances the likelihood of an arms race ending in war tends to vary inversely with the length of the arms race and directly with the extent to which it is quantitative rather than qualitative.[30]

Huntington's reasons for holding war to be most likely early in an arms race are essentially a jitteriness in the initial stages of an arms race, when (1) the side challenged may try preventive war to "nip the challenge in the bud," and (2) the challenger in realizing this (or suspecting this) may be seized with fear and

---

[29] This idea will be examined in detail later in the study.
[30] Huntington, "Arms Races," p. 55.

preempt. The link-up, in short, between preparations for war and war itself is through a "reciprocal-fear-of-surprise-attack" mechanism, and Huntington sees the passage of time as psychologically soothing. However, this need not necessarily be so. Over time, the sum of differences between power and grievance may increase, and hence each side's nervousness and propensity to start a war may grow. The point here is that the risk of war may depend not only on the exogenously determined psychology of either side, but on the course of the arms race as well.[31]

The monograph is best known for its distinction between qualitative and quantitative arms races. Proceeding on the assumption that scientific developments are universally known and applied to weaponry with only short time lags, Huntington deduces that a qualitative race tends toward equality of armaments since with each new "ultimate" weapon system any previous imbalance is eliminated or very largely reduced. Therefore, "insofar as the likelihood of war is decreased by the existence of an equality of power between rival states [that is, if grievances are equally distributed], a qualitative arms race tends to have this result."[32] On the other hand, qualitative arms races tend to be less of a drain on the resources of the country participating, and they therefore tend to reduce incentives for agreement on arms limitation.

To an extent, Richardson's weakness is Huntington's strength, and vice versa. Strong and rich in the detail of the relations perceived, Huntington's analysis lacks structure. Primitive in its detail, Richardson's account suggests a structure and an illuminating menu of questions. A synthesis of the two will be sought in later chapters of this study.

---

[31] An arms race in unprotected, quick-reacting ICBM's is the obvious example.

[32] Huntington, "Arms Races," p. 76. This obscures the possibility that even a brief lag in development of AICBM's might provide great incentive for the first possessor to attack.

Boulding's Model

Where Richardson brought the skill of the mathematician to bear on a study of arms races, and Huntington the skills of political science, Professor Boulding, in *Conflict and Defense*, brings the skills of economics, that is to say, the skills of a theory of choice. Boulding's contribution has been, essentially, to introduce the preference functions or indifference curves used by economists into the Richardsonian analysis. This allows one to view Richardson's equations of equilibrium, or more complex variants thereof, as describing each side's utility-maximizing response to the threat from its adversary. Thus each side may now be viewed as responding "rationally" to any situation posed by a rival; that is, as acting so as to make the best of the situation, taking national objectives and costs into account.

The economist is familiar with reaction process in the theory of oligopoly, especially the theory of price war. The political scientist meets the reaction process in the concept of the arms race which is very similar to the price war.[33]

This is a major step in the elaboration of an arms-race model. As Professor Schelling observes it allows for bargaining, for "negotiation of mutually preferred positions and decisions consciously oriented toward the reaction of the other side."[34]

Two points are noteworthy if Richardson processes can be described as a sequence of mutually interacting, economic— that is utility-maximizing—choices: (1) at once a very great body of economic theory awaits application to the arms-race problem,[35] and a translation of ideas from one context to the other may prove fruitful and suggestive; (2) since we can view

---

[33] Boulding, *Conflict and Defense*, p. 25.
[34] Thomas C. Schelling, "War Without Pain, and Other Models," *World Politics* 15:471 (April 1963).
[35] Especially Stackelberg's pioneering efforts in duopoly theory.

the arms race as a sequence of choices, a theory along these lines may have something to say to the choice makers. This book is an effort toward making such a translation.

The Burns-Schelling-Hoag Contribution

We have suggested that the arms competition may be viewed as a sequence of mutually interdependent choices made by each side in the race, where any such choice resolves the conflict between the contribution of arms to national objectives and the drain of such armaments on national resources. But how do armaments contribute to national objectives? Professors Burns, Schelling, and Hoag have all commented on the relation.[36]

The first observation to be made is that "national objectives" are multidimensional. Possible desiderata include: an ability to attack and defeat, an ability to deter attack upon one's self, and an ability to defend against attack on one's self. The second observation to be made is that the manner in which one side's forces counter another's, and the efficiency with which a side's forces contribute to that side's potential to attack, deter, or defend, both depend upon technology.

Schelling's example is well known. Suppose our purpose is deterrence and we calculate we need 100 missiles as a retaliatory force surviving the enemy's countermissile attack to deter such an attack in the first place. Then, if any one of his missiles has just a 50–50 chance of killing ours; (1) we need to build 200 if the enemy has 200; (2) 400 if the enemy has 800; (3) and only 800 if the enemy has 2400. "The larger the initial number on the 'defending' side, the larger the *multiple* required by the attacker in order to reduce the victim's residual supply to below some 'safe' number" (assuming the attacker fires all his missiles

[36] Arthur Lee Burns, "A Graphical Approach to Some Problems of the Arms Race," *Journal of Conflict Resolution* 3 (1959); Schelling, "Surprise Attack and Disarmament," in *The Strategy of Conflict*, Ch. x; Malcolm W. Hoag, "On Stability in Deterrent Races," *World Politics* 13 (July 1961).

at once, or if not at once with no information on subsequent salvos as to the success of earlier ones).[37]

Hoag applies similar reasoning to cases in which technology shows relative favor to the side with numerically inferior forces, and next to the side with numerically superior forces. In doing so he demonstrates that, if the object is to deter, the entire character of an arms race can be altered by technology. As in Schelling's example the technological environment is summarized in a single concept, the *ratio* between "Enemy Forces" and "Own Forces" required to deter the enemy.

In an ingenious effort to translate Huntington's historical findings into diagrammatic terms Burns employs this notion of ratio between forces and extends it to treat the attack-deter distinction mentioned earlier. Burns' contribution to our conceptual inventory may be shown graphically. In Fig. 4 let axes x

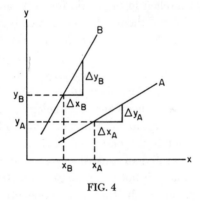

FIG. 4

and y represent X's and Y's forces as before. Suppose that for X to attack Y successfully, X must dispose of x_B, if Y's forces are y_B. The line B describes how, in order to attack, X must

---

[37] Schelling, *Strategy of Conflict*, p. 236. This argument assumes we are satisfied with 100 missiles surviving *on the average*. See pp. 87ff. for a description of cases in which we insist on 100 surviving with odds of 10 to 1 or better in our favor.

respond to Y's forces of whatever level if the ratio $\Delta y_B/\Delta x_B$ is constant. Imagine next, that X wishes only to deter Y. For $y = y_A$, X must dispose of x_A forces. If $\Delta y_A/\Delta x_A$ remains constant, then the curve A shows the ratio at which X must match Y so as to maintain adequate deterrence. Accordingly, it is cheaper for X to maintain a deterrence than an attack posture. Suppose, however, the curve A is now taken as indicating attack requirements, and B deterrence requirements. Obviously the roles are reversed, and for X an attack posture is far cheaper than a deterrent posture. The question of which of the two combinations (attack-cheaper-than-deterrence, or attack-dearer-than-deterrence) in fact obtains can only be resolved with reference to technology, costs, and force configurations.[38]

The chapters to follow are an effort to synthesize and elaborate the several ideas implicit in the works reviewed aforegoing. The main inspiration of the theory devised comes from Richardson and Boulding. The ideas of an interdependence between each side's arms levels, of a reaction curve, and the selection of a level of armaments as a rational economic choice are obviously central to the entire analysis. The debt to Burns-Schelling-Hoag is equally obvious in the role given to technology and the survivor-attacker ratio in the argument. The obligation to Huntington is less direct and much in the nature of a restraint on any pretentions of having presented an exhaustive treatment of arms races. The model, essentially, is not designed to handle the two aspects of arms build-ups on which Huntington concentrates. First, the question of the influence of all the interacting decisions upon the likelihood of war is not adequately addressed. The model could handle a part of the question by concentrating upon the

---

[38] The obvious example is the safe, vulnerable, clustered missile force for which attack is cheaper than defense and the ratio of own to enemy missiles (similarly configured) is less than 1, versus the hard, invulnerable, dispersed missile force for which attack is more expensive and the ratio greater than 1.

changes in postattack potential utilities, as the arms race progresses, for comparison with prewar utilities. Still this should handle only a small portion of the problem, which is closely related to the possibilities of initiating a war by mistake, inadvertence, or irrational decision[39]—a possibility excluded from the model presented here (irrational *response* with a constant probability is necessary to the argument, but irrationality, mistake, and so on, are allowed to enter only *after* the first-strike is over and the war has already begun).

Secondly, the structure of a qualitative arms race has not been explored. The introduction of something minor, like improvements in accuracies or yields can be easily dealt with (as a once-over shift in the technological constraints), but our system is not adaptable to describing the competition arising from some utterly new weapon with new costs and payoffs. It should be noted in defense of this shortcoming that it is a necessary price if one is to have much detail in theorizing about actual decisions and contemporary issues.

One very general feature of the arms race and of the sequence of economic choices of which it is comprised which our theory illustrates is the fruitlessness of a search for absolutes in security. Whether a side seeks a retaliatory or a first-strike capability the constructions of chapters to follow illustrate the inherent probabilistic nature of the deterrent or intimidation potential so sought. The missile-war example illustrates that it is a technological fact that no matter how much in resources is allocated to defense, some risk of failure inheres in the mechanism of the arms competition.

In the same way the theory developed in subsequent chapters indicates no clear line between quality and quantities of weapons. A large number of low-quality weapons is substitutable

---

[39] These three are conceptually distinct ways for a war to start; and there are other ways.

for a smaller number of high-quality weapons. Trade-offs exist between quality and quantity. It can make sense to refrain from pushing research and development to its extreme and costly limit and instead to allocate the resources so saved to greater numbers of those less-than-perfect strategic weapons.

If there is one central message in this study of arms races and the role of information, it is embraced by the adage "know thy enemy." Two decades of military competition with the U.S.S.R. should teach us we are participating in a *process*, in a phenomenon with a structure. Each of the two sides in the cold-war conflict has expectations and desires. The growth in weapons stockpiled by both sides is a one prime manifestation of unilateral attempts by and the accompanying frustrations of both adversaries to achieve inconsistent ends.

"A requirement for successful negotiation of a stabilized deterrence agreement is that each side understand, in a fairly sophisticated way, the security requirements of the other."[40] This is so not only because arms agreement without such understanding will probably never be achieved. Equally important, without such understanding an arms agreement, if reached, could easily lead to positions, less preferred, more dangerous, possibly even more expensive than the situation obtaining before the negotiations. A disarmament pact which makes all parties worse off is possible. And the utility of understanding an adversary's security needs remains even in the absence of arms control. To the contrary such knowledge is equally rewarding to the aggressive participant in the arms race. The enemy reacts to our moves. A grasp of the mechanism of this reaction allows one to plan for it, to use it, and to benefit by it.

[40] John B. Phelps, "On the Role of Stabilized Deterrence," in *Arms Reduction Program and Issues*, ed. David H. Frisch (New York: Twentieth Century Fund, 1961), p. 88.

II · PREREQUISITES FOR A THEORY
OF THE ARMS RACE

The intent of this study is to develop a theoretical structure for the explanation of the arms race. We seek a theory that will explain the selection of the level and quality of armaments on each side as a rational choice which balances the contribution such armaments make to national objectives against the costs they entail. We therefore need some specific idea as to how arms contribute to objectives. What is sought in this chapter first is a mechanism for generating the phenomenon we propose to study—namely, the arms race. This entails postulating plausible reasons on each side for viewing weapons as a source of security and strength and, hence, establishing plausible motives for accumulating arms.

To understand why a nation amasses the tools of war, one must reflect upon war itself. More specifically, the manner in which opposing arsenals influence the *outcome* of war must be explored. This, in turn, demands some notion of the structure of war as a dynamic process.

It is commonplace that the appallingly large accumulation of nuclear materials over the past decade has shifted our attention, especially in recent years, away from the possibilities for all-out thermonuclear exchange and toward the alternative of limited conflict. A strategy of flexible response, counterforce retaliation, and controlled application of punishment via violence suggests that our theory of war must admit limits, and constraints in strategic exchanges between the great powers.[1]

There are essentially two reasons for believing that war could be thermonuclear yet limited in violence and extent. The first reason is technological. While the fact is well known, it can hardly be overemphasized that among the prime targets for a rational attacker's missiles must be the missiles of the defender. It is a fundamental characteristic of the accumulation of armaments in the form of missiles in today's world that each side's inventory is of service in two different ways. Each missile is potentially both an attacker in a first strike against the opponent's missile force and a target for, and a possible survivor from, an attack by the enemy. Characteristically, missiles are located away from population centers. The emplacement of United States missiles under the ocean in Polaris submarines is a case in point. As a result, a counterforce missile strike can in principle occur with relatively limited damage to the population and other assets of basic national value.[2] Another characteristic of the missile force today is that it is dispersed and highly protected. The result of this is that when any single attacking missile is aimed at a single defending missile site, the probability that the attacker will destroy the defender is less than 1. From this it follows that if two opposing missile forces are equally matched (or nearly so) and if both are protected and dispersed, then neither side can completely disarm the other with a counterforce first-strike. (The possibility that one booster may carry two or more independently guided warheads may reverse this.)

[1] Both scholars and planners of recent years have paid increasing attention to the so-called strategy of limited retaliation, a possibility recognized as early as 1959 by Herman Kahn in *On Thermonuclear War* (Princeton, N.J.: Princeton University Press, 1960), p. 126.

[2] A counterforce war would be a moral catastrophe. But if airfields are excluded as targets, destruction to population would be confined to downwind fallout casualties—with deaths much reduced from a counter-city exchange.

Furthermore, it should be noted that technology is progressing so as to make a sequence of counterforce blows more plausible. This derives from the fact that we approach a proficiency in pinpointing the locations of enemy missile sites and in targeting them exactly with ever increasingly accurate missiles. When we add to this an enhancement in the yields of warheads and a reduction in their fallout-producing components—a potentially attainable if not presently extant situation—a counterforce attack (or retaliation) with air bursts, and minimum collateral damage to population, becomes increasingly possible.

The second reason why the possibility of less-than-all-out missile exchange deserves a place in our theory is that the rational self-interest of the attacking side must lead it to strike with something short of its full strength—*given the technological conditions outlined above.* This can be best illustrated by an extreme example. Suppose, to the contrary, that the attacking side did employ its entire missile force in launching a first-strike counterforce (or countervalue) attack. Imagine that the attacker shot every missile he had at his victim. What situation obtains at the end of this first strike? Suppose that initially before the attack the two sides were at approximate parity in numbers and yields of missiles. In that case, once the attack is over, the attacker will find that he has expended all of his missiles to destroy something less than all of his victim's missiles (or none of his missiles if the first strike was countervalue). In short, the attacker will find that he has initiated a process of unilateral disarmament at his own expense. Whatever satisfaction the attacker may find in the pain or loss of value imposed upon his victims, he also will find that he has expended all his missiles in firing at his enemy and that therefore he in turn is himself the helpless victim of threat and possible retaliation from his adversary. (Fallout shelters plus extensive active defenses against missiles and bombers could make the attacker a much less helpless victim.) This is a well known example, and as such it proves that in one case at least a potential attacker need think only one step in advance to perceive that all-out and unlimited attack would work to his own disadvantage. This is an extreme illustration of the fact that in order to calculate the advantage a side may perceive in possessing weapons, we need some understanding of how a war may proceed when each side weighs the advantages and disadvantages of various courses of action—some understanding of how the weapons might find use.

WAR AS A SEQUENCE OF COUNTERFORCE EXCHANGES

A major treatise on war as a theoretical process should have to dwell in some detail upon the distinction between a *counterforce* military operation—in which the immediate objective is to destroy an enemy's military forces in being—and a *countervalue* operation—in which the immediate objective is to hurt or punish the enemy, his people, and his wealth. We do not propose to linger over the definitions. Indeed, in the long run any enemy possession may have a military worth. Instead we shall simply assume outright that war is divisible into two phases: (1) counterforce, (2) countervalue. The progress of thought about conflicts over the past decade and, in particular, about manipulation of adversary's *costs* in contrast to his military *capabilities*[3] has given rise to these categories—to be used here for analytic purpose.

A countervalue campaign may be undertaken for various ends. (1) The attacker may simply take pleasure in the suffering of his enemy; (2) the attacker may physically eliminate his enemy as a rival for world power; (3) the attacker may demonstrate an ability and/or intent to punish his enemy further and thereby induce a change in the victim's actions, decisions, or

[3] See especially Glenn H. Snyder, *Deterrence and Defense* (Princeton, N.J.: Princeton University Press, 1961).

intentions. A countervalue campaign is undertaken or threatened to secure some end desired for itself. A counterforce campaign, in contrast, is of use not because it effects some desirable end, but rather because of the new more preferred options for potential subsequent countervalue strikes or threats thereof that it creates. Our assumption is that missile wars begin with one or more counterforce exchanges, that an end to the counterforce phase signals either (1) a countervalue phase, or (2) a negotiated settlement, and that the objective of each side during the counterforce phase is to optimize its prospects for subsequent negotiations or countervalue exchanges.

Begin with the supposition that the world is composed of only two powers or, at least, that prospective war is to be fought between only two adversaries. Call these two adversaries Side X and Side Y (X and Y are capital letters to denote the countries themselves). Next, suppose that each side possesses military forces of a magnitude which can be reduced to a unidimensional index number. The magnitude of these forces on each side we define by x and y. If we were to assume that each side possessed only intercontinental missiles and that on each side these missiles were of a single homogeneous yield, accuracy, reliability, and vulnerability, and so on, then the letters x and y simply denote the numbers of missiles in the inventory of each side. Each side knows that, if war does occur, it may either attack first or be attacked first. In order to describe the significant variables in the counterforce phase of a war Table 1 is now introduced.

Table 1. Measures of strength in a counterforce duel

Attacker	Post-attack strength of	
	X	Y
X	v_{xx}	v_{yx}
Y	v_{xy}	v_{yy}

The magnitude of a side X's forces before a war has been defined as x and of side Y's as y. The forces side X would have remaining if X attacked Y, that is, the initial inventory, x, less the number used by X in the attack is denoted by v_{xx}; the number X would have surviving Y's attack by v_{xy}; v_{yy} the force level Y would have after first attacking X's missiles and v_{yx} the number Y would have surviving if X attacked Y's missiles (with all but v_{xx} of his, X's forces).[4]

This definitional scheme suggests what will be a further important assumption in our analysis. We assume that it does make sense to speak of one side striking first and the other side striking second. It can be plausibly argued that both sides, given the sophisticated intelligence capability now at their disposal, would strike simultaneously or virtually so. Nevertheless, it will aid our analysis to suppose that war is a sequence of strikes first by one side, then by the second, then again by the first, and so on. Even if this should be proved to be factually unrealistic, it is of value for heuristic purposes—that is, for understanding in slow motion what in the heat of war might be telescoped into a few hours or days. In other words, we suppose that the national decision-maker on each side, with the information as to enemy capabilities and his own national objectives available to him, decides on that basis to what extent he will commit his own military forces. He then acts upon this decision. Having so acted, he waits for the enemy's response. War, therefore, as we conceive it, is a sequence of such actions and reactions, first by one side and the next.

It may be objected that one side, if it strikes first, has every reason not to wait for the reaction of the enemy; that whoever can acquire target location information first will shoot second; and that this is more likely to be the side which struck first.

---

[4] For the moment we treat v_{xy} and v_{yx} as uniquely determinate numbers, a simplification corrected later on.

Target surveillance is presumably more swift, and reliable for the attacker than the defender, whose military machine has suffered a damaging blow. To account for this, the argument to follow may be interpreted as allowing one side two or three turns without interruption and then the other side the same. For simplicity of illustration a one-turn-by-one example is developed below; the principles are no different; a general framework for a missile duel with wider applicability will result.

Determination of Post-Strike Strengths: Techniques of Analysis

Imagine that the prewar inventories of weapons on both sides are fixed. The account could easily be generalized for variable initial forces. Let the values of x and y be given as x_o and y_o respectively. If, as in Fig. 5 we plot post-attack residuals

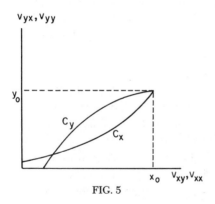

FIG. 5

(either survivors or inventory held back) along the two axes, Y's residuals along the ordinate and X's residuals along the abscissa, we can indicate prewar stocks by the point (x_o, y_o) as shown. Suppose that each side's forces consist solely of ICBM's.

Now imagine that X attacks Y. Side X can attack Y's missile force (strength y_o) with only one single missile, leaving himself with $v_{xx} = (x_o - 1)$, or with his entire force of x_o, leaving himself $v_{xx} = 0$; or X can attack with some number between 1 and x_o. The curve C_x shows how Y's number of surviving missiles varies with the intensity of X's attack. It is a technological fact (demonstrated later in this chapter) that each additional missile X shoots at Y causes less of a reduction in v_{yx}, Y's residual of survivors, than did the previous X-missile.[5] The shape and curvature of C_x and C_y derive from the fact that there is some probability that a missile will miss its target through misfire or inaccuracy. The curve C_x shows all the possible combinations of v_{xx} and v_{yx} open to X if he attacks when $x = x_o$ and $y = y_o$. Similarly, C_y shows the combinations of v_{xy} and v_{yy} open to Y if he attacks X first. The curves will be symmetric if $x_o = y_o$ and the two sides' missiles are qualitatively identical. These two curves, in brief, describe the technology available to side X and side Y in a missile war. The curves show respectively the highest destructions attainable by side X against Y's missile force if X strikes first and the highest destructions Y can attain against X's missile force if Y strikes first.

On the assumption that it is side X which attacks first concentrate on C_x of Fig. 5. First it should be noted that beginning at the point (x_o, y_o) the slope of C_x denotes the rate of exchange that side X must pay in sacrificing its own missile inventory to reduce the number of survivors on side Y. If it were the case that on each side missiles were positioned such that no single enemy attacking missile could possibly destroy more than one defending missile site, then the slope of the curve C_x could never exceed the value 1. Moreover, the slope of the curve C_x

---

[5] This assumes side X achieves complete surprise in the attack; furthermore, it assumes X has no trans-attack intelligence, that during the course of his attack he has no means of telling which of his missiles had, in fact, successfully destroyed the enemy's missile sites and which had not, that he is unable to fire some missiles, identify enemy survivors and shoot more at them. Side X must fire everything he fires at once, causing some enemy missiles to be "killed" more than once. Then the race for target intelligence begins.

reaches a *maximum* value at the point (x_o, y_o), and declines continuously as the curve approaches the ordinate.

That is, C_x and C_y show that from the point of view of the attacker, each additional enemy missile site destroyed is more expensive in terms of attacking missiles required for its destruction. In the language of economics, the marginal costs of destroying the enemy's strategic inventory are increasing as one expends greater numbers from one's own arsenal of missiles. It would seem that this technological fact finds realistic application beyond the simplified model of a missile duel described here. More specifically, the notion that an attacker must pay increasing marginal costs to destroy each additional unit of its adversary's military force would have general application according to an argument as follows: we have in fact a nonhomogeneous collection of strategic weapons. In particular, our inventory of strategic weapons is heterogeneous in its vulnerability to attack from enemy strategic systems. The same is true of the Soviet's. The Titan ICBM, the strategic bomber, the Minuteman Missile, and the Polaris submarine come to mind. If we assume that the attacker finds no particular disadvantage to targeting one system over the other—such as the collateral damage to population caused—then, in undertaking a first-strike, an enemy would target first the most vulnerable strategic weapons (or those with the largest warheads) and only later the least vulnerable strategic weapons (or the smallest). He would do this because such a strategy would allow him to achieve the highest destruction (to those victim's weapons which in turn can threaten him) for any given expenditure from his own strategic arsenal. He does this by foregoing the destruction of targets for which he should have to pay the highest price. As a result, for the level of abstraction dealt with here, the curve C_x is a plausible representation of side X's cost schedule for attacking side Y, under the assumption that side Y has a variety of types of strategic weapons which X should like to destroy.

The second point to be mentioned by way of a generalization of Fig. 5 is that the initial point labeled (x_o, y_o) need not be restrictively interpreted as showing pre-strike inventories alone. Indeed, the point (x_o, y_o) *can* be taken as characterizing the prewar strategic weapons inventories on either side, but it also can be taken as representative of the *residual* inventories existing on both sides at any point during the sequence of attack, counterattack, counter-counterattack, and so on. In other words, the technology of increasing marginal costs obtains whether we take as our starting point the initial prewar inventories or the residual inventories obtaining at intermediate points during the course of the counterforce war. Figure 6 is a diagrammatic illustration of this fact.

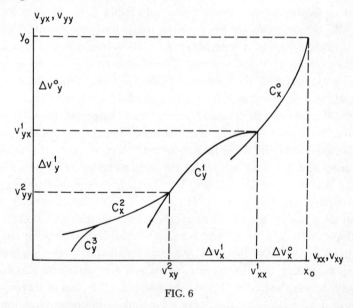

FIG. 6

In that figure the point (x_o, y_o) designates the initial prewar stocks of missiles on sides X and Y respectively. This illustrates the case in which X attacks first. With due regard for his position after attacking Y's missile sites, the decision-maker on side X decides to expend less than his total inventory, that is, less than x_o. In fact, the decision-maker for side X decides to expend $\Delta v_x{}^o$ in his initial attack against Y's missile sites. In doing so side X reduces side Y's inventory of missiles by $\Delta v_y{}^o$. Thus at the end of the first stage in the sequence, where side X has attacked and side Y has not yet responded, X possesses $v_{xx}{}^1$ of its own missiles remaining, and side Y has had all but $v_{yx}{}^1$ of its missiles destroyed. The force levels on each side at the end of the first stage in nuclear exchange are indicated by the point at those two coordinates. In proceeding from the initial prewar inventory to the inventories obtaining at the end of the first stage in the war, side X, as attacker, was constrained by a marginally increasing cost curve. We do not as yet offer any explanation for why side X decides to fire just $\Delta v_x{}^o$ of its own initial inventory in its first strike against side Y. That is, for the present, we do not state why side X fires just so many missiles, no more and no less. For purposes of argument and illustration simply assume that the situation at the end of X's initial attack is as indicated in the figure.

Now turn your attention to side Y. It is now Y's turn to attack, if it wishes. Being in possession of missiles in the amount $v_{yx}{}^1$, Y, is constrained by the curve labeled $C_y{}^1$. $C_y{}^1$ indicates that if it does attack, Y must pay increasing marginal costs for every additional of X's missiles which it destroys. Assume for the sake of illustration that side Y does in fact decide to counterattack by expending $\Delta v_y{}^1$ of the missiles it had remaining after the initial attack by X. In counterattacking against X's residual missiles with the indicated expenditure of its own missiles side Y can kill an additional $\Delta v_x{}^1$ of X's missiles. Thus, at the end of the second stage in this sequential war, the military strengths of each side are as at the point $(v_{xy}{}^2, v_{yy}{}^2)$.

Once again it is X's turn to counter-counterattack if it so wishes. In considering whether it should attack once again, X is constrained by the curve $C_x{}^2$. Similarly, if after a second attack by X, Y decides to fire back a second time, it is constrained by the curve $C_y{}^3$. Evidently the diagram can be extended for a fourth or fifth or further counterforce exchange—until the counterforce phase of the war terminates.

Determination of the Degree of Attack or Counterattack

We shall now try to explain how it is that one side having decided to attack the other, selects one particular level of counterforce attack, no more and no less. Restrict your attention to side X. How does X decide how many missiles to shoot if he attacks; that is, how does he select a point on the curve $C_x{}^o$?

The mechanism of this selection and its structure can be clarified by the introduction of a preference function, or diagrammatically of indifference curves. The indifference curve is a tool familiar to the economist. An indifference curve is defined as follows: all the points along any one of such curves have the property that they give rise to a single level or degree of utility. In comparing one indifference curve with another, it is always possible to recognize which has the higher degree of utility (it is in general not possible to attach a single meaningful quantity to that degree of utility). Many varieties of preference structure can be imagined. For illustration let us pause over three possibilities.

First, in considering attack, X may be interested solely in the absolute number of his victim's survivors—the lower that number the better. This type of preference function is shown in Fig. 7 as a set of straight parallel lines with utility increasing in the direction of the arrow. To reduce v_{yx} to as low a figure as possible and thereby achieve the most preferred position, X will shoot his entire arsenal, x_o.

Second, X may be only concerned with the ratio of his own to his victim's residuals—the higher that ratio the better. Figure 8

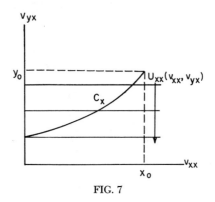

FIG. 7

shows such a preference function with utility increasing in the direction of the arrow. In this case X will not shoot his entire stock; he will only shoot $x_o - v_{xx}^o$, since this allows him to reach the highest ratio possible when starting from (x_o, y_o) and constrained by C_x.

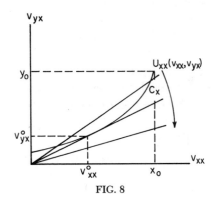

FIG. 8

Third, X may be interested in a combination of low v_{yx} and high v_{xx}/v_{yx}. Figure 9 shows such a utility function and the resulting selection of (v_{xx}^o, v_{yx}^o) by X.

The foregoing cases describe possible preferences of X when he ponders attacking Y. Continue to pay attention to X, but now

59

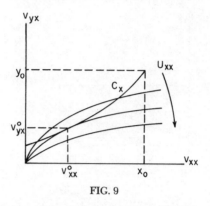

FIG. 9

imagine Y attacks. Side Y will choose one of the combinations (v_{xy}, v_{yy}) to which he is constrained by C_y of Fig. 5. Assume X knows Y's preferences, his technology, and therefore his best choice $(v_{xy}{}^o, v_{yy}{}^o)$ and let us ask why did X decide to buy x_o missiles in the first place. In choosing x_o, when confronted by y_o, side X in effect picked $v_{xy}{}^o$ potential survivors from potential attack. Side X's preferences for v_{xy} and v_{yy}, and therefore part of the explanation for how he happened to decide on x_o, again allow for three interesting cases.

First, X may be interested only in the value of $v_{xy}{}^o$, the absolute number of missiles he has surviving—the higher the better. Figure 10 shows a preference map consistent with this

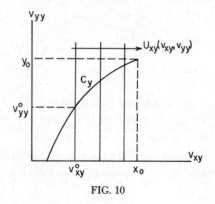

FIG. 10

60

assumption. Y picks a point on the constraining curve C_y, a point $(v_{xy}{}^o, v_{yy}{}^o)$ which maximizes utility (Y's indifference contours not shown). As a result X ends up with a utility, $U_{xy}{}^o$ corresponding to his indifference curve through that point.

Second, X may desire only a high v_{xy}/v_{yy} ratio. No diagram is given since the preference for pure ratios is shown by Fig. 8.

Third, X may want a combination of high v_{xy}/v_{yy} and high v_{xy}, as in Fig. 11.

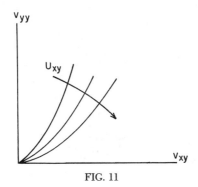

FIG. 11

These are three of many plausible directions which X's preferences could take if he attacks or if he is attacked. An exactly similar approach can provide a logical structure for analysis of Y's choice of missiles to be fired. Note that a side may display preferences of one sort when it ponders attack and of another sort when it considers being attacked. These preference functions, whatever their shape, summarize a great deal of information. They summarize a side's views on the general nature of future war. In particular, they contain a side's concept of the comparative value of relative and absolute strength. More specifically they indicate the extent to which a side expects a series of counterforce blows with bargaining preeminent or as an exercise in vengeance, retribution, and annihilation. The preference functions on both sides embody the connection between the counterforce and countervalue phases in the war.

61

Yet an attempt to devise realistic preference functions should draw us deep into a theory of war and the unexplored reaches of the theory of deterrence, of threat, of bargaining. We wish to avoid this. Ours is a study of the arms race. For the moment therefore we shall proceed with a technical analysis based upon preference functions selected for expository convenience—relegating to a footnote some preliminary considerations relevant to the determination of such preferences.[6] Later we shall truncate our theory of war by introducing a set of assumptions—assumptions that will generate an arms race and thereby allow us to advance to the body of our study.

[6] The first observation to be made here is that the two utility functions are interdependent. For consider the factors which contribute to a determination of $U_{xx}(v_{xx}, v_{yx})$, in particular the factors influencing the relative importance of ratios vis-a-vis absolute values. The weight given by X to v_{yx}, that is, the shape of the function, will be influenced by how X thinks Y would *use* the $v_{yx}{}^i$ he would have remaining. Side X could know what Y plans if he could observe Y's preference function $U_{yx}(v_{xx}, v_{yx})$ because Y's plan is reflected in the shape of this function. If Y's plan is to retaliate, then the absolute value of v_{yx} must count high therein, and if v_{yx} weighs heavily, Y plans to retaliate. If, on the contrary, the ratio v_{yx}/v_{xx} counts highly and the absolute values v_{yx} only slightly, then one should suppose Y plans to bargain and negotiate. What decides which alternative Y inclines toward? These two factors, at least, count: First, if $v_{xx}{}^i$ is large, Y should hesitate to strike back at X's cities since X still holds Y's population hostage; if $v_{xx}{}^i$ is low, this restraint is correspondingly diminished. Second, if the ratio $v_{xx}{}^i/v_{yx}{}^i$ is low, Y has less temptation to retaliate against cities, since he is in a superior bargaining position anyway. These two factors are sufficient to demonstrate interdependence between U_{xx} and U_{yx}. Others might be mentioned. If armed conflict is going on elsewhere and Y, the victim, is losing badly, he may be strongly tempted to retaliate against cities, industry, population, and so on, either because this may physically reduce X's war-making potential or because it may persuade X to negotiate a settlement. Or again the greater the collateral damage to Y's population, industry, and so on, caused by X's counterforce first strike, the more would Y be inclined to punition, and the less has Y to lose from a third, city targeted response from X, to his (that is, Y's) counter-city retaliatory second strike. These last two factors mentioned are exogenous to our model. The first two factors are endogenous.

We have reasoned, in effect, that $U_{xx}(v_{xx}, v_{yx})$, and therefore X's selection of (v_{xx}, v_{yx}) is dependent upon $U_{yx}(v_{xx}, v_{yx})$. In turn, U_{yx} depends on the (v_{xx}, v_{yx}) chosen by X. If now we were to call X the victim and Y the attacker, the exact same argument as above, with x and y interchanged, would apply—which is to say U_y depends on U_x and vice versa.

Counterforce Turn Taking

Having set forth the logic according to which a single side will select its own optimum level of counterforce attack or counterforce retaliation, we can now proceed to consider a sequence of decisions where each decision is a single optimized choice as just outlined. This demands that we question the extent to which one side foresees or anticipates the reaction of an adversary to its own actions. How, in consequence, and to what extent does the first side alter its behavior in order to take advantage of, profit by, or accommodate to this foreknowledge of its rival's reactions? For the moment and as a first step in the analysis, let us assume complete naïvete on the part of each side in the missile exchange. Assume that neither side anticipates the reactions of its rival. Each side simply attempts to maximize utility in the fashion explained in the foregoing paragraphs.

As an example of such a sequence of naïve utility-maximizing decisions, we turn for a simple illustration to an analysis of the case in which the utility functions of both sides are straight lines through the origin. That is, we assume that both sides are interested only in the ratio of own to enemy missile inventories existing at any point during the missile exchange. As the arrows in Fig. 12 indicate, it is further assumed that the utility functions of X and Y can be described by the identical set of straight lines through the origin, with utility increasing in a clockwise direction for side X and a counterclockwise direction for side Y.[7]

Let the initial stock of missiles be given as the point (x_o, y_o). Imagine that the prewar relation between the two sides is one of parity in numbers of missiles, that is, that the point (x_o, y_o)

[7] This particular assumption makes the counterforce duel a zero-sum game. It has been introduced however, not for this reason; but rather merely to simplify the geometry.

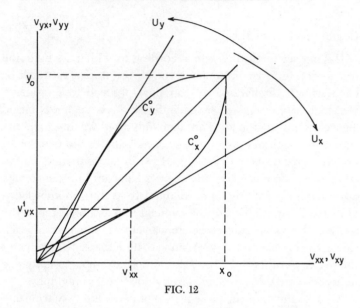

FIG. 12

lies along a straight, 45-degree line through the origin. Then the curves $C_x{}^o$ and $C_y{}^o$ show the combination of residuals on either side open to sides X and Y respectively if they undertake an initial counterforce strike. $C_x{}^o$ and $C_y{}^o$ show the technological constraints as initially allowing the attacker to destroy more than one enemy missile with one attacking missile. That is, at the point (x_o, y_o) the slope of $C_x{}^o$ is greater than 1, and the slope of $C_y{}^o$ is less than 1—with the result that the curves cross and reintersect closer to the origin. What is the outcome if side X attacks first? According to our assumption, side X enjoys no foresight. It therefore will simply compare the utility of all positions along the curve $C_x{}^o$. The highest utility attainable by X occurs at the point $(v_{xx}{}^1, v_{yx}{}^1)$. Side X will therefore fire missiles at side Y, proceeding along $C_x{}^o$ up to that point but not beyond.

Now turn your attention to side Y and to Fig. 13. Let us assume that the *shape* of side Y's technological constraint is independent

64

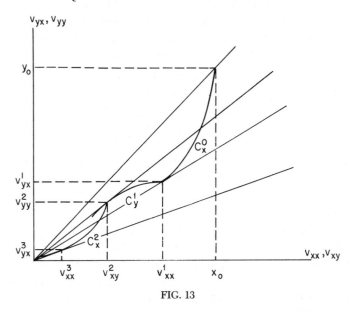

FIG. 13

of the initial inventory point. Consequently, the curve C_y^1 is a simple rigid translation of C_y^0.

This is probably a false assumption for two reasons. First, as stated previously, the attacker is likely to expend those weapons first in which he enjoys the highest comparative advantage over his enemy. For example, *ceteris paribus*, he will shoot his most vulnerable weapons early in the initial counterforce attack, thereby presenting his victim with relatively invulnerable targets when the victim contemplates counterforce retaliation.[8] In general he will attack so as to reduce the enemy opportunity for improving the ratio $v_{\text{enemy}}/v_{\text{own}}$ when the enemy retaliates. Second, if the attack serves to improve the ratio of forces in favor of the attacker—if in Fig. 13 $x_0/y_0 < v_{xx}^1/v_{yx}^1$—then

[8] Such a strategy demands some anticipation of enemy reaction on the part of the attacker, contrary to the immediately foregoing assumptions.

65

the victim must spread his retaliating forces more thinly over the remaining targets of the attacker when he strikes back.[9] The first of these tendencies will cause the curve $C_y{}^1$ to rotate counterclockwise such that the initial marginal costs to Y increase from (x_o, y_o) to $(v_{xx}{}^1, v_{yx}{}^1)$. Symbolically:

$$\frac{dC_y{}^1(v_{xx}{}^1)}{dv_{xx}} > \frac{dC_y{}^o(x_o)}{dv_{xx}}.$$

The second tendency has the opposite effect on $C_y{}^1$. Nevertheless it will be assumed here that the one cost curve is a rigid translation of the other. This assumption may exaggerate the extent of the sequence of counterforce exchanges.

The question to be settled next is whether starting from the point $(v_{xx}{}^1, v_{yx}{}^1)$ side Y in its turn will choose to expend some of its residual stock of missiles in order to reduce X's residual further. Without specific data the answer to this is indeterminant. The answer depends on the slope of C_y as compared to U_x at the point $(v_{xx}{}^1, v_{yx}{}^1)$. In Fig. 13 the slopes of the two curves at that point are such that side Y can indeed improve its utility by making a counterforce retaliation against side X. For the configuration of curves shown in Fig. 13, Y would maximize the utility available to it by choosing point $(v_{xy}{}^2, v_{yy}{}^2)$. Again it is X's turn to decide whether he wants to continue the counterforce battle from point $(v_{xy}{}^2, v_{yy}{}^2)$. Whether or not X decides to continue the battle depends upon the relative slopes of X's technological constraint and utility contour at the point $(v_{xy}{}^2, v_{yy}{}^2)$. The curves in Fig. 13 are drawn for the case in which X does wish to continue the battle and for a second time expends

---

[9] This suggests what is a simplifying assumption made throughout this chapter, namely that missiles are infinitely divisible such that ½ or ⅒ of a missile can be programmed for an enemy missile site. If we insist that missiles come in discrete units only, then the victim does not spread his retaliating missiles more "thinly"; he simply fires at a lower proportion of the attacker's sites when he retaliates or else doubles up his attackers against only a fraction of the attackers' sites. See p. 84.

missiles in reducing Y's residual inventory. X maximizes utility for the second time by choosing the point (v_{xx}^3, v_{yx}^3).

This example suggests the following conclusions: First, it is possible that a sequence of counterforce exchanges can extend over two or three or more cycles; and second, because of the sequential nature of the exchange, one side could in fact reduce to zero the residual inventory of the side of its opponent.

Now consider another example. Suppose the initial resource point (x_o, y_o) is as shown in Fig. 14. In Fig. 13 the two sides began with prewar inventories of equal magnitude; in Fig. 14 side X

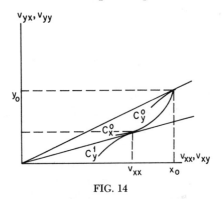

FIG. 14

begins with a substantial advantage. The advantage to X is so great, in fact, that subject to the assumptions of naïveté mentioned earlier, side Y never would initiate a first strike in the hope of improving the ratio of Y's to X's missiles at the end of the first round in the exchange. This is so because the shape of side Y's technological constraint will allow side Y only to achieve less preferred positions (utility below that obtaining at the point (x_o, y_o)) even if he attacks first. This is shown by $C_y{}^o$ in Fig. 14. A *fortiori* if X should take the initiative and strike first choosing the point (v_{xx}^1, v_{yx}^1), side Y could not thereafter improve its utility further. This is also shown in Fig. 14, where Y's technological constraint originating at the point $(v_{xx}{}^1, v_{yx}{}^1)$ also will allow Y to achieve only less preferred positions than what obtains at that point. This example shows that if the ratio of military forces between sides is the sole measure of the goodness of outcome of a sequential, turn-by-turn exchange of strategic weapons, then the best interests of the victim of a first-strike counterforce attack may lead that victim to refrain from counterforce retaliation. The greater the victim's prewar disadvantage in numbers or magnitude of strategic systems, the more vulnerable he is to counterforce attack in response to which in his own best interests he is constrained from retaliating. To the extent that our assumptions are realistic, the foregoing analysis supports the intuition that the greater a side's initial advantage the less need that side worry about losing its advantage either at the outset of a missile exchange or at any point during the course of a sequence of exchanges.

Let us extend the preceding analysis of the dynamics of turn-by-turn nuclear exchange to the case for which the preference functions of either side are other than straight lines through the origin. Further, we shall relax the simplifying assumption that the utility function of one side is a mirror image of the utility function of the other. This requires two indifference maps plotted on the same diagram, one expressing the preferences of side X and the other the preferences of side Y. Each point in the quadrant is then characterized first by the degree of utility available to each side at that point and second by the marginal rate of substitution between own and enemy survivors on the indifference curve of each side going through that point. Turn your attention to Fig. 15. That figure shows (1) an initial inventory point (x_0, y_0), (2) the trade-off schedule between own and enemy missiles which side Y should have to follow if, from the initial endowment of strategic forces, side Y were to strike X in a counterforce attack first, and (3) a set of utility contours for side Y. Let us now concentrate attention on the utility contours. In particular, note that at some point along each single

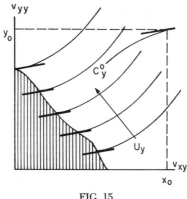

FIG. 15

indifference curve the marginal rate of substitution of own for enemy residual missiles is as shown with the heavy line in the figure. That line denotes the slope of the utility contour at that point. Observe further that all the slopes so marked with the heavy line, one along each utility contour, are of the same value, and that this value is the same as the slope of Y's technological constraint at (x_o, y_o). At these points the marginal rate of substitution of own for enemy survivors equals the initial marginal cost—at the beginning of any[10] attack by Y—which side Y must pay in terms of its own missile force to reduce the enemy missile force. It follows that if side Y should find itself situated at any point at which the marginal rate of substitution is as indicated by the heavy lines, then in further attacking or counterattacking against X's residual missile force, Y could only worsen its position or decrease its utility. Every such point has been connected by a line in Fig. 15, and the area beneath that line toward the origin has been shaded. From the foregoing it follows that if side Y should find itself within that shaded area after one or more reciprocal exchanges, then Y's

[10] Recall the assumption that $C_y{}^i$ whatever its starting point is of the same shape as $C_y{}^o$—$C_y{}^i$ being a rigid translation thereof.

69

most preferred course of action is to avoid continuing the exchange. If side X can manipulate Y into that area, then in doing so X will be assured of a stable outcome to the counterforce phase of the missile exchange. X knows that once inside that area side Y will refrain from further reactions. Exactly analogous opportunities are open to Y. This is shown in Fig. 16.

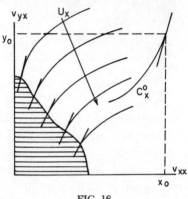

FIG. 16

The shaded area in Fig. 16 indicates all those combinations of residuals, after one or more reciprocal exchanges in the missile war, from which side X has no incentive to reinitiate further attack. The outermost border of the shaded areas in Figs. 15 and 16, therefore, might be considered as a barrier to further effective counterforce strikes in the sequential nuclear exchange. Figure 17 shows these two barriers and the two shaded areas beneath each on one diagram—with underlying indifference maps, initial endowments, and cost schedules eliminated for simplicity. The reader can observe that a portion of the area is doubly shaded. Within that area neither side X nor Y has incentive to further a counterforce missile exchange. Thus, the outermost boundary of that area is a line which, if reached, will signal the end of the missile duel. This is so since along that heavily lined boundary it is in the best interest of both sides, regard-

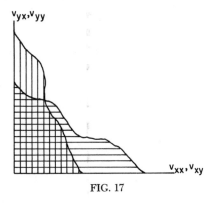

FIG. 17

less of the action of the other, to discontinue further attack or counterattack. It may occur to the reader to ask whether, in fact, such a boundary will exist and whether anything short of total destruction of one side's missile force by the other will signal an end to the missile exchange. In answer to such a question, it can only be stated that the existence or nonexistence of such a boundary depends upon the shapes of the two utility functions in question and upon the shapes of the two cost curves,[11] and upon the crucial assumption of *rationality*.

Let us continue our analysis of the course of reciprocal missile exchanges with one further complication. We wish to allow for the fact that one side, in evaluating a variety of actions or responses, may take into consideration the fact that his adversary in turn will respond to his own actions; that is, we now shall relax the assumption of complete naïvete and investigate how one side might turn to its own advantage its knowledge or expectation of the reaction of an adversary to its own acts. For ease of illustration, we revert to the case in which the indifference contours of either side are straight lines through

[11] If the counterforce game is zero-sum with a saddle point, one point on the boundary of Fig. 17 will result; if non-zero-sum then more than one point on the boundary is candidate for solution.

71

the origin. Again both sides have identical utility contours except for the order and magnitude of their numbering.

The next diagram is Fig. 18—to be used to explore and to illustrate how side X might anticipate the reaction of side Y to his, X's initial attack, and in doing so, improve his prospects throughout the course of the missile duel. Starting with initial

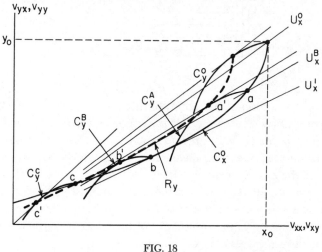

FIG. 18

strategic inventories of (x_0, y_0), the utility attainable by side X is that of the straight utility contour through the origin and the initial resource point. In Fig. 18 this utility is denoted as $U_x{}^0$. If side X were to be completely naïve and ignore the prospects of a retaliation on the part of his enemy to his own first strike, then in accordance with arguments of foregoing paragraphs he would continue to fire missiles until it reached the utility contour $U_x{}^1$. At the point of tangency between the straight line $U_x{}^1$ and the cost curve, side X maximizes its utility subject to the assumption that no further displacements from that point occur. But we now suppose that X has reason to believe that some further

72

displacement will occur from any initial stopping point which he, X, might select. In order to project the anticipated effects of this displacement, X must consider and evaluate all the possible reactions of Y to all of his own possible actions. He must evaluate those in the light of his own preference function and then pick the action which will lead to the reaction by side Y which maximizes his, that is, X's utility. The procedure for X to follow is illustrated in Fig. 18. Side X has the choice of stopping along his cost curve at any point. A number of such possible terminal points have been selected and labeled a, b, and c. From each such point the technological constraint to which side Y in its turn would be subjected is drawn. After X attacks, the option is open to Y to take its turn in the missile exchange and to move along its own technological constraint. Side Y will exercise this option and fire its own missiles in counterforce retaliation up to the point that maximizes its own utility. Corresponding to X's options, a, b, and c, are Y's "best" choices, a', b', and c'. (The graphics of the illustration have been considerably simplified by the assumption that the preference function of side X is the mirror image of Y's preference function—that both therefore can be represented by one set of straight lines through the origin.) Of course, Y will only optimize its own utility at a', b', c' . . . if it, unlike X, remains totally naïve.

The possible effects on side X of a totally naïve reaction on the part of Y to X's initial counterforce attack are summarized by the dotted line passing through all points a', b', c' . . . This is the naïve "reaction curve," as we shall call it, of side Y. It has been labeled R_y. If X looks no further than this initial naïve reaction by Y, the rational thing for X to do is to inspect all points along the curve R_y and to pick the one that allows X to reach the highest of its own utility contours. This is indicated in Fig. 18 by the point labeled b'. To attain $U_x{}^B$, X should proceed along $C_x{}^o$ to point b, Y will then follow $C_y{}^B$ to b'.

The process of anticipating actions and reactions need not stop here. X could carry his anticipations one step further. He could consider his own reaction to side Y's reaction to his own initial first strike. That is, side X can anticipate that he, X, will react in his own turn to side Y's naïve reaction to his own initial counterforce attack. This next step in the process of anticipating reactions is shown in Fig. 19. There the curves of Fig. 18 have

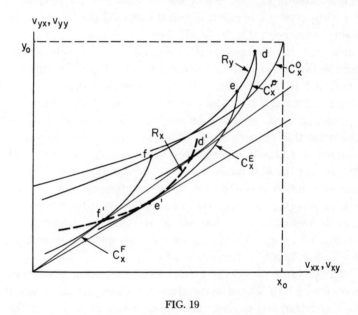

FIG. 19

been all surpressed but the reaction curve R_y and the initial cost curve applicable to X, C_x^o. The curve R_y again shows the optimal but naïve reaction of Y to a variety of levels of first attack by X. At each point on R_y side X again has the option of beginning a second round of missile exchanges, of undertaking a second counterforce attack. Therefore, from each point on the curve R_y, d, e, and f, for example, a cost curve according to which X must trade-off its own for enemy missiles can be drawn. Cost curves $C_x{}^D$, $C_x{}^E$, and $C_x{}^F$ are shown. Each of this family of cost curves in turn is tangent to one contour of X's utility function at some point (d', e', and f' shown). These points of tangency have been connected by the line labeled R_x. This line traces out the optimum responses by X to each of the optimum but naïve responses of side Y—responses derived in turn from each of the possible initial attacks by X. If X carries all his calculations this far, he can optimize his utility at the end of the third round in the missile exchange by choosing the point labeled e'. Let it be observed that to achieve point e' and the corresponding utility, side X in all likelihood should have to select a different level of attack on its initial strike from that implied by point b' of Fig. 18.

It now may be useful to mention several further extensions of this type of analysis without going into detailed examples. First, it seems clear that the progression from Fig. 18 to Fig. 19 can be continued indefinitely, subject to the assumption that side Y reacts in a naïve fashion. The foregoing paragraph develops tools for analysis capable of describing the outcome of ever greater foresight by X. Next, it seems that this type of analysis can allow for slightly different behavioral assumptions with regard to side Y. For example, one might suppose that Y is not naïve. Viewing the situation from the point of view of side X, we could suppose that X credits Y with foresight one stage in advance—that is, we can suppose that X credits Y with the sort of foresight of which Fig. 18 was an example. X could then analyze the behavior of Y under the assumption that Y believes X to be naïve although X is in fact sophisticated. In doing this, side X should have to consider all possible levels of first attack against Y. At each of these levels of attack he then would analyze the reactions of side Y. As Y attempts to anticipate the reactions of X whom he, Y, believes to be naïve, Y will pick the optimum utility available to him under the assumption that X remains naïve. Of these optima, side X in turn can select the one which is most favorable to him. This sort of analytical procedure therefore can provide X with information as to whether or not he should attempt to persuade Y that he, X, is naïve or sophisticated.

POTENTIAL WAR AS PROBABLE RETALIATION: SIMPLIFICATIONS FOR THE STUDY OF ARMS RACES

Our theory of war, being, as it is, only a side-calculation for the greater problem of the arms race, has become somewhat complex. For the purposes of this study, we now propose to reduce the complexity by making a number of simplifying assumptions. While we shall thereby leave unexplored important and interesting trade-offs as they exist in reality, our heuristic purpose —to explore the arms race as a series of interacting economic decisions—will be advanced.

We shall therefore eliminate all but a few of such trade-offs by a list of assumptions. It is to be emphasized that an exhaustive description should have to include all variables. The assumptions are as follows:

(1) If X attacks Y, his resulting utility is expressed as U_{xx}^{i}. This index $U_{xx}^{i} = U_x(v_{xx}^{i}, v_{yx}^{i})$ may be interpreted as containing and combining the satisfactions (positive and negative) which X derives from (a) the damage to X's society (as *foreseen* by X) from Y's retaliation—possibly a probability of retaliation times disutility of being retaliated upon; (b) the improvement or deterioration in X's bargaining position vis-a-vis Y (as X foresees it); and (c) the damage to Y's society. Still this determination alone will not explain a decision on the part of X to attack. This can be done only by introducing X's utility before he

attacks (if he should) for comparison.[12] Imagine X's pre-attack utility—call it "$U_x{}^o$"—is well in excess of $U_x{}^i$; X is happy, and to attack Y would only make him less so. Now suppose X is gravely threatened or provoked by Y. Two cases merit consideration. Side Y may present X with a *fait accompli*, an irreversible loss in utility. Then $U_x{}^o$ will fall, and X might reckon that by deliberately attacking Y with complete surprise he could improve his position, that is, achieve $U_x{}^i > U_x{}^o$. Secondly, Y may initiate a course of action which if completed will prove harmful to X. Side X may attack to reverse the action or forestall its completion. Again X's decision is contingent upon $U_x{}^i > U_x{}^o$.

(2) When a side attacks, it will retain some fraction of its initial stock of missiles in reserve for post-attack bargaining. This fraction is independent of the size of the initial inventory. This assumption provides the victim with a motive for bargaining rather than retaliating. The assumption further eliminates the apparent anomaly which would arise if no missiles were held back by the attacker such that the side to strike first would completely disarm itself, only partially disarm the victim, and, in so doing, presumably would lose the war. The situation in which all missiles are fired—when the fraction withheld is zero—may be considered a limiting case. In subsequent chapters, when no difference in principle arises from imagining the fraction withheld to be negligible, and when an explanation can be simplified by supposing so, we shall make that assumption.

(3) When a side is the victim of a counterforce attack, it *may* respond by retaliating against the cities of the attacker with all the surviving missiles at its disposal. This is the chance that the

---

[12] Side X might attack, of course, because he thinks Y is about to attack him. But this merely removes the question one step to: "Why would X think Y would attack?"—which includes as a subquestion: "Why would Y attack?" We are concerned with explaining why a side might deliberately decide to attack from "aggressive," not "self-defensive," motives.

victim will be irrational in his response to attack, that in short, he will lose control. *There is some probability that the victim will lose control, become irrational, and retaliate upon the attacker's cities. This probability is known by both victim and attacker and is assumed to remain constant for the purposes of this model.* These assumptions imply that if X attacks, both X's and Y's utility indices $U_{xx}{}^i$ and $U_{yx}{}^i$ can be measured by $v_{yx}{}^i$ alone (for each fixed (x_o, y_o)).[13]

Within the context of these simplifying assumptions what is the value of possessing missiles? Imagine that along with the arms race a cold war is in progress. Each side threatens, provokes, challenges, and subverts the other. A successful challenge promises the challenger an increase in prewar utility, and the challenged a decrease in utility (pre-attack). The potential loser of the challenge inspects his own utility index, comparing its level if he accepts the cold-war loss to its level if he attacks. If the challenger—say, Y (that is the potential victim of an attack from the party challenged, X)—would have a high number of missiles surviving X's attack, then X will conclude it is preferable to accept the loss and not attack. An attack against Y would only further reduce X's utility through the probability-of-retaliation-times-disutility-of-retaliation-if-it-comes mechanism. If, to the contrary, Y would have a low v_{yx} such that $U_x{}^o <$ $U_x{}^i$, then X would attack in response to Y's provocation. Therefore the higher the number of potential survivors Y has, the more successfully he can provoke X. It is probably fair to assume that as the expected intensity of retaliation by Y increases, X's potential disutility increases but at a decreasing rate. This articulates the idea that while one may see a terrific difference between

[13] That is, since the probability of massive, countercity retaliation is fixed by the above assumption, prospects for bargaining—and hence the significance of ratios of own to enemy residual weapons—do not enter into the evaluation of U_{xx} or U_{yx}. The model is driven by the magnitude of retaliation, that is, by v_{yx} if X attacks, and by v_{xy} if Y attacks.

having 1 and 21 cities obliterated, if the difference is between 200 and 220 cities, one is less discriminating. Therefore, similarly the utility to Y of securing greater numbers of surviving missiles—a utility measured by the extent of successful provocation short of war—is an increasing function with a decreasing first derivative,[14] as for example in Fig. 20. In a similar manner

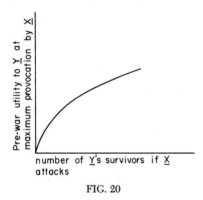

FIG. 20

the larger the number of X's survivors if Y should attack, the more provocative can X be without risking a deliberate attack by Y. In short, the deterrent value of a side's missile inventory in our model is that it allows the deterrer to be provocative in the cold war. At the same time a missile inventory is potentially an attacking force. The attacker, by reducing the number of the adversary's surviving missiles, will force his potential victim to be *less* provocative. In summary, an increase in a missile inventory: (1) as a deterrent, allows its possessor to be more provocative, and (2) as a potential for striking first, forces the adversary to be less so.

Again, what the preceding assumptions and interpretations in effect accomplish is to reduce the number of variables

[14] In effect this assumes the cold war, mutual provocation game is constant sum, *so long as war does not break out.*

affecting the utilities and therefore decision processes of both rivals. Side X should want to keep v_{xy} above some minimum level, and Y to keep v_{yx} above some minimum. At the same time X benefits from a low v_{yx}, and Y from a low v_{xy}. *Missiles are fabricated and installed, weapons and vehicles are tested, and secrecy is imposed for the effect upon these two desiderata: (1) ability to attack successfully thereby forcing a rival to be docile, (2) ability to deter thereby allowing one's self to be provocative.* It is a well-known feature of the present arms race that these two goals may conflict; both nevertheless are desired.[15]

The Role of Risk in the Model

This account should have completed our theory of potential war as a scaffolding from which to inspect the arms competition were it not for the technical fact central to a missile exchange which forms the basis of the next section. That fact is that v_{xy} or v_{yx} cannot be predicted as unique numbers; they can only be predicted as probability distributions. In truth, the number of missiles, $v_{xy}{}^o$, X would have surviving if his inventory, x_o in size, were attacked by y_o of Y's missiles, follows a binominal distribution. Therefore $v_{xy}{}^o$ can take on any value from 0 to x^o with a probability. Consequently, even with perfect knowledge on either side, risk is inherent. This will require some small modification of the theory outlined to this point.

We shall assume each side to be "conservative"—or as having an aversion to risk. Side X, as deterrer, now insists upon a

[15] Our entire model of the arms race hinges upon the assumption that a side desires to increase its own z and to decrease its enemy's value of z. By introducing a set of assumptions we have in effect rigged our model of a missile war to generate this conclusion. This gives our arms race model the character of a first approximation, and the reader should interpret it as such. An argument can be made, however, to the effect that in the context of recent history—of preoccupation with all out attack and all out response—our naïve index of the value of strategic forces (that is, the residuals on either side from all out attack) is of descriptive merit.

$v_{xy}{}^o$ and a low probability that $v_{xy}{}^o$ will fall below that figure. Side X's aversion to risk can be explained as follows: if Y attacks (with counterforce targeting), collateral damage to X is substantial; nevertheless X plays the game of mutual provocation. But X is not sure of Y's utility function; for all X knows, Y may be reckless. Therefore X feels it necessary to promise Y that if Y attacks, and if X in return chooses to retaliate (with countervalue targeting), Y can be 90-percent sure (or any high confidence) he will at least suffer the damage from $v_{xy}{}^o$. Now consider Y's point of view, Y the attacker. There appear to be two plausible approaches for Y to take. First, Y may be a risk averter. When Y compares the loss in utility from losing X's cold-war challenge with the loss from X's, k-percent probable retaliation against his cities, he may wish to be very confident (say 90 percent, for example) that X's retaliatory blow, if it comes, is not beyond some intensity. If this is so, Y will then think of the pay-off from his missile inventory as the reduction in survivors he can impose upon X with high assurance that *no more* than this number will survive.[16] (Side X is interested in having *no less* than some number survive.) In the remainder of this study, it will be assumed that both X and Y are risk averters in this sense.

The reader should note, however, that other possibilities exist. For example, Y may observe that X is a risk averter. Side

---

[16] Reducing an opponent's confidence he can deter may make him less provocative, but it may also provide him with a motive for preemptive attack—especially if the rules of the game as outlined here are imperfectly understood or agreed upon. Whether in fact it is advantageous or disadvantageous to so reduce an opponent's confidence depends on whether the enemy's motive to attack is considered profit-oriented (that is, oriented toward cold-war gains) or self-defensive (that is, preemptive in response to an imminent attack). The self-defensive motive (so defined) does not figure in this model. In fact, which of these motives is paramount will be strongly influenced by the relative destruction to one's society arising from (1) collateral damage when one is the victim of the enemy counterforce attack, compared to (2) the damage arising from an enemy retaliation against one's cities following one's own first (preemptive) attack against his missiles.

Y can then take advantage of this knowledge by putting on the appearance of recklessness. Side X then will be reinforced in his risk aversion, and Y can impose greater docility on X by lowering the *minimum number of missiles that X is highly confident will survive Y's attack*. This is cheaper in terms of y missiles required than lowering the *maximum number Y can be highly confident will survive*. This covers one case, Y's taking advantage of X's aversion to risk by appearing reckless. It can work in reverse as well.[17] The potential victim may, by giving the pre-

[17] It is more plausible to assume the potential attacker will be reckless, since he has much to gain from it and little to gain in terms of post-attack utility from being conservative. This is shown in Fig. 21. On the abscissa is plotted the number of

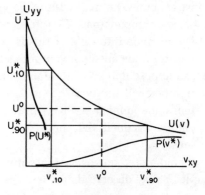

FIG. 21

missiles the victim of a counterforce attack has surviving. The ordinate represents the utility accruing to the attacker if the victim fires all his surviving missiles in retaliation against the attacker's cities. The curve $U(v)$ shows the attacker's marginally decreasing loss in utility from $\overline{U}$ (after the attack but before retaliation) as a function of number of retaliating missiles. The curve $P(v^*)$, with its own scale now shows the cumulative probability that $v \leq v^*$. The curve $P(v^*)$ is symmetric about v^o, the value which v is equally likely to surpass or fall short of. The curve $P(U^*)$ then shows the corresponding cumulative distribution on U. Now consider two points on the curves $P(v^*)$ and $P(U^*)$. The value v_{10}^* indicates the minimum number of survivors that the victim is assured will survive a counterforce attack with only 10 percent chance of failure. In other words, the victim (say, X) knows tense of recklessness, force Y to be "conservative." Again, the assumption of this study will be that both are risk averters, which is to say we disregard these two possibilities.

TECHNOLOGICAL PREREQUISITES

Among the reasons for choosing a missile exchange model for this study of the arms race is that quantitative relations can be precisely specified. Relatively simple mathematical relations exist among the variables, x, y, v_{xy}, v_{yx}. The previous chapter has discussed how v_{xy} and v_{yx} can contribute to national objectives. We can only get at the costs of achieving those objectives by relating (v_{xy}, v_{yx}) to (x, y), and we do need to get at the costs to have an economic model. The purpose of this chapter is to specify the cost schedules by examining the relations among the four variables.

For notational simplicity we shall now drop the second subscript on the v's, since no ambiguity arises, and the reader must remember when we refer to one side as surviving that the other is assumed to be the potential attacker. Furthermore, to simplify the analysis we make the following asumptions:

(1) Both sides position their missiles such that no more than one can be destroyed by a single attacker.

---

that if Y attacks his x_o missiles with y_o of Y's missiles, nine times out of ten he, X, will have more than $v_{10}*$ surviving. Therefore both attacker and attacked would know that, nine times out of ten, Y's utility will fall below $U_{10}*$. By similar reasoning $v_{90}*$ and $U_{90}*$ indicate that only one time out of ten will X's survivors exceed and Y's resulting utility fall below those figures. Suppose, as we have said, Y is conservative; he therefore, in considering an attack, takes $U_{90}*$ as a measure of his utility if he attacks X. But for every increase in risk Y assumes, he is rewarded by a greater increase in utility. For X, the victim, the case is the reverse. For every decrease in utility to Y, he must pay with increasing loss in confidence. Therefore, unless Y has a much greater aversion to risk than X, it is reasonable to suppose Y will accept a lower confidence (of success) level than X.

(2) An attacked missile is either destroyed or it survives. No missiles are only damaged to be repaired later.

(3) The missiles of either side are identical in range, accuracy, yield of warhead, and reliability.

(4) An attacker will target the defender's missiles so as to minimize expected survivors.

(5) The attacking side achieves complete surprise. None of the victim's missiles escapes damage by virtue of being fired back in retaliation (counterforce or counter-city) before the attacker's missiles arrive. The victim "rides out" the attack.

(6) All the attacker's incoming missiles that is, 100a percent) must be launched before the attacker can reconnoiter to discover which of the victim's missiles have survived.

(7) No re-cycle capability is allowed. Those missiles of the attacker that fail at launch or in flight are deemed out of use. No re-programming is allowed. The attacker cannot replace those missiles that fail at launch or in flight with other missiles programmed for the same target.

The fourth assumption implies that the attacker target each of the defender's missile sites with an equal number of missiles, such that for all defending sites, the probability that the site will survive is the same. This targeting strategy both minimizes expected survivors and minimizes the probability that any given number of defender's sites will survive. Such a targeting scheme is impossible insofar as it implies that fractions of attacking missiles are programmed for each defending site. The error resulting from such an assumption is an overestimate of the number of defenders destroyed.[18] The error is more serious if the ratio of attacking to defending missiles is less than one. However, the continuity assumption seems a decent approximation. It will simplify our formulae; it is susceptible to correction later.

---

[18] Glenn A. Kent, *On the Interaction of Opposing Forces under Possible Arms Agreements*, Occasional Papers in International Affairs, no. 5 (March 1963), Center for International Affairs, Harvard University, p. 32.

The rest of this chapter is largely algebraic. We shall conclude this section therefore with a diagrammatic preview for the reader less interested in mathematical proof than in the general outline of the study.

We can refer to the variables x and y as "costs," or to z_x and z_y as "returns" since, as in the economic analogy of production, so in our model, costs are incurred for the returns they generate. As explained on p. 81, z_x is defined as the maximum or minimum value of v_x—whichever is appropriate—with a high assurance of success; and similarly for z_y and v_y. We shall illustrate the cost-return relations of side Y; they are exactly symmetrical for side X.

Suppose side X has a fixed stock of missiles, of size x_i. Then as side Y increases its stock of missiles, that is, incurs costs, measured by the magnitude of y, two things happen:

(1) The number of Y's *own missiles* to survive with a high assurance increases. Figure 22 shows this relation. As z_y increases y must increase, but at an ever decreasing rate. In other words, marginal costs of increasing the deterrent fall with such increases.

(2) The number of X's *missiles* that side Y is highly assured

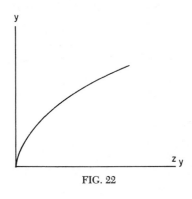

FIG. 22

85

will be *killed* rises, and correspondingly numbers of x_i surviving decline. As shown in Fig. 23 the marginal costs in terms of y are increasing.

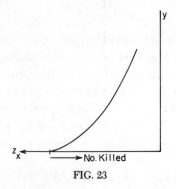

FIG. 23

In summary the marginal costs of increasing one's own deterrent power decline with greater own-stocks, while the marginal costs of decreasing an adversary's ability to retaliate against one's self mount.

The Mathematics of a Missile Duel[19]

First Approximation. Our simplifications of the real situation allow us to represent the missile-exchange relations in a model in which the result of a first strike by one side is *the outcome of a number of independent trials.* Let us restrict our attention to side Y as defender, and side X as attacker. At each of Y's sites, y in number, there is some probability, r, that that site will survive the attack by its share of the missiles which X actually shoots. Remember that X spreads his attackers equally over y targets. In this first approximation we assume arbitrarily that r is constant (see the second and third approximations for greater

[19] Robert D. Bower, "Fundamental Equations of Force Survival," *Air University Quarterly* 10: 82–92 (Spring 1958), provides the basis for the initial relations in this section.

realism). Then the number of survivors out of the total y sites follows a binomial distribution:

$$p(v_y) = \binom{y}{v_y} r^{v_y}(1 - r)^{y-v_y}, \tag{4}$$

with mean yr, and variance $yr(1 - r)$. If the values of y and v_y are fairly large, the distribution can be approximated by the normal curve. In particular, the probability that less than some value z_y survive is approximated by

$$P(v_y \leq z_y) \doteq \frac{1}{\sqrt{2\pi}} \int_{-\infty}^{t_\alpha} e^{-t^2/2} \, dt, \tag{5}$$

where $t_\alpha \equiv (z_y - yr)/[yr(1 - r)]^{1/2}$. Here, z_y is to be interpreted as the smallest number of surviving missiles the defender figures (in the way described earlier) he must have in order to retaliate and thereby deter attack. The value of $1\text{-}P$ denotes the confidence with which the defender can expect at least z_y or more to survive. Earlier we assumed that Y wishes to maintain some low value of P for whatever value of z_y is selected, since P represents the probability that Y will be *unable* to retaliate with sufficient force. If side Y operates under the assumption that the value of r is fixed, regardless of its own choices, then Y has available to it only a choice of y, the number of its own missiles to install. By increasing y, the same value of z_y is attained at a lower value of P, or a higher value of z_y at the same probability.

Second Approximation. The foregoing can now be elaborated to account for the fact that the value of r, probability of survival of a single defender's missile, depends upon the numbers of missiles on both sides. Denote by $(1 - s)$ the probability that a single of Y's sites will be destroyed when side X programs a single missile for that site. Within the value of $(1 - s)$ are collapsed the following factors: the probability that X's missile will fail before impact; the yield and accuracy of X's missiles; the vulnerability to blast of Y's missile site. Denote by the letter

87

a the fraction of X's total inventory of x missiles which X actually shoots. Thus X shoots ax missiles.

Then the probability that Y's site survives the attack by a single missile is given as s. If X programs two missiles for one of Y's sites the probability of survival is s^2. In general if X spreads its attackers evenly over Y's defenders, the probability of survival at any one of those sites is

$$r = s^{ax/y}. \tag{6}$$

All factors influencing this probability are collapsed into s, except numbers of missiles on each side. The probability that less than some minimum number survive, z_y, is approximated now by:

$$P(v_y \leq z_y) \doteq \frac{1}{\sqrt{2\pi}} \int_{-\infty}^{t_\alpha} e^{-t^2/2} \, dt, \tag{7}$$

where now $t_\alpha \equiv (z_y - ys^{ax/y})/[ys^{ax/y}(1 - s^{ax/y})]^{1/2}$.

As before, side Y is supposed to desire some small value of P for its choice of z_y. The formula indicates that for given s and x each possible choice of y allows for different trade-offs between z_y and P. By increasing y a lower probability is attainable with the same z_y, or a higher z_y with the same P. The effect is more pronounced than in the first approximation because of the appearance of y in the exponent.

Third Approximation. It remains to account for the remaining variables heretofore subsumed in the value of s. In this paragraph the influence of yield, accuracy, and hardness of defending missile sites is explicitly allowed for. We begin with notation:

W, yield of attacking missiles warhead in megatons;
C, accuracy of the attacking missile (circular error probable: the radius within which 50 percent of the missiles will impact) in thousands of feet;

K, vulnerability of the defender's site, the maximum distance at which a 1-megaton attacker will destroy the target.

Then it is known that s, the probability of survival of a single site attacked by one missile, is

$$s = 0.5^{W^2\ ^3K^2/C^2} \tag{8}$$

and

$$r = 0.5^{axW^2/3K^2/C^2y}. \tag{9}$$

The probability that less than some z_y survive is

$$P(v_y \leq z_y) \doteq \frac{1}{\sqrt{2\pi}} \int_{-\infty}^{t_\alpha} e^{-t^2/2}\ dt, \tag{10}$$

where this time

$$t_\alpha \equiv \frac{z_y - y(0.5)^{axW^2/3K^2/C^2y}}{[y(0.5^{axW^2/3K^2/C^2y})(1 - 0.5^{axW^2/3K^2/C^2y})]^{1/2}}.$$

For any combination of (W, K, C) side Y as before controls the choices between z_y and P by selecting various values of y.

The Cost Schedules in the Missile Duel

The Costs of z_y: Own Survivors from Enemy Attack. In each of three representations of the missile-survival equations considered above, side Y is taken as paying a cost, y, to obtain some number of missiles surviving with a specified probability. This section examines this cost as a function of z_y given a probability, α. As explained earlier we *assume* a side is concerned only with one fixed confidence limit, α. The z_y secured is always measured with reference to that value of α.

If one assumes the unit money costs of Y's missiles are constant, then the relations developed will represent resource allocations necessary to secure $(z_y | \alpha)$. *Whenever the term z_y*

henceforth appears, it should be interpreted as $z_y | \alpha$. To avoid notational clutter we shall omit the probability "α," leaving it to the reader to supply it mentally.

First Approximation. For any fixed $P(v_y \leq z_y) = \alpha$, the upper limit of the standardized normal integral is fixed, call it t_α. For a low probability of failure t_α is negative:

$$t_\alpha = \frac{z_y - yr}{[yr(1 - r)]^{1/2}} < 0. \tag{11}$$

Therefore

$$z_y = t_\alpha[yr(1 - r)]^{1/2} + yr \tag{12}$$

and

$$\frac{dz_y}{dy} = \frac{t_\alpha[r(1 - r)]^{1/2}}{2y^{1/2}} + r. \tag{13}$$

Thus, as pictured in Fig. 24, marginal costs of z_y in terms of y are constantly decreasing and asymptotic to the value $1/r$; or put otherwise, marginal product z_y, in terms of y is increasing and asymptotic to r. In Fig. 24 $r_1 < r_2 < r_3$. Figure 24 may be viewed as portraying costs under an assumption that the enemy reacts in a special way to increases in one's own missile force.

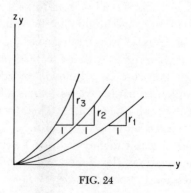

FIG. 24

In short, if X matches Y in a constant ratio—with $s^{ax/y} = r$ therefore constant—increases in deterrence are obtainable at decreasing marginal costs.

Second Approximation. If it is now allowed that s, x, and y enter explicitly into the formulation and assuming as before continuous rather than integer programming, then from Eq. 7 the upper limit of the integral is:

$$t_\alpha = \frac{z_y - ys^{ax/y}}{[ys^{ax/y}(1 - s^{ax/y})]^{1/2}} < 0 \tag{14}$$

or

$$z_y = t_\alpha[ys^{ax/y}(1 - s^{ax/y})]^{1/2} + ys^{ax/y}, \tag{15}$$

and

$$\lim_{y \to \infty} \frac{dz_y}{dy} = 1. \tag{16}$$

That is, under the assumption the adversary does nothing in response to increases in y, such increases "buy" increasing increments in z_y, as shown in Fig. 25, where each slope is asymptotic to 1, and $(s^x)_1 < (s^x)_2 < (s^x)_3$.

Third Approximation. Evidently if the s in Eq. 15 is expanded to

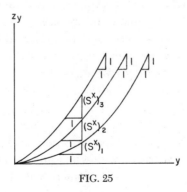

FIG. 25

account explicitly for the variables, yield, hardness, and accuracy, and these are assumed fixed, the costs of z_y will follow the same pattern as in the foregoing figure. But to increase z_y side Y now has open the alternative of hardening its missile sites rather than adding new ones. From Eqs. 9 and 11,

$$z_y = t_a[y0.5^{axW^{2/3}K^2/C^2y}(1 - 0.5^{axW^{2/3}K^2/C^2y}]^{1/2}$$
$$+ y0.5^{axW^{2/3}K^2/C^2y}. \quad (17)$$

Larger values of K indicate more vulnerable missile sites. As shown in Fig. 26 decreases in K buy increasing increments of z_y for fixed values of y.

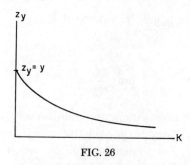

FIG. 26

Costs of z_x: Enemy Survivors from Our Attack. It was stated once (see pp. 76–80 for a complete discussion) that in addition to a capability to deter, expressed as a value of z_y, side Y might also want to be able to intimidate, threaten, or perhaps attack side X, and that this could be achieved by building so many y missiles that the number, z_x, which X could be assured would survive an attack by Y would fall below the level at which Y is deterred by X. $z_x | \alpha$ indicates the minimum number of survivors on side X from a surprise attack by Y, and the associated probability of failure. Earlier we stated it as an assumption about a potential attacker that he would seek to reduce the *maximum* enemy survivors with a low probability of failure. In our terminology a 10-percent chance that the maximum of

$v_x > z_x$, is a 90-percent chance that the minimum of $v_x < z_x$. Therefore side Y as attacker seeks something like $(z_x | 0.90)$. Side Y can reduce the numbers z_x in a variety of ways. The most obvious of course is simply to build more missiles. Alternatively, Y can increase the accuracy and/or warhead yield of its weapons. The relation is given by Eqs. 8 and 14; now, however, it is Y who can only fire $100a$ percent of his initial stock of y. Therefore:

$$0 < t_\alpha = \frac{z_x - xs^{ay/x}}{[xs^{ay/x}(1 - s^{ay/x})]^{1/2}}; \; s = 0.5^{W^{2/3}K^2/C^2}. \tag{18}$$

or

$$z_x = t_\alpha[xs^{ay/x}(1 - s^{ay/x})]^{1/2} + xs^{ay/x}. \tag{19}$$

It turns out that,

$$\lim_{y \to \infty} \frac{dz_x}{dy} = 0. \tag{20}$$

It can be demonstrated that if a *reduction* in z_x is taken as a return, and an increase in y, W or $1/C$ is taken as a cost, then as z_x varies from a maximum $(z_x = x)$ to $(z_x = 0)$, marginal costs are continuously increasing as pictured in Fig. 27. To repeat, we have assumed that a potential attacker, X, seeks a high value of α in $z_x | \alpha$; such as $z_x | 0.90$.

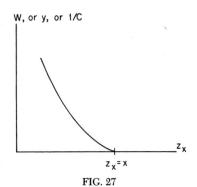

W, or y, or 1/C

z_x

$z_x = x$

FIG. 27

III · THE CHOICE OF ARMAMENTS:
AN ECONOMIC DECISION

Strategic forces cost money; they are a drain both on the limited defense budget, and upon the national economy as a whole. The decision on the quantity and quality of missiles to build is therefore an economic one; it is a decision to allocate limited resources among competing ends. An arms race is correctly thought of as a sequence of such decisions by one side and then the other. The first elements of a theory to describe these decisions have been set forth in Chapter II. The purpose of this chapter is to formulate the logic of these basic decisions. This will be done by combining the two elements of the preceding chapter. Specifically, a theoretical structure is required to describe the single decision by one side as to how large and what type of force to build when all other factors and, in particular, the adversary's forces are held constant. In the following account side Y is taken as the side deciding while X (for reasons to be explained later) makes no changes in its forces.

Following the argument of Chapter II it is assumed that nation Y's motives for building missiles, whether fixed or mobile, land or sea launched, surface or sub-surface launched, and all other related systems can be summarized by (1) the desire for a high retaliatory capability of one's own and (2) a low retaliatory capability for one's adversary. These two desiderata are attained by Y to the extent z_y is high and z_x is low; and Y's procurement of missiles both will raise z_y and lower z_x simultaneously. Chapter II has shown how increases in y lower z_x and raise z_y.

94

How does Y decide how many missiles to procure? Imagine that in arriving at an answer to this, the decision-maker for side Y telescopes time into a single instant. He foresees all future national income of his country and all future cost streams attributable to each missile he decides to procure; he foresees all future accretions to his utility from z_y and z_x. Let the decision-maker discount all these costs and returns to the present.[1] He then will continue to allocate money to increase numbers, yields, accuracies, and reliabilities and to decrease the vulnerabilities of his own missiles until the last addition to his utility arising from higher z_y and lower z_x just equals the utility lost in parting with that last dollar. At this point, he will refrain (1) from changing his total expenditures on the arms race and (2) from altering the particular number-yield-accuracy-reliability-vulnerability combination chosen, since to do so could only lower his over-all utility. The remainder of the chapter is devoted to illustrating the application of this rule and to developing its implications.

The principles involved in making the decision on size and composition of forces can be retained and the exposition simplified by making the following assumptions:

(1) For a missile of given yield, accuracy, vulnerability, and reliability, the unit costs are constant. This allows us to count money in units of missiles, and thereby to avoid a separate cost of fabrication (maintenance, replacement and so on) when measuring the drain of a missile force on national resources.

(2) The total national utility is determined by z_y, z_x and

---

[1] Our model is timeless, or in the argot of economics, "comparative static." The model does not address such problems as inventory optimization, maintenance, replacement, and obsolescence, and optimum patterns for phasing systems in and out of the arsenal. For purpose of analysis the decision-maker is assumed to have this information in foreseeing future cost streams. For heuristic purposes we assume that when this has all been calculated, it turns out that the average unit cost of a missile is constant.

national income or wealth. This allows us to write the national utility function as

$$U(z_y, z_x, \hat{y}), \tag{21}$$

where $\hat{y}$ is the amount of *wealth retained* after y missiles are procured. We shall now further assume that the contribution of each component in utility is independent of the values of the others. That is,

$$U(z_y, z_x, \hat{y}) = f(\hat{y}) + g(z_y) + h(z_x). \tag{22}$$

(3) Lastly, we shall assume, as suggested in Chapter II, that the marginal utility of z_y to Y is positive and decreasing, that is,

$$\frac{\partial U}{\partial z_y} > 0, \frac{\partial^2 U}{\partial z_y{}^2} < 0; \tag{23}$$

that the marginal utility of z_x is negative and increasing, that is,

$$\frac{\partial U}{\partial z_x} < 0, \frac{\partial^2 U}{\partial z_x{}^2} > 0; \tag{24}$$

and also that the marginal utility of income is positive and decreasing, that is,

$$\frac{\partial U}{\partial \hat{y}} > 0, \frac{\partial^2 U}{\partial \hat{y}^2} < 0, \tag{25}$$

where $\hat{y}$ is resources remaining after allocations to missiles. $\hat{y}$ is measured in units of the numbers of missiles which it could buy.

It is to be emphasized that these assumptions are not to be taken as necessary to our decision theory, nor as factually unassailable. Rather they are convenient and heuristically advantageous.

The limitations of two dimensions in diagrams and the insights to be gained by a partial analysis now lead us to treat the problem of choice of forces first, as if the only contribution of missiles were to enhance one's own deterrent ability, and second, as if their only contribution were to diminish an opponent's deterrence. This accomplished, we shall combine the two. In each case the basic approach is through a timeless, indifference-curve analysis, consistent with our assumption about telescoping time to the present.

The Choice of Forces for Deterrence: Numbers

We begin with the case in which not only the enemy's forces are fixed by assumption, but also all the characteristics of one's own missiles are given except the numbers which one chooses. This is the choice to be explained. Figure 28 shows two axes

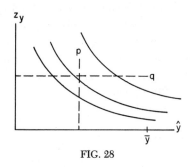

FIG. 28

z_y and $\hat{y}$. The point $\overline{y}$ on the abscissa indicates the total wealth available to Y if nothing is spent on missiles. Therefore, the amount allocated to missiles is

$$y = \overline{y} - \hat{y}. \tag{26}$$

An indifference map showing equally preferable combinations of $\hat{y}$ and z_y along any contour has been added to the figure. An indifference map gives graphical expression to Y's utility or preference function. Since this section is restricted to utilities deriving from only two variables, wealth retained, and numbers of one's own survivors from enemy attack—the preference function is of the form

$$U_y(\hat{y}, z_y) = f(\hat{y}) + g(z_y).$$

The curvature and spacing of the indifference curves are consistent with the properties

$$\frac{\partial U}{\partial \hat{y}} > 0, \frac{\partial^2 U}{\partial \hat{y}^2} < 0,$$

$$\frac{\partial U}{\partial z_y} > 0, \frac{\partial^2 U}{\partial z_y^2} < 0.$$

Utility increases as one proceeds out from the origin; but along any line such as $p(q)$ in the figure, utility contours are more widely separated at higher values of $z_y(\hat{y})$. Along any constant utility curve, the rate at which money is willingly sacrificed for greater z_y, as shown by the slope of the curve, is low when z_y is large, and $\hat{y}$ small, and is high when $\hat{y}$ is large and z_y is small. Now consider Y's decision-maker. Before allocating any resources to missiles he sees his position as at the point $(\bar{y}, 0)$. His utility corresponds to the value of the indifference curve through that point. He also knows, from Eq. (15), that he can exchange these resources for surviving missiles according to the formula:

$$z_y = t_a[(\bar{y} - \hat{y}) \, s^{ax_o/(\bar{y}-\hat{y})}(1 - s^{ax_o/(\bar{y}-y)})]^{1/2}$$
$$+ (y - y) \, s^{ax_o/(\bar{y}-\hat{y})}, \quad (27)$$

in which the transformation

$$y = \bar{y} - \hat{y}$$

has been made to accommodate the change of origin. The subscript on x_o indicates the particular magnitude of the opponent's forces.

This cost schedule appears in Fig. 29 together with the postulated utility function. The cost curve begins at the point $(y, 0)$, where no allocation is made to missiles, and proceeds upward to the left, approaching a slope of -1,[2] as greater resources are allocated to missiles, with less left for other pur-

[2] See Fig. 25 for verification of this slope.

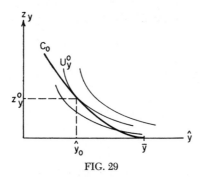

FIG. 29

poses. The curve is labeled C_o to indicate Y's possibilities for increasing z_y when $x = x_o$. The reader should recognize C_o as a mirror image of the cost curves of Fig. 25.

It is known that the marginal costs of z_y are declining. Alternative resource uses should be foregone and money allocated to the purchase of z_y up to the point at which

$$\text{Marginal cost of } z_y = \frac{\text{Marginal utility of } z_y}{\text{Marginal utility of } \hat{y}}.$$

In Fig. 29 this point is reached at the coordinates $(z_y{}^o, \hat{y}_o)$. At this point Y attains $U_y{}^o$, the highest U_y available when he is constrained by the curve C_o.

Y's decision can be formulated in simple mathematical terms. Suppose, for ease of illustration, that

$$U(\hat{y}, z_y) = a \log (\hat{y} + 1) + b \log (z_y + 1), \qquad (28)$$

and simplify Eq. (27) to

$$z_y = F(\overline{y} - \hat{y}) \text{ or } G(\hat{y}, z_y) = 0. \qquad (29)$$

Then side Y's choice can be formulated as the solution to the problem:

Max: $a \log (\hat{y} + 1) + b \log (z_y + 1),$
 subject to: $G(\hat{y}, z_y) = 0.$

99

The solution is found by forming the function

$$V = a \log (\hat{y} + 1) + b \log (z_y + 1) + \lambda\, G(\hat{y}, z_y), \quad (30)$$

where λ is the Lagrange multiplier. Differentiating,

$$\frac{\partial V}{\partial \hat{y}} = \frac{a}{\hat{y} + 1} + \lambda \frac{\partial F}{\partial \hat{y}} = 0,$$

$$\frac{\partial V}{\partial z_y} = \frac{b}{z_y + 1} + \lambda = 0, \quad (31)$$

$$\frac{\partial V}{\partial \lambda} = G(\hat{y}, z_y) = 0.$$

At the maximum,

$$\frac{dF}{d\hat{y}} = \frac{a}{b} \frac{z_y + 1}{\hat{y} + 1}, \quad (32)$$

and Y should continue to procure missiles until the rate of increase in z_y reaches this value.

The Choice of Forces for Threatening Attack: Numbers

The second part of the missile allocation problem springs from the more aggressive of the motives for building missiles, namely, from the desire to threaten attack credibly, in the face of an enemy's provocations and thereby to forestall such provocations.[3] Our measure of the ability of one side to do this is the number of missiles potentially surviving on the other side from attack by the first. Accordingly, Fig. 30 shows two axes labeled $\hat{y}$ and z_x. We now wish to consider only the utility arising from expenditure on missiles by virtue of the reduced enemy retaliatory potential. Therefore, we limit Y's utility to

[3] It should be noted that the distinction between an aggressive and deterrent psychology tends to vanish in our model. After all, the "aggressive" side only attacks first because he was provoked. With this caveat to the reader we shall continue to use "deterrent" in connection with one's efforts to improve one's own z and "aggressive" with the effort to reduce the enemy's z, rather than to coin a new term.

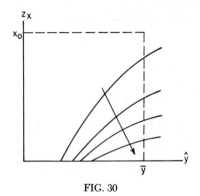

FIG. 30

$$U(\hat{y}, z_x) = f(\hat{y}) + h(z_x). \tag{33}$$

Again $\bar{y}$ shows Y's total initial resources measured in units of missiles that could be bought at constant unit cost. However, if Y retains all its resources for uses other than armaments, then every missile X builds is a potential survivor. If X procures x_o missiles, he will have that many survivors. Thus Y must be viewed as located at $(\bar{y}, x_o)$ before allocating funds to his own missiles.

The preference map shown in Fig. 30, with utility increasing in the direction of the arrow, is consistent with the conditions: [4]

$$\frac{\partial U}{\partial \hat{y}} > 0, \frac{\partial^2 U}{\partial \hat{y}^2} < 0;$$

$$\frac{\partial U}{\partial z_x} < 0, \frac{\partial^2 U}{\partial z_x{}^2} > 0.$$

[4] The conditions

$$\frac{\partial U}{\partial \hat{y}} > 0, \frac{\partial^2 U}{\partial \hat{y}^2} < 0,$$

$$\frac{\partial U}{\partial z_x} < 0, \frac{\partial^2 U}{\partial z_x{}^2} > 0$$

also allow for the preference map shown in Fig. 31.

101

In Fig. 32 the cost curve from Chapter II, Eq. 19,

$$z_x = t_\alpha[xs^{a(\bar{y}-\hat{y})/x_0}(1 - s^{a(\bar{y}-\hat{y})/x_0})] + xs^{a(\bar{y}-\hat{y})/x_0}, \qquad (34)$$

or more simply

$$z_x = \phi(\bar{y} - \hat{y}), \text{ or } H(\hat{y}, z_x) = 0, \qquad (35)$$

is drawn from the initial point $(\bar{y}, x_0)$. Y's decision can now be formulated as the solution to

$$\text{Max } U(\hat{y}, z_x)$$

subject to

$$H(\hat{y}, z_x) = 0.$$

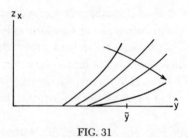

FIG. 31

Proof:

The rate of change of the slope of the indifference curve is:

$$\frac{d^2 z_x}{d\hat{y}^2} = \frac{-1}{(\partial U/\partial z_x)^3}\left[\frac{\partial^2 U}{\partial \hat{y}^2}\left(\frac{\partial U}{\partial z_x}\right)^2 - 2\frac{\partial^2 U}{\partial z_x \partial \hat{y}}\frac{\partial U}{\partial \hat{y}}\frac{\partial U}{\partial z_x} + \frac{\partial^2 U}{\partial z_x^2}\left(\frac{\partial U}{\partial \hat{y}}\right)^2\right].$$

The independent utility assumption of Eq. 22 entails

$$\frac{\partial^2 U}{\partial \hat{y}\partial z_x} = 0.$$

The total expression may be positive or negative. If positive the curves have the shape as drawn in the accompanying Fig. 31. In such a case the argument for reaching a maximum utility follows the identical form as given by Eq. 37.

We shall in fact later in the study for purpose of illustration draw the curves for $U_y(\hat{y}, z_x) = K$ as straight lines.

102

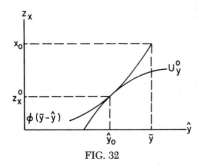

FIG. 32

As an example, assume U_y is of the form

$$U(\hat{y}, z_x) = a \log (\hat{y} + 1) - c \log (z_x + 1). \quad (36)$$

At the solution,

$$\frac{d\phi}{d\hat{y}} = -\frac{\partial U/\partial \hat{y}}{\partial U/\partial z_x} = \frac{a}{c} \frac{z_x + 1}{\hat{y} + 1}, \quad (37)$$

or

$$\text{Marginal cost of } z_x = \frac{\text{Marginal utility of } z_x}{\text{Marginal utility of money}}.$$

This point is shown in Fig. 32 as $(z_x{}^0, \hat{y}_0)$.

The Choice of Numbers for Deterrent and Threat Potential

The principles of choice are unchanged, but less easily illustrated when the utility arising from higher z_y and lower z_x are counted simultaneously. Side Y's decision maker wishes to maximize

$$U(\hat{y}, z_y, z_x) = a \log (\hat{y} + 1) + b \log (z_y + 1)$$
$$- c \log (z_x + 1), \quad (38)$$

subject to

$$z_y = F(y - \hat{y}),$$
$$z_x = \phi(\bar{y} - \hat{y}).$$

103

The solution,

$$V = a \log (\hat{y} + 1) + b \log (z_y + 1) - c \log (z_x + 1)$$
$$+ \lambda_1 [z_y - F(\bar{y} - \hat{y})] + \lambda_2 [z_x - \phi(\bar{y} - \hat{y})], \quad (39)$$

$$\frac{\partial V}{\partial \hat{y}} = \frac{a}{\hat{y} + 1} - \lambda_1 \frac{\partial F}{\partial \hat{y}} - \lambda_2 \frac{\partial \phi}{\partial \hat{y}} = 0,$$

$$\frac{\partial V}{\partial z_y} = \frac{b}{z_y + 1} + \lambda_1 = 0,$$

$$\frac{\partial V}{\partial z_x} = \frac{-c}{z_x + 1} + \lambda_2 = 0,$$

requires that missiles be procured up to the point that[5]

$$\text{MU of money} = \frac{\text{MU of } z_y}{\text{MC of } z_y} + \frac{\text{MU of } z_x}{\text{MC of } z_x}.$$

Since acquisition of missiles adds to Y's utility in two independent ways, *it will profit Y to procure more missiles than if its national objectives were advanced by either high z_y or low z_x alone.*

The Choice Between Quantity and Quality

So far, it has been assumed that Y has a single standardized missile of unalterable yield, accuracy and hardness. (Hardness is a technical term for invulnerability.) We shall now relax that assumption and illustrate the results for one case. Suppose Y is concerned with deterrence. On the one hand, he can build unprotected missiles installing them in the open air. Ignore the fact that in doing so Y might positively tempt attack by X. Suppose X's proclivities for attack are unchanged and attend to the economics of the case. Figure 33 shows a cost curve, C_1, indicating how many unprotected missiles, $\bar{y} - \hat{y} = y$, must be

---

[5] MU meaning "marginal utility," and MC meaning "marginal cost."

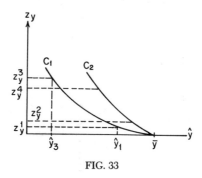

FIG. 33

procured to attain various z_y when $x = x_1$. Now, on the other hand, imagine that hardened missile silos come in one variety. Reference to Chapter II, Fig. 25 and Eq. 17 will verify that the cost curve for hardened missiles would look something like C_2. Next assume that each hardened missile costs exactly twice as much as an unprotected missile. This means that Y can take any number of missiles along curve C_1 and trade them in for half that number on C_2. This diagram can now be used to illustrate rational choice between quality and quantity. Consider point $(z_y^1, \hat{y}_1)$. Side Y spends $\bar{y} - \hat{y}_1$ on soft missiles. If Y takes one-half of this money and spends it on missile silos, he will have $(\bar{y} - \hat{y}_1)/2$ missiles left. This results in z_y^2 missiles surviving. Evidently Y should make the change since for the same total budget he gains in numbers surviving. $z_y^2 > z_y^1$. In contrast, consider the point $(\hat{y}_3, z_y^3)$. Y spends $\bar{y} - \hat{y}_3$ on missiles. By allocating $(\bar{y} - \hat{y}_3)/2$ to silos, Y comes up with z_y^4 survivors. It does not pay. $z_y^4 < z_y^3$. If all preferred points such as $(\hat{y}_1, z_y^2)$ and $(\hat{y}_3, z_y^3)$ are connected up, a new curve results. This is shown as C_* in Fig. 34.

This example serves to illustrate two points. First, the optimum allocation between quantity and quality depends on the magnitude of the missile force. It is intuitively obvious that this also depends on the size and character of the opponent's forces.

105

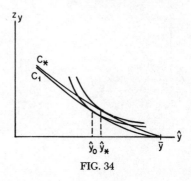

FIG. 34

Secondly, the optimum total budget itself depends upon the trade-offs between quantity and quality. In Fig. 34 it is shown that the optimum budget can be higher or lower after the new trade-off is introduced. $\hat{y}_*$ may fall short of or exceed $\hat{y}_o$.

IV · SECRECY AND THE ECONOMIC MODEL

As already postulated two motives can explain one's decision to build strategic forces in the form of missiles; one, the desire to deter and thereby be in a position to provoke via a retaliatory capacity, the other, the desire to intimidate, threaten, and limit an enemy's provocation. It is a fact of technology that strategic forces—whether missiles or bombers, land or sea launched—satisfy both these needs in varying degrees. A U.S. missile is both a potential survivor from Soviet attack and a potential attacker of Soviet missiles. This, basically, explains why efforts to distinguish offensive from defensive weapons explain so little. The same weapon serves both functions, is both offensive and defensive.

It seems clear that if one side acts upon the assumption that the parameters of the opponents' weapon systems remain fixed and if this is a true assumption, then that side can buy increases in its capacity to retaliate, and thereby to deter, for decreasing increments in expenditure. Such a tendency would be reinforced by possible economies of scale in the fabrication of missiles. On the other hand, if one side wishes to reduce the opponents' survival/retaliatory capability, then it must pay increasing marginal costs for each further reduction. Economies of scale in fabrication may neutralize this over some range, but marginal costs after some point must increase.

This characterization of the missile duel is based upon the assumption that each side, whether attacker or defender, acts with certain knowledge of his own and his opponent's weapons parameters—their numbers, yield, accuracy, and vulnerability to destruction. But suppose this were not so. Imagine side Y could only guess at the numbers, yield, and accuracy of the missiles of side X, his potential attacker. The purpose of this chap-

107

ter is to explore these possibilities. Within the framework of the basic theoretical-decision model of Chapter III in which the opponent's actions are given and unchanging, we seek to describe the effects of such imperfect information upon the choices of the decision-maker. In the first part of this chapter imperfect information will be treated as imposed by fiat. Secrecy will be taken as a new, additional parameter—that is, the decision-maker will not be permitted to improve his information by allocating funds to intelligence acquisition, a possibility to be introduced separately later in the chapter. In this first section a side is supposed to possess all the information it does have free of charge, and to be unable to improve its information at any price.

Strategic weapons, we have said, are at once offensive and defensive. Sub-systems, however, which serve the strategic weapons may be of defensive or offensive character, in the sense of augmenting a second strike as opposed to a first-strike capability. The Ballistic Missile Early Warning System, for example clearly is intended to increase the number of bombers surviving a Soviet first launch and thereby to augment retaliatory capability. Foremost among the auxiliary systems which add to first- or second-strike capabilities are intelligence-gathering systems. Information can be valuable because it improves a side's first-strike ability or because it improves a side's second-strike capability, or both. This chapter also addresses the problem of how to evaluate the information so obtainable. Although we will not in the first section of the chapter permit information to be actively sought, we do ask, and attempt to answer, how much such information would be worth if it were obtained. As a prerequisite this requires an assessment of the relevance of one's intelligence about various elements in the enemy's force structure. Categories of intelligence are established as follows:

(1) Locations of enemy missiles; (2) Numbers of enemy missiles; (3) Missile characteristics—(a) Uncertainty by the Defender, (b) Uncertainty by the Attacker.

Digression on Costs and Value

In general, the value of a thing can be measured by the amount of a second thing a person would willingly forego so as to gain the first. The cost of a thing is measured by the amount of a second thing that must be foregone if the first thing is to be had. Such are the familiar concepts of economics. They are equally applicable to analysis of a race to build missiles in general and, in particular, to such a race when information is allowed to enter as an explicit variable. In this context, the value of information is measured by the number of missiles that can be saved when the information is available, over the number necessary when it is not available—where in both cases some specified level of utility is held constant. The cost of information in the same context would be the number of missiles one should have to sacrifice to release funds to pay for the information acquisition. (To be technical the value of an increment of information is the amount of any other element in the implicit utility function that can be foregone while remaining on the same indifference contour—or in the limit the marginal rate of substitution between information and the other element contributing to security.)

All this is true if an accretion in information actually would enhance one's objective utility. But suppose it does not. What if it only raises a side's appreciation of its security? An example will help to resolve this. Suppose a defender possesses only a single means of buying potential survivors, namely by installing missiles of a given size, vulnerability, and so forth. In this case, one value of intelligence would be to inform the defender if his budget was large enough. But if his budget were absolutely limited and if there were only one absolutely rigid system for achieving a retaliatory capacity, *and if the objective were to maximize true potential retaliation for the fixed budget* then the entire budget should be used in buying that one available kind of missile. With no funds allocated to intelligence the defender would be partially (or totally) ignorant of his own capability to retaliate but the true capability would be as great as possible, for that fixed budget. One use of *knowing* this capability is that one can then decide whether it is enough or not, and thus decide whether or not to alter the budget. If the budget were absolutely fixed, such knowledge would serve by its costs to have reduced funds spent on missiles (that yield survivors which deter). In short, if my enemy is deterred by what my *actual true number* of survivors would be if he attacks, then the increase in my appreciation of these numbers will not add to the deterrence. If this is so, then intelligence only is of value if it tells whether enough money is being allocated over all for deterrence.

But now consider not the enemy's proclivities for attacking me, but *my own inclinations to provoke* an enemy. It will be remembered that in Chapter II war at the choice of the attacker arose only in reaction to excessive provocation by the victim, or deterrer. My level of provocation is decided not by what my true deterrent power is but by my appreciation of that deterrent power. If this is so, an enhanced appreciation of my own deterrent-originating utility will allow me to provoke my rival more efficaciously and to remain obstinate in the face of enemy threats.

In fact, within the model of war developed in Chapter II it is the subjective appreciation of deterrent capability that allows one to provoke. Our characterization of the value of intelligence in the first paragraph of this section is valid, subject to the proviso, that the "same indifference contour" means an indifference contour, based on a subjective appreciation of one's own and enemy's potentially surviving weapons.

Varieties of Imperfection in Information: And Their Measurements

In some cases the effects of secrecy on the part of one adversary upon the information available to the other may be described in probabilistic terms. The secrecy of the adversary may force the first side to estimate, rather than know and be certain of, the characteristics of the adversary's forces. Such estimates are inherently probabilistic; they can be represented as probability distributions. Examples are our guesses at the size of the enemy's missile force, the reliability of his missiles, their yields, or accuracies. In this study we shall assume that when our misinformation can be identified as uncertainty—which is to say, can be characterized as probabilistic—the true value of a variable or parameter corresponds to the mean value of our estimate. This is not a necessary assumption but it will simplify our calculations, with no loss in analytic value; the principles illustrated will have a general validity.

When secrecy causes a probability distribution to enter one's calculations, and therefore uncertainty to arise or to increase in its significance, there seems to be no unambiguous ordinal (not to say cardinal) measure of this uncertainty. As between distributions of the same shape, some index of dispersion—say, variance—may serve as an ordinal scale. When comparing uncertainties arising from different varieties of distributions, however, even this ordinal scale collapses.[1] Specifying a scale of

[1] For example, Fig. 35 shows three distributions, a, b, and c. Suppose (var a) = (var b) > (var c). While we might agree that more uncertainty arises in b than in

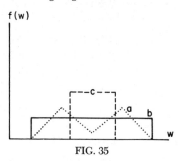

f(w)

FIG. 35

c and that this is adequately expressed by (var b) > (var c), what appeal is there in saying that equal uncertainty exists in a and b simply because (var a) = (var b)? We shall evade this problem when calculating the effects of uncertainty by considering only distributions of one type, namely rectangular. See Appendix A.

measurement for uncertainty is fortunately only a terminological convenience. Since neither cardinal nor ordinal scales are needed for the determination of optimum allocation to intelligence, failure to find such measure need cause no concern.

A second possible effect of an enemy's secrecy is not to create uncertainty, but simply to give rise to ignorance; a good example is secrecy over locations of missiles. For some locations the Soviets are likely to be certain and correct in their knowledge of our missiles. For others (presumably Polaris), they may be not uncertain at all; they may be totally ignorant. In such cases an ordinal measure of ignorance is obvious—*viz.* the number not located—and a cardinal measure is unnecessary.

SECRECY AS A PARAMETER IN THE
BASIC ECONOMIC MODEL

A treatment of imperfect information as a parameter is of value in two ways. First, an understanding of the effects of a parametric variation is contained within and is a necessary element of an analysis of secrecy as a variable. Secondly, there is a good reason to suppose that in reality some secrecy cannot be overcome at any cost. Some intelligence may be impossible to obtain with the existing technology; some information may be attainable but only with an unacceptable time lag. Our negotiators must often regard Russian secrecy as a parameter rather than as a variable that we can overcome by allocating funds to intelligence.

Location of Enemy Missiles

Knowledge of the location of enemy missiles is a necessary condition for a first-strike capability. It is also true that a policy of counter-missile retaliation—to use one's own missiles surviving an opponent's first strike to carry out a second-strike against his unused missiles—would require intelligence as to location.

Counter-missile retaliation also implies a high value on knowledge as to which of the enemy missiles have been fired. In fact an effective intelligence capability in this direction may allow for a missile exchange consisting of a series of pure counterforce blows (with clean weapons to eliminate fallout casualties perhaps). In this context the concept of deterrence via retributive punishment may vanish. But because to do otherwise would carry us into the dynamics of a missile war itself, we shall limit our attention to the contribution of knowledge of locations to a side's ability to threaten *initial* attack, and shall refrain from considering explicitly the effect of such knowledge on the ability to retaliate against missiles, important as this second role may be. The tools we develop could be easily turned to this second problem.

It is worth noting that each stage in a sequence of counter-missile exchanges, might be viewed as the initiation of new war, with both sides partially disarmed. In that case our analysis of the first war and the role of secrecy over location there should in principle apply to the initiation of the "second war," and the "third," . . . In our model, one side deters another by virtue of the probability it will retaliate against his *cities* if he attacks the first's missiles. In contrast, if the attacker, Y, also is deterred by his victim's, X's, ability to retaliate against Y's residual missiles v_{yy}—which is to say that each phase in such an exchange or each "new war" depends upon the attacker's idea of the initiation of the "subsequent wars"—then, of course, knowledge of locations of an enemy's, Y's, missiles enhances X's posture as a *deterrer*. Plausible as this may seem, no analysis of the contribution to one's own deterrent ability of a knowledge of enemy locations will be undertaken in this study. By an exactly analogous argument the value to one's self of secrecy over the location of one's own missiles, whether accomplished by putting the weapons on Polaris submarines, or by closing one's borders and airspace to foreigners, by installing a large number of dummy sites or mounting the missiles on rail, will be studied for its effect in augmenting one's retaliatory power without concomitantly increasing the ability to attack first.

The question of what is meant by knowing the location of an adversary's missiles has no exact answer; there may always be doubt as to geodetic accuracy. There is however a qualitative difference between having usable, if inaccurate, coordinates and having no coordinates at all. The primary purpose of intelligence here considered is to obtain some coordinates, precise specification being more a refinement. Such secrecy over the location of one side's missiles may be illustrated graphically. The secrecy of course has an effect both upon the position of the side withholding the information, the defender in this case, and upon the side from which the secrets are withheld, the attacker.

Effects on the Deterrer. Figure 36 shows the effects upon the defender, Y, who is interested in maintaining a retaliatory force.

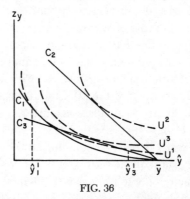

FIG. 36

The reader is referred to Figs. 25 and 29 for the general rationale of the diagram. The lines labeled C_1, C_2, and C_3 show how, starting from resources $\bar{y}$, the defending side must give up wealth to secure z_y missiles surviving (with some given confidence level $(1 - \alpha)$ percent assumed) under different circumstances as follows:

114

(1) Curve C_1 shows costs of z_y under the assumption that the enemy has a given and known number of missiles of known fixed characteristics and that the enemy knows the locations of all of the defender's missiles. As described in Chapter II the marginal costs of z_y are constantly decreasing and asymptotic to the value 1.

(2) Curve C_2 (a 45° line) shows the costs of z_y under the assumptions that the attacker has no knowledge at all of location of the defenders' missiles, and that imposing this total secrecy is costless to the defender. Such might be the case in the U.S.S.R., where secrecy pervades the society and where releasing location secrets would not effect savings in the unit costs of missiles. Accordingly, curve C_2 indicates that the first and each additional missile built adds one more survivor to z_y. Marginal costs are constant and of value 1 from the start. The situation (not shown) in which some fraction of the defender's missiles are kept hidden from enemy eyes (no security precautions are perfect) would result in a hybrid between C_1 and C_2, a curve of the same general shape as C_2 but with marginal costs approaching 1 more rapidly.

(3) The curve C_3 represents still another case, one in which indeed all missiles are of location unknown to the attacker, but where this secrecy advantage costs the defender. A good example is the Polaris-missile-carrying submarine. If a Polaris could be located it could be killed. But the Polaris cannot be located; therein lies its advantage. Missile for missile, a Polaris-armed submarine probably cost more than does Minuteman; and this is shown by drawing the curve C_3 with higher (although constant) marginal costs.

Now introduce a utility function as in Fig. 28

$$U_y(\hat{y}, z_y) = f(\hat{y}) + g(z_y).$$

Two questions may be asked: (1) How does secrecy over the location of its missiles affect the utility of the defender? and (2) How does it affect the resources allocated to missiles and resulting retaliatory capacity? Figures 36 and 37 indicate two possibilities. Clearly in both cases the secrecy alternative at no extra

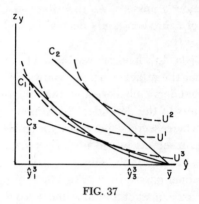

FIG. 37

costs (curve C_2) allows the defender to attain a higher utility contour, by spending less money and securing a higher z_y than in the no-secrecy case (C_1).

A comparison between C_1 and C_3 is less unambiguous. An expensive but hidden missile system, C_3, may (Fig. 36) or may not (Fig. 37) be preferred to C_1. If C_3 (C_1) is chosen, fewer (more) missiles will be built and fewer (more) will survive. Virtually any result could be arrived at by varying the proportions in which C_1 and C_3 or C_1 and C_2 may be combined.

The value of secrecy to the side keeping the secrets, in this case Y, can be measured as $\Delta \hat{y}$, the amount by which the defender should have to be compensated to remain indifferent between keeping his missile sites hidden and announcing their locations for a payment.[2] Consider Fig. 36. If the defender has

---

[2] If the defender releases his missile site coordinates to the attacker and if some of those hitherto secretly located missiles are near the defender's cities, the defender in giving up his secrets may raise the collateral damage to himself if the attacker actually attacks. As we have not explicitly calculated the effects of collateral damage elsewhere in the study, we ignore them here as well.

no secrets, he is constrained by C_1. He will spend $(\bar{y} - \hat{y}_1^1)$ on missiles and optimize utility at U_y^1. If, on the other hand, Y possessed a system characterized by C_3, he could maintain the same utility, U_y^1, by spending only $(\bar{y} - \hat{y}_3^1)$. The difference,

$$(\bar{y} - \hat{y}_1^1) - (\bar{y} - \hat{y}_3^1) = \Delta\hat{y} > 0,$$

is what Y could save if he kept his secrets, and remained at U_y^1. This measures the worth of these secrets to Y. Figure 37 shows a perverse case. Side Y would willingly increase his expenditure from $(\bar{y} - \hat{y}_3^3)$ to $(\bar{y} - \hat{y}_1^3)$ if, starting with the expensive secret system, he could announce his locations. In this case Y's secrets have a negative value to him:

$$(\bar{y} - \hat{y}_3^3) - (\bar{y} - \hat{y}_1^3) = \Delta\hat{y} < 0.$$

Effects on the Attacker. The second aspect of secrecy over location is the effect upon the would-be attacker who is totally or partially ignorant of the locations of the missiles he would attack. Consider Y to be the attacker. Figure 38 shows curves

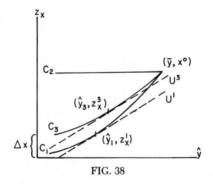

FIG. 38

C_1, C_2, and C_3, in this case representing costs to the attacker of reducing the defender's retaliatory potential. For illustration utility contours are drawn as straight lines (the broken lines). A general explanation of the diagram is given in Figs. 27 and

32.[3] The curve C_1 shows the cost of decreasing the defender's survivors, it being assumed the attacker knows all locations. Marginal costs increase without limit as efforts are made to be in a position to destroy all the defender's missiles. Curve C_2 shows the effects of spending money on missiles when the opponent has his missiles completely hidden; utility is lost via a loss of money and none is gained via reduction in z_x.

Curve C_3 illustrates a case in which some number, shown as Δx, of the defender's missiles are concealed. *The result is to raise marginal costs at every point on the cost curve, and to rotate the curve C_1 clockwise.*[4] From this it follows:

(1) The potential attacker, at his new optimum $(\hat{y}_3, z_x{}^3)$, must settle for lower utility; $U_y(\hat{y}_3, z_x{}^3) < U_y(\hat{y}_1, z_x{}^1)$.

(2) The number of potential survivors increases; $z_x{}^3 > z_x{}^1$.

(3) Depending upon the relative slopes the attacker may spend more $(\hat{y}_3 < \hat{y}_1)$ or less $(\hat{y}_3 > \hat{y}_1)$ at the new optimum.

(4) Some level of secrecy, that is, some value of Δx will cause Y to cease expenditures altogether. This occurs when

$$\frac{dF_\sigma(\overline{y}, x^o)}{d\hat{y}} \leq \frac{\partial U(\overline{y}, x^o)/\partial \hat{y}}{\partial U(\overline{y}, x^o)/\partial z_x},$$

where F_σ is the cost function with the effect of secrecy included.

The value to the attacker of intelligence as to site location may be developed by considering a mixed system in which some of the defender's missiles are hidden and some of known location, and where all missiles are equally vulnerable once their location is known. (Since a Polaris submarine carries sixteen missiles, once located it is probably more vulnerable missile for missile than a hardened silo. This illustration therefore very

[3] To simplify the diagrams the contours for $U_y(\hat{y}, z_x)$ will be drawn as straight lines, rather than concave as in Chapter III. The principles dealt with can be illustrated with equal validity and greater clarity by doing so. See pp. 101–102.

[4] This anticipates the analytic and numerical evaluation of the effects of uncertainty on the cost curves, which is contained in Appendix A.

likely underestimates the value of information about the location of submarines.) Figure 39[5] shows a number of cost curves for the attacker for a total of x_o defending missiles of which x_i

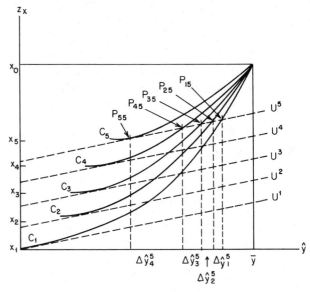

FIG. 39

are hidden ($x_1 = 0$). If x_5 of the defender's x_o missiles are hidden, then the attacker is limited by cost curve C_5, and similarly for x_4, C_4, and so forth. The figure is drawn for the case in which

$$(x_5 - x_4) = (x_4 - x_3) = (x_3 - x_2) = (x_2 - x_1).$$

The utility contours are drawn for the case of a high marginal utility of lowering z_x and low marginal utility of money relative to this. Suppose the defender does in fact have x_5 missiles con-

[5] Here the indifference curves are drawn as parallel straight lines. Thus, for this illustration we assume that the optimally chosen value of $\hat{y}$ increases with secrecy by X.

cealed. Obviously if the attacker could uncover the locations of $(x_5 - x_4) = \Delta x_4$ missiles he would find himself on curve C_4. Curve C_4 intersects the initial utility contour, U_5, at a point labeled P_{45}. As between the points P_{55} and P_{45} the attacker is indifferent since both lie on the same contour. The attacker therefore should be just willing to pay $\Delta \hat{y}_4{}^5$ for locating $(x_5 - x_4)$ missiles, $(\Delta \hat{y}_4{}^5 + \Delta \hat{y}_3{}^5)$ for locating $(x_5 - x_3)$ missiles, $(\Delta \hat{y}_4{}^5 + \Delta \hat{y}_3{}^5 + \Delta \hat{y}_2{}^5)$ for locating $(x_5 - x_2)$ missiles and so on. Along one single indifference curve the marginal value of increases in intelligence is decreasing. For example along U_5:

$$\left[\frac{\Delta \hat{y}}{\Delta x}\right]_4^5 > \left[\frac{\Delta \hat{y}}{\Delta x}\right]_3^5 > \cdots > \left[\frac{\Delta \hat{y}}{\Delta x}\right]_1^5.$$

Remember,

$$\Delta x_4 = \Delta x_3 = \cdots = \Delta x_1.$$

The value, however, of finding the location of $(x_5 - x_4)$ missiles when the initial cost curve is C_5 is less than the value of finding $(x_2 - x_1)$, missiles when the initial curve is C_2. In short *if each bit of information is exploited by allowing the budget to increase, then each additional piece of intelligence is of greater value than the last.* This whole tendency is the more pronounced, the flatter the utility contours in Fig. 39. If the contours were steeper than the cost curve C_1 at the upper-right corner of the box, then no missiles would be bought by the potential attacker and intelligence about enemy missile locations would be worthless.[6]

Number of Enemy Missiles

It is plausible to assume that each side knows exactly how many of its own missiles it possesses. There may be some considerable uncertainty on the part of the possessor of the missiles

---

[6] This valuation of intelligence is illustrative. If the indifference curves are shaped differently, then application of similar reasoning will result in different conclusions.

as to how many would be ready to launch at any specific time; the distribution of missiles out for repair may have an appreciable spread. But the potential attacker can be assumed not to know each particular value of this distribution of his enemy's missiles as it occurs over time. The potential attacker therefore must view each of his opponent's missile sites as a target. Therefore, the potential victim knows with certainty how many targets he presents to his attacker.

Uncertainty over the number of missiles possessed by one's opponent is a different matter. Conceptually, there is an overlap between secrecy (or conversely information) about numbers of enemy missiles and their locations. If a side knows the locations of *all* its opponent's weapons, it probably knows the number of enemy missiles. This need not be true necessarily; it is conceivable one should know where the adversary's sites are, accurately enough to target, without being sure whether one or two or more missiles are located at that site. For a gross generality, nevertheless, there is more to be said for than against the proposition that if one knows enemy locations one knows enemy numbers.

Effects on the Attacker. Assuming no uncertainty exists on the part of the potential attacker over the number of missiles per located missile site or missile-site complex, it remains possible that the number of untargeted missiles remains in doubt. In terms of Fig. 39 this is to say that, for example, the value $(x_0 - x_5)$ may be known while uncertainty exists over the value of x_0 and therefore of x_5. The attacker is interested in reducing the potential enemy survivors. He is uncertain how many will survive because they cannot be targeted—this in addition to the uncertainty inherent in the binomially distributed outcome of survivors from the missiles actually targeted. Imagine, for simplicity of illustration, that the attacker can express his doubts as a distribution about the true value of enemy unlocated missiles. Assume that the risk that in fact my enemy may have a large number of hidden missiles will reduce my inclination to attack in the face of provocation by him.[7] If the attacker judges his position conservatively, he will take the upper limit of his estimate (or the upper decile)[8] as the true value. In Fig. 40, x_o

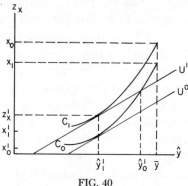

FIG. 40

indicates the true total number of defending missiles, and $x_o{}^1$ the true number of hidden missiles; x_1 is the attacker's conservative estimate of the total, and $x_1{}^1$, of the hidden. The attacker therefore sees himself limited by C_1 and settles for $z_x = z_x{}^1$ and expenditure $(\bar{y} - \hat{y}_1{}^1)$. A knowledge that in fact only $x_o{}^1$ missiles remained unlocated, rather than $x_1{}^1$, would allow the attacker to reach curve C_o. As in Fig. 39 the value of this information is $(\hat{y}_o{}^1 - \hat{y}_1{}^1)$.[9]

---

[7] The opposite argument is possible here: the attacker may not be deterred by missiles he doesn't know about. Thus the potential victim may be obliged to forego provocation unless he shows the attacker his hidden missiles. If this is true the attacker should pretend he doesn't know of his victim's hidden missiles, and the victim, thinking the attacker is not deterred, will back down on his provocation so as to forestall attack. The argument of the text above illustrates the effects of hiding missiles if the attacker is unable to carry through this pretense.

[8] In fact a new trade-off exists here requiring a new computation of the entire cost schedule C_o. So this "conservative" reaction must be taken as an approximation.

[9] In this case the value of the information is purely psychological since Y does not change its expenditures on attaining curve C_o. But if this allows Y to forestall X's provocations then Y benefits objectively. Also, expenditure would vary as between C_o and C_1 if the indifference curves of Fig. 32 were used for illustration. See also the argument on pp. 109–110.

Effects on the Defender. For the defender, interested in securing a strategic force which survives attack—the number of survivors desired depending on the cost—uncertainty over the size of the enemy's missile force raises costs everywhere along the schedule. This is demonstrated in Appendix A. The way in which such costs are raised is determined by the extent or magnitude of the uncertainty, by the values of the other variables in the system, and by the true value of the uncertainly known variable. (The reader is reminded that "numbers" surviving means the lower bound of missiles expected to survive attack with a high confidence.) Figures 41 and 42 illustrate in principle the effects upon the defender of uncertainty over the number of attacking missiles.

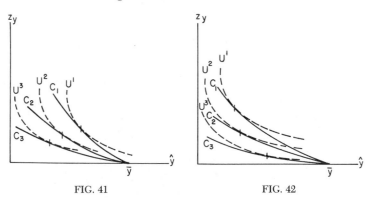

FIG. 41   FIG. 42

The exact shape of the cost curve depends upon which variables are fixed parametrically and at what values. In Figs. 41 and 42 the curve labeled C_1 represents costs under the assumption of complete information. Curves C_2 and C_3 indicate the cost schedules for increasing uncertainty over enemy numbers, the greater the uncertainty, the more the downward shift in the cost curve. Greater uncertainties may result in the selection of an optimum at which expenditures (that is, numbers of missiles) have increased, while numbers of survivors, z_y, have decreased.

This is shown in Fig. 41. In Fig. 42 both expenditures and numbers surviving decrease with greater uncertainty. A theory of the value of information can now be constructed which will apply generally to all such uncertainties.

Figure 43 repeats three cost curves; C_1 for the case of per-

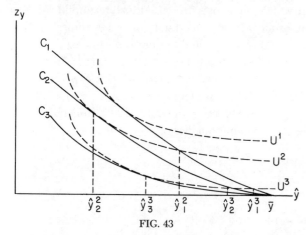

FIG. 43

fect knowledge, C_2 for some uncertainty, C_3 for greater uncertainty. It should be noticed that as uncertainty increases from situation C_1 to C_3 the utility-maximizing solution occurs at continually decreasing values of z_y, and first at increasing then at decreasing values of $(\bar{y} - \hat{y})$. That is, first more then less money is spent on buying z_y. As in previous examples, the value of the information obtained in decreasing uncertainty from one level to the next is measured as the savings realizable in $\hat{y}$ if one stays on the same indifference curve after as before acquiring the new information. In Fig. 43 starting from situation 3, curve C_3 is tangent to U^3 at a point requiring $(\bar{y} - \hat{y}_3^3)$ in resources to be spent on missiles. If information now becomes available such that C_2 is the new cost curve, the defender can retain utility U^3 by spending only $(\bar{y} - \hat{y}_2^3)$ on missiles. The difference $(\hat{y}_2^3 - \hat{y}_3^3)$, is the value of the information obtained in

124

moving from C_3 to C_2. Similarly $(\hat{y}_1{}^3 - \hat{y}_3{}^3)$ indicates the value of information obtained in moving from C_3 to C_1, the state of perfect knowledge. The value of information obtained when the starting point is the utility maximizing solution obtaining at the tangency of C_2 with U^2, is of course different. Starting from $\hat{y}_2{}^2$ attaining complete knowledge is worth $(\hat{y}_1{}^2 - \hat{y}_2{}^2)$, the savings made possible by the introduction of C_1 while remaining on curve U^2.

Missile Characteristics

Uncertainty over the characteristics of the missiles on either side for some parameters affects the attacker exclusively, and for other parameters affects only the defender. The parameters to be dealt with are yield, and accuracy of the weapon, and the hardness or vulnerability of its silo or site.

For the defending side, the side buying deterrence, and therefore potential survivors, the parameters of interest are the yield and accuracy of the attacker's missiles and the vulnerability of its own sites. For the potential attacker, who wishes to reduce the defender's deterrent, the parameters of interest are his own yield and accuracy, and his opponent's vulnerability. In other words, if one is attacker and the other defender, both are interested in the same information. On the other hand, one side, when attacker, profits from information about different parameters from when it is defending. In both cases, however, information about one's own missile characteristics as well as about the adversary's is significant.

The Defender's Uncertainty. The effect of uncertainty on the part of the defender, whether over the yield or accuracy of incoming attackers, or over the hardness of his own missile sites is qualitatively similar to the effect of uncertainty over enemy numbers.[10] The magnitude of the effects of uncertainty depends

[10] See Appendix A for a verification of this and other assertions about changes in shape of cost curves resulting from uncertainty.

upon all the variables in the missile-duel equations. Figure 44 diagrams the effect of uncertainty over yield, accuracy, and hardness of one's own sites. Curve C_1 represents the cost curve under conditions of complete certainty. C_2 and C_3 show the change in costs due to increasing uncertainty. For a given value of z_y both total and marginal costs are greater, the greater the uncertainty.

The question of whether the *value* of improvements in information (that is, of decreases in enemy secrecy) is increasing or decreasing depends upon two factors.[11] First is the relative positions of the various costs curves under different degrees of uncertainty. As shown in Appendix A, the general tendency is for increasing uncertainties over variables in the missile exchange equations to increase the cost of z_y more than proportionately all along the cost curve—that is, for the curve C_2 to diverge from C_1 *less* than does C_3 from C_2. The second determining factor concerns the shapes of the cost curves relative to the utility contours.

From the first factor it follows that from any single initial position of uncertainty, that is, starting from some curve to the left of C_1, such as C_2 or C_3, the first reductions in secrecy are the most valuable. From the second of the above factors it follows that as between initial starting points the first accruals of information may be of more or less value as the initial equilibrium point is one of greater uncertainty, depending on the shape of the cost curves relative to the utility function. If, as in Fig. 41, increases in secrecy on the part of the enemy cause increasing amounts to be spent on deterrence, then the information obtained in narrowing uncertainty from situation C_3 (at tangency to U^3) to C_2 (while remaining on U^3) is of greater value than that obtained from *starting at* C_2 (that is, at the tangency

[11] The reader may discern the need for a definition of "equal increment of information" here, but if he will suspend judgment until the next paragraph, the operational meaning of this proposition will become clear.

between C_2 and U^2) and going to C_1 (while remaining on U^2). In other words, the more uncertain the defender is to start with in Fig. 41, the more it pays to spend the first dollar on intelligence. If, on the other hand, the situation is as depicted in Fig. 42 where increases in uncertainty raise costs to the point that less will be spent on deterrence, then the less one is uncertain to start with, the more it pays to begin to collect intelligence.

The Attacker's Uncertainty. The potential attacker in the missile duel may be uncertain about the accuracy and yield of his own weapons, or the hardness of the targets he is attacking. The direction of the effects of such uncertainty depends on the confidence level desired by the attacker. Figure 45 shows two solid curves $C_{0.90}$ and $C_{0.10}$. Both curves indicate the costs an

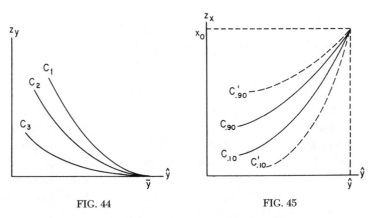

FIG. 44   FIG. 45

attacker must pay to reduce his victim's survivors if he knows yield, accuracy and vulnerability with certainty. The curve $C_{0.90}$ shows how Y must give up $\hat{y}$ to be 90-percent sure no more than z_x of X's initial x^0 missiles will survive. Curve $C_{0.10}$ shows how he must pay out to be 10-percent sure (90-percent sure) that no more (no less) than z_x survive. The same figure shows two broken curves, $C_{0.90}'$ and $C_{0.10}'$. These curves portray the effects of uncertainty. It is an assumption of this study

127

that the potential attacker is a risk averter. Our attention is limited to cases represented by $C_{0.90}$ and $C_{0.90}'$, therefore.

This being the case, it is clear that uncertainty raises the costs to Y of lowering z_x. For the same y, z_x is higher when uncertainty is introduced, and for the same z_x, $\bar{y} - \hat{y}$ must be increased once uncertainty enters. Refer to Fig. 39. It will be seen that the effects of uncertainty are similar to the effects of concealment of missiles. In fact the mechanics of illustrating uncertainty about yield, accuracy, or vulnerabilities are so similar to the illustration of the effects of hiding missiles that to present them here would amount to pure repetition. The reader may wish to reinterpret the argument supporting Fig. 39, as relating to uncertainties about missile characteristics.

SECRECY AS A VARIABLE
IN THE ECONOMIC MODEL

Now we extend the preceding analysis by allowing for the fact that a side can reduce or limit the imperfections in its information by directing its resources into an intelligence acquisition and evaluation apparatus. This is what is meant by saying secrecy is a variable. If this is so, the degree of misinformation under which a side labors can no longer be taken to be a datum as was done earlier. This degree now will vary with the effort of the malinformed side. Instead we shall take as a datum the degree and character of the severity with which the side withholding information imposes security precautions.

Intelligence-Hardware Optimization: The Defender

Figure 46 illustrates how the theory developed thus far can be extended to account for the defender's decision to divert funds from hardware to intelligence for a given, fixed budget. As in the preceding diagrams, initial resources are shown as $\bar{y}$. Curves C_1, C_2, C_3, and C_4 indicate how missiles alone buy z_y for side

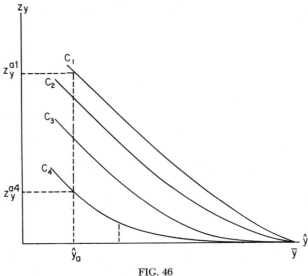

FIG. 46

Y, under conditions of increasing uncertainty; each such cost curve corresponds to a different degree of uncertainty on the part of side Y. Each cost curve refers to the same value of $x = x_o$, the true numbers and true characteristics of X's potentially attacking missile force. In other words, each curve, C_1 through C_4, corresponds to a different parametric variation on the uncertainty of side Y, the case treated earlier in this chapter. It is demonstrated in Appendix A that as uncertainty increases, the cost curves shift from C_1 toward C_4.

Next, assume that the curve C_1 shows the costs with perfect knowledge. Assume C_4 shows the costs under a maximum-secrecy or maximum-uncertainty situation. That is, assume some meager information is available to the defender absolutely free. Now consider the value $\hat{y}_a$ representing resources remaining if the total missile-duel budget of side Y is $\bar{y} - \hat{y}_a$. If Y knew all the characteristics of X's missiles, he would know that by spending $(\bar{y} - \hat{y}_a)$ entirely on his own missiles, he would be

129

$100(1 - \alpha)$ percent confident that no fewer than $z_y{}^{a1}$ would survive attack by X. But in fact X maintains a shroud of secrecy about his arms preparedness and only varied and conflicting reports filter through to Y. Side X's security precautions are so good that if Y plays only a passive role in being informed of X (in contrast to actively seeking information) he is very uncertain. In that event spending $(\bar{y} - \hat{y}_a)$ entirely on missiles will only allow him to be $100(1 - \alpha)$ percent confident that $z_y{}^{a4}$ of his missiles will survive. Side Y is not in a position to *know* he is warranted to predict $z_y{}^{a1}|(1 - \alpha)$, even though he in fact is so warranted.

Let it be asked: "Can side Y improve its situation while remaining within the fixed budget $(\bar{y} - \hat{y}_a)$?" See Fig. 47. Assume

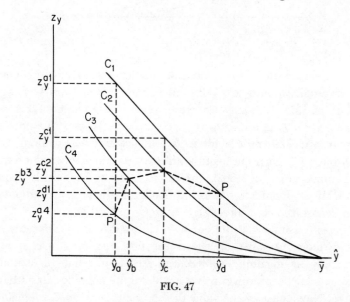

FIG. 47

that the potential attacker maintains the degree of his security precautions constant. Then, side Y, by reducing the number of missiles procured (or their accuracy or some other costly feature) and by taking the funds thereby released and spending them on reducing its uncertainty, can increase the number of survivors *it knows* (with assurance $1 - \alpha$) would survive. Imagine the defender begins working within the same budget, $(\bar{y} - \hat{y}_a)$ to take funds away from missiles and to spend them on intelligence. Suppose that to reduce uncertainty to C_3, $\Delta\hat{y}_b = (\hat{y}_b - \hat{y}_a)$ must be spent, leaving Y, $(\bar{y} - \hat{y}_b)$ to buy missiles. With $(\bar{y} - \hat{y}_b)$ to be spent on missiles Y can secure $z_y{}^{b3}$ survivors, with assurance $1 - \alpha$. Next assume that by increasing intelligence allocation by $\Delta\hat{y}_c = (\hat{y}_c - \hat{y}_b)$ and thus reducing funds available for missiles to $(\bar{y} - \hat{y}_c)$, Y can reduce uncertainty to C_2 and thereby attain $z_y{}^{c2}$, at a total budget (missile plus intelligence) of $(\bar{y} - \hat{y}_c + \hat{y}_c - \hat{y}_a) = (\bar{y} - \hat{y}_a)$. Lastly, by spending $(\hat{y}_d - \hat{y}_a)$ on intelligence, and $(\bar{y} - \hat{y}_d)$ on missiles, $z_y{}^{d1}$ is attainable. The marginal costs of proceeding from C_4 to C_1 are shown as $\Delta\hat{y}_b, \ldots, \Delta\hat{y}_d$. Since $\Delta\hat{y}_b < \Delta\hat{y}_c < \Delta\hat{y}_d$ marginal costs may be said to be increasing.[12] The reader should now imagine a large number of "C" curves, and a large number of small incremental transfers from missiles to intelligence; then the broken curve with end points P–P, can be imagined as smooth and continuous. At a total budget of $(\bar{y} - \hat{y}_a)$, Y can choose any point on the curve P–P. It is consistent with our model of war (Chapter II) to suppose Y will choose the highest point on P–P, for to do so maximizes the z_y side Y *knows* have a $100(1 - \alpha)$ percent chance of surviving. In Fig. 47 the highest z_y attainable for a budget of $(\bar{y} - \hat{y}_a)$ is $z_y{}^{c2}$.

If Y decides to spend only $(\bar{y} - \hat{y}_c)$ on missiles and devote the remainder of the budget, that is $(\hat{y}_c - \hat{y}_a)$, to intelligence, then the true number he would be warranted to predict would survive declines from $z_y{}^{a1}$ to $z_y{}^{c1}$. In making the decision to divert resources to intelligence Y knows that his "objective" deterrent capability will decline, but he does not know by how

---

[12] This is speaking metaphorically since the idea of an objective definition of "equal information increment" has been rejected. See p. 111.

much. Side Y knows neither the value $z_y{}^{a1}$ nor $z_y{}^{c1}$ nor the difference between the two. He simply knows two such values exist and that $z_y{}^{a1} > z_y{}^{c1} > z_y{}^{c2} > z_y{}^{a4}$. Since in our model the pay-off to Y of an ability to retaliate, is the derived ability to provoke X without fear of attack, and since in this context it is the retaliatory ability *of which one is aware* that allows one to provoke, it follows that Y should maximize the value of $(z_y \mid \alpha)$ *that he knows,* and therefore that he will pick the highest point on P–P, as stated above.

The logic supporting allocations to intelligence from budgets of a given size now understood, we can proceed to vary the budget. For clarity, the notation will be changed slightly. Figure 48

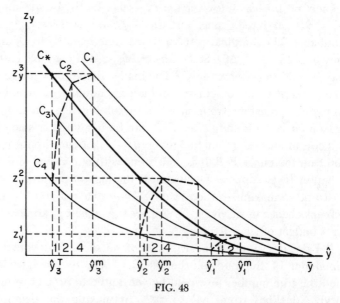

FIG. 48

shows a set of Y's cost curves for a given $x = x_o$, C_1 for all parameters known with certainty, and for increasing degrees of uncertainty $C_2 > C_3 > C_4$, where C_4 is assumed to represent the maximum uncertainty possible. It is then assumed that for

$x = x_o$, and *regardless of the value of y*, the marginal costs of decreasing uncertainty from C_4 to C_3 are $\Delta\hat{y} = 1$, for decreasing uncertainty from C_3 to C_2 are $\Delta\hat{y} = 2$ and for decreasing uncertainty from C_2 to C_1 are $\Delta\hat{y} = 4$. Then, following the foregoing argument, if the budget for deterrence is fixed at $(\overline{y} - \hat{y}_1^T)$, the maximum number of survivors is shown as $z_y{}^1$, requiring $(\overline{y} - \hat{y}_1{}^m)$ to be spent on missiles and the remainder $(y_1{}^m - \hat{y}_1{}^T)$ to be spent on reducing uncertainty. Therefore the point $(z_y{}^1, \hat{y}_1{}^T)$ shows the maximum in surviving missiles obtainable for the corresponding fixed budget. By similar constructions, as suggested by the broken lines in the figure, the points $(z_y{}^2, \hat{y}_2{}^T)$ and so on, show the maximum in survivors for other fixed budgets. As the total budget for deterrence expands, the assumption of an unchanged marginal-cost schedule for intelligence acquisition implies that the amount expended on reducing uncertainties expands also. But if complete certainty can be attained at a finite cost, some budget $(\hat{y}_3{}^T$, in Fig. 48) will mark the point after which all additional funds will go for hardware. The points $(z_y{}^1, \hat{y}_1{}^T)$ and so on, are joined by a curve labeled C_* in the figure. This curve shows the maximum survivors attainable at each budget level, subsuming the intelligence-hardware allocation-optimization. The curve C_* crosses the curves C_2, C_3, . . . , and at every such point of intersection is steeper than the curve it intersects—or of equal slope, but not less steep. At high budget levels the curve C_* becomes parallel to C_1.

Now imagine that side X, for reasons as yet unexplained, increases security precautions, and suppose that as a result the marginal costs to Y of going from C_4 to C_3 increase to $\Delta\hat{y} = 2$, of going from C_3 to C_2 increase to $\Delta\hat{y} = 4$, and of going from C_2 to C_1 increase to $\Delta\hat{y} = 8$. In other words, we assume marginal costs double. Figure 49 shows the derivation of the maximum survivor curve under this new situation. In Fig. 49 as in 48, $x = x_o$. It can be seen from a comparison of the two figures that the curve C_{**}, which obtains when the marginal costs are

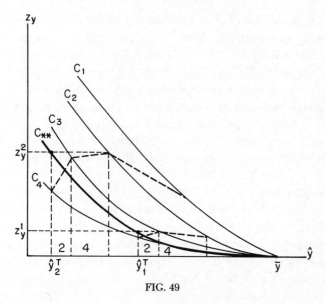

FIG. 49

higher, lies below the curve C_*. In fact a whole set of such curves may be presumed to exist, each one corresponding to the "degree" of security enforced by side X. This is shown in Fig. 50, where C_* and C_{**} are included. It should be recalled that each curve in Fig. 49 refers to one identical value of $x = x_0$. Figure 50 therefore describes the effect of increases in security imposed by X upon Y, or of increases in uncertainty imposed upon Y, with all other parameters in the opponent's (X's) missile force constant.

Figure 51 in contrast shows the effect of increases in x by side X, when X maintains a fixed standard of secrecy, but Y is allowed to optimize its own allocation between intelligence and hardware. The figure shows a set of cost curves for no uncertainty—denoted by $\sigma = \sigma_0$—and for varying x as $(x_0 | \sigma_0)$, $(x_1 | \sigma_0)$, $(x_2 | \sigma_0)$, etc. It is known from Chapter II that $x_0 < x_1 < x_2$. The diagram also shows a second set of curves labeled $(x_1 | \sigma_1)$, $(x_1 | \sigma_1)$, $(x_2 | \sigma_1)$ where σ_1 is now to be taken to refer to the fact that some fixed level of security precautions has been

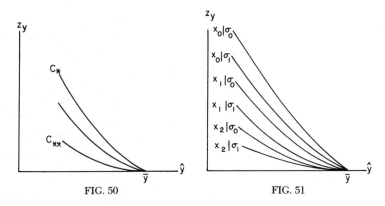

FIG. 50   FIG. 51

introduced by side X. Against this threat, side Y optimizes its hardware and intelligence effort. In Fig. 51 it is assumed that the marginal costs of gathering intelligence do not vary with the size to an opponent's force. From this assumption it follows that the cost curve $(x_2 | \sigma_1)$ is below $(x_1 | \sigma_1)$. (This may in fact be a tenuous assumption.)[13]

[13] As another example, it could be plausibly argued that as the size of the enemy's missile force increases, it becomes increasingly difficult for him to conceal the numbers and/or characteristics of his missiles, so that after a point the defender's (Y in this case) costs are reduced because his intelligence problem is reduced by more than his difficulty in maintaining survivors is increased. If this were so, a set of cost curves could take on the appearance of Fig. 52, where increases in x first

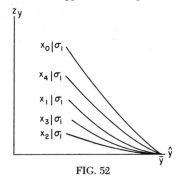

FIG. 52

shift the cost curve down but eventually shift it up again because Y is allowed to optimize his allocation between discovering X's secrets and building missiles.

135

The Deterrer's Optimum Choice: Missiles and Intelligence

How does the inclusion of uncertainty as a variable, which can be reduced or eliminated at a cost, effect a potential victim's decision as to how much to spend in total on the arms' race and how to divide that amount between missiles and intelligence? The general answer is that it depends on the victim's preferences. This section explores some specific possibilities. In doing so it will prove awkward if not impossible to refrain from crossing the line between "one-sided" and "two-sided" models in a small way.

Figure 53 shows two cost curves C_3 and C_*. Curve C_3 obtains when maximum uncertainty exists and nothing is allocated to intelligence by Y. Curve C_* is the optimized intelligence hardware curve of Fig. 48. Suppose the marginal utility of $\hat{y}$ to Y were constant, and the marginal utility of z_y were decreasing. If this were so Y's utility map would look something like Fig. 53. When C_3 obtained, U^3 was reached by spending $(\bar{y} - \hat{y}_3)$ on missiles and nothing on intelligence. With C_*, U^* is attained by spending a total of $(\bar{y} - \hat{y}_*)$ on missiles plus intelligence. Obviously the allowance for allocation to intelligence results in Y's choosing a lower total budget and *a fortiori* a lesser number of missiles.

Next imagine the marginal utility of z_y to Y were constant and of $\hat{y}$ were decreasing. Figure 54 illustrates this case. Evidently, the total budget expands from C_3 to C_*. Whether the number of missiles increases is another question. Not only may the increase in the total budget $(\hat{y}_3 - \hat{y}_*)$ be spent entirely on intelligence, but the original allocation to hardware may be diminished as well.

These two extreme examples establish limits for the case in which marginal utilities of both $\hat{y}$ and z_y are decreasing as in our Chapter III model. It is clearly possible that once Y optimizes his allocation between missiles and hardware, he will end up at

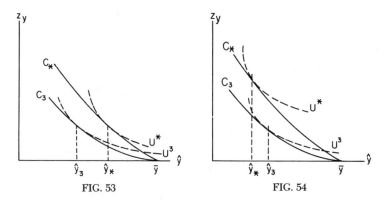

FIG. 53   FIG. 54

a lesser number of *missiles* than if he did not; but it is not necessary.

This reasoning suggests another interesting implication for the attacker X. Suppose the attacker knows that Y, the defender, will choose $(\bar{y} - \hat{y}_1^T)$ missiles in response to C_1 and will choose $(\bar{y} - \hat{y}_2^T)$ missiles in response to C_2, where as shown in Fig. 55, $\hat{y}_1^T > \hat{y}_2^T$. C_1 represents complete certainty and C_2 maximum uncertainty on the part of the defender. Imagine that the attacker has settled upon $x = x_o$ as the number of his attacking missiles and wishes to maintain security precautions which will minimize the number of *missiles* built by Y, that is, $\bar{y} - \hat{y}_1^m$. (Perhaps X desires his own missiles, solely as an attack force and therefore wants y as low as possible.) If he, X, has no secrets at all, then Y can attain cost curve C_1 at no expense in intelligence effort and will choose $(\bar{y} - \hat{y}_1^T)$ missiles. If X makes it extremely costly for Y to improve his intelligence and decrease uncertainty, Y will spend all his defense budget on missiles and choose $(\bar{y} - \hat{y}_2^T)$ of them. If X allows Y to attain complete certainty at a cost just slightly less than $(y_2^m - \hat{y}_2^T)$, then Y will (1) devote these resources to intelligence (2) improve his z_y slightly over the complete uncertainty case, and (3) considerably reduce the number of *missiles* to $(\bar{y} - \hat{y}_2^m)$

137

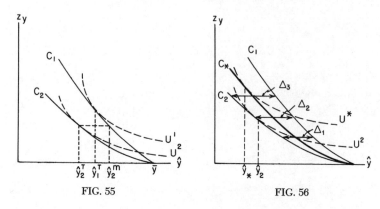

FIG. 55   FIG. 56

from $(\bar{y} - \hat{y}_2{}^T)$ while maintaining total budget at that latter level. Through a judicious use of the diligence with which he keeps his secrets, in other words, side X can expand Y's total *budget* beyond what it would be if he, X, kept no secrets while simultaneously *contracting* the number of *missiles* that Y installs. Therefore X, if he can only maintain secrecy at a cost to himself, has some optimum between building his own x, and keeping it a secret from Y just how many x he has and of what yields, accuracies, reliabilities, and so forth. It should be noted that side X cannot *assure* itself that Y—in response to X's secrecy—will reduce the number of missiles below the number that would be chosen in the complete-certainty case unless X successively increases the cost to Y of going from C_2 to C_1 from Δ_1 to Δ_2 to $\Delta_3 \ldots$, as shown in Fig. 56. If, in contrast, X holds Y's marginal cost of intelligence schedule invariable, as would be shown by (say) the heavy curve (C_*) in Fig. 56, then Y might increase both total budget and numbers of missiles (over the values obtaining under complete certainty) in moving from maximum uncertainty, C_2, to the optimized intelligence hardware curve C_*. This latter possibility is suggested by $\hat{y}_* < \hat{y}_2$. The curves C_*, C_{**}, ... , to repeat, are based on the assumption that X keeps a fixed degree of security precautions and therefore would not assure X that Y had the minimum in *missiles* for the budget level that he, Y, selects.

Intelligence-Hardware Optimization: The Attacker

The last sections dealt with potential retaliators who were allowed to respond to the secrecy imposed by the adversary by allocating resources to intelligence, and thereby to decrease the uncertainty under which they operate. We shall now deal with the exact analogue for this for the case in which each side is a potential attacker, wishing to reduce the numbers of his adversary's surviving missiles. We cannot construct a detailed model for every possible type of uncertainty. In this and the next section we shall restrict the analysis to the case of uncertainty by the attacker over locations of the defender's missiles.

The results of an optimum allocation of money between missiles for attack and intelligence for target acquisition, when the total missile-duel budget is fixed, are shown in Fig. 57. Suppose that out of a total of x_o enemy missile sites x_4 are concealed, and $(x_o - x_4)$ are at locations known at no cost. Let the budget be limited to $(\bar{y} - \hat{y}_a)$. If nothing is spent on intelligence, Y reduces X's survivors to z_x^{a4} at this fixed budget.

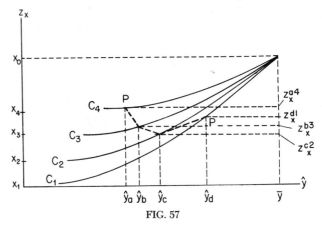

FIG. 57

139

Suppose the cost of acquiring $(x_4 - x_3)$ target locations is $\Delta\hat{y}_b = (\hat{y}_b - \hat{y}_a)$. Then diversion of $\Delta\hat{y}_b$ of resources away from hardware to intelligence will allow the attacker to reach $z_x{}^{b3}$. To obtain the location of $(x_3 - x_2)$ missiles, a further $\Delta\hat{y}_c = (\hat{y}_c - \hat{y}_b)$ of the limited budget must be allocated to intelligence; this allows $z_x{}^{c2}$ to be reached. The diversion of an additional $\Delta\hat{y}_d = (\hat{y}_d - \hat{y}_c)$ to intelligence allows $z_x{}^{d1}$ to be reached. In short, for a fixed budget $(\bar{y} - \hat{y}_a)$ side Y can choose any point on the curve P–P in Fig. 57. In the limit this can be imagined to be a smooth curve. The potential attacker will allocate money to intelligence so as to attain the lowest point on P–P. In Fig. 57 this is shown as $(\hat{y}_c, z_x{}^{c2})$.

Now turn to Fig. 58. Suppose that the costs of uncovering $(x_4 - x_3)$ missiles is $\Delta\hat{y} = 1$; of uncovering $(x_3 - x_2)$ is $\Delta\hat{y} = 2$; of uncovering $(x_2 - x_1)$ is $\Delta\hat{y}_c = 3$. If the initial budget is $(\bar{y} - \hat{y}_1{}^T)$, then as Fig. 58 shows the best allocation is $(\bar{y} - \hat{y}_1{}^m)$ to missiles and $(\hat{y}_1{}^m - \hat{y}_1{}^T)$ to intelligence, since at this allocation $z_x = z_x{}^{1*}$ is a minimum for the budget assumed. Therefore the point $(\hat{y}_1{}^T, z_x{}^{1*})$ is one point on the cost curve C_*. Curve C_* passes through all other points similarly derived from all other

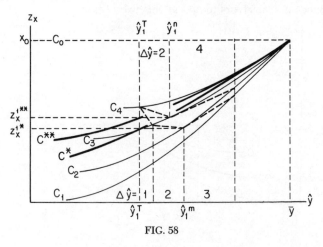

FIG. 58

140

possible fixed budgets, when marginal costs are $\Delta\hat{y} = 1, 2, 3$. Now assume the defender takes a great deal more care in hiding his missiles, to the point that marginal costs are doubled for the attacker. Then $z_x = z_x{}^{1**}$ is the minimum number of surviving missiles attainable at the budget $(\bar{y} - \hat{y}_1{}^T)$, and the amount $(\bar{y} - \hat{y}_1{}^n)$ should be allocated to missiles and $(\hat{y}_1{}^n - \hat{y}_1{}^T)$ to intelligence. The curve C_{**} is drawn through as such points where marginal costs are twice those for C_*.

The following observations now seem appropriate with reference to Fig. 58: with a linear or concave (to the point $(\bar{y}, o)$) utility function assumed, it is likely, although not necessary, that as the schedule of marginal costs of discovering locations increases, or as one moves from C_* to C_{**} and finally to C_0, utility is optimized at lower values of total budget. Also as secrecy increases, or the marginal-cost schedule to the attacker of uncovering the locations of the defender's x_0 missiles increases, the attacker will allocate smaller and smaller fractions of any fixed budget to intelligence. Therefore just as in the preceding section of this chapter, where the attacker could control in part the defender's response to his potentially attacking missile inventory, the analogy exists here for the defender who controls the security precautions surrounding the locations of his x_0 missiles. As X increases secrecy, the attacker's, Y's, response is to reduce his total budget but to *reduce by more*, his intelligence effort. As X makes it easier for Y to find the location of his missiles, Y will spend a greater total budget but also increase the proportion going to target-location acquisition. Therefore, at some point (perhaps, one of the "corners" of complete secrecy, or perfect knowledge) the *number of missiles* (not the total budget outlay) that Y, the potential attacker, builds is minimized. For the defender, X, to be assured that the attacker builds a minimum number of *missiles* (not a minimum total-defense budget), he must increase his security precautions, that is, increase the marginal-cost-of-uncovering locations, to side Y, as Y's total budget grows.

V · THE ARMS RACE:

AN INTERACTION PROCESS

To this point, we have restricted our attention to the problem of explaining how a single side chooses an optimum in hardware and intelligence in our simplified version of the missile-arms race. This has been done under the assumption that the optimizing side confronts an unchanging situation, that the enemy's forces and other parameters in the missile-duel equations are fixed. Put otherwise, the chapters preceding are an effort to answer the question, "What is my best choice if my opponent chooses x_1? If he chooses x_2?, and so on."

In this chapter and the one to follow we shall introduce the facts that my "best" choice can influence or change the adversary's "best" choice, which in turn may lead me to a new "best" position. In short, we shall introduce the interactive character of the arms race into our theoretical description. Further, we shall consider the possibility that one side *discovers* that what it thought "best" no longer is because the rival's "best" response alters the situation, and that the one side makes this discovery *in advance* and is able to utilize it to its own advantage.

The previous chapters have examined the arms race from the viewpoint of side Y exclusively. Chapter V in contrast, must, in its description of arms races, embrace the viewpoint and self-interest of both sides X and Y simultaneously. Indeed, this is *the* central feature of the arms race, which demands explanation beyond that afforded in Chapters II, III, and IV. The essential technique of Chapter V will be to place two models, such as were developed in Chapter III adjacent to one another, and to allow them both to vary simultaneously. This is done without allowing any imperfection in information to enter. The results will be compared with "duopoly theory," in the hope that likenesses and distinctions between the two will add to our understanding of the arms race.

INTERACTION MODELS OF THE MISSILE RACE: PERFECT INFORMATION

An interaction model, in the sense intended here, is one in which it is recognized that each side's decision-variable or variables influence the other's choice of value of its own decision-variable, and in which this mutual interdependence is explicitly taken into account.[1] The purpose of this chapter is to develop the theme of mutual interaction and interdependence by extending the model constructs of Chapters II and III. Our development of the logic of choosing a missile force by one side allows for a variety of such interdependencies.

Interactions with z Fixed

The simplest such model can be represented by the equations

$$z_y = t_a[ys_y^{x/y}(1 - s_y^{x/y})]^{1/2} + ys_y^{x/y}, \tag{40}$$

$$z_x = t_a'[xs_x^{y/x}(1 - s_x^{y/x})]^{1/2} + xs_x^{y/x}. \tag{41}$$

Equation 40 will be recognized as identical with Eq. 15, an equation which shows how side Y's survivors z_y, vary with y, and x, given t_a and s_y, if X fires all of his missiles. Equation 40

---

[1] While the two adversaries may or may not recognize this interdependence, the fact of interdependence is explicitly formulated in the analyst's model. Whether the adversaries—one or both—recognize this or not is of determining influence in interpretation of the model. Three cases arise: one, both, or neither may recognize their mutual interdependence. Each of the three will be considered in this chapter. "Decision-variables" in our model are numbers and characteristics of missiles.

may be viewed as specifying how Y must build y missiles to insure some minimum survivors for itself, or how X must build x missiles to reduce Y's survivors surviving below some maximum $(z_y | \alpha)$. Equation 41 specifies exactly the same information for z_x, y, x, t_α', and s_x. The interactive character of an arms race derives from the fact that both equations must be satisfied simultaneously. (Note that t_α (t_α') will have different values depending on whether Eq. 40 (41) specifies the behavior of side X or Y. For simplicity of illustration this difference is ignored in the remaining analysis of this section.)

Suppose, for example, that both sides X and Y are motivated exclusively by a desire to deter, and further that each side, as a matter of policy independent of cost considerations, sets particular values of z and t_α which it must achieve. Then Eq. 40 indicates the value of y that side Y must choose so as to maintain $(z_y | \alpha)$ at the desired level for each value of x. Side X chooses x for reasons not yet mentioned. It is known from the first numerical approximation of Appendix A that as both sides increase their forces proportionately, z_y increases. Therefore, at constant z_y the potential attacker (X in Eq. 40) must increase his forces always more than in proportion to the defender. This is illustrated by the curves in Fig. 59, which show y vs. x for vari-

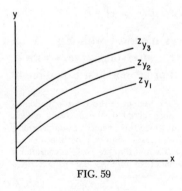

FIG. 59

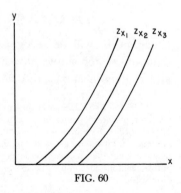

FIG. 60

ous given z_y from Eq. 40. All are concave from below. As Fig. 59 shows, when $x = 0$ side Y picks some positive y depending upon the value of $z_y | \alpha$ declared a policy objective. In the figure $z_{y_1} < z_{y_2} < z_{y_3}$.

Next, an analogous interpretation can be given to Eq. 41, which specifies how side X, wishing only to deter, will increase x less than in proportion to increases in y, for any z_x and t_α'. Figure 60 then shows that some positive value of x is chosen by X even when $y = 0$. Also

$$z_{x_1} < z_{x_2} < z_{x_3}.$$

The central elements of the interactive process can now be exposed by combining Eqs. 40 and 41. Suppose side Y picks one particular level of z_y, and X picks one particular level of z_x. That is, one equal z_y curve from Fig. 59, and one equal z_x curve from Fig. 60 obtain simultaneously. This is shown in Fig. 61 where

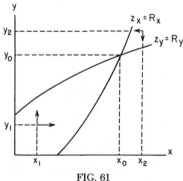

FIG. 61

it is seen that one particular pair (x_o, y_o) allows both sides to achieve the desired z at once. From any point, such as (x_1, y_1) side X will increase x and Y will increase y. From a point such as (x_2, y_2) both sides will decrease their decision variables as indicated by the arrows. Thus, it is seen the point (x_o, y_o) is one of stable equilibrium, that is, a pair of values of the decision-variables x and y away from which neither side will move once they are achieved, and toward which both will ultimately tend once displaced therefrom. Because side X will always attempt to adjust x so as to reach the curve z_x for every value of y, this curve may be called X's "reaction curve" and is labeled R_x. Similarly R_y is Y's "reaction curve."

Now suppose, in contrast to the assumption governing the foregoing, that both sides are concerned only with their potential for attack. In that case Eq. 40 represents the reaction curve of side X, and Eq. 41 of side Y, and the possibilities for both sides to attain a satisfactory position at once are radically altered. Figure 62 shows an example where side Y insists upon some maxi-

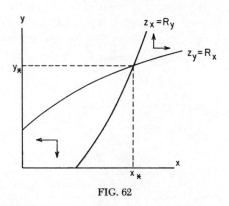

FIG. 62

mum level of z_x and side X upon some maximum level of z_y. Only the point (x_*, y_*) is an equilibrium point, but it is unstable. A movement away from that equilibrium is self-reinforcing and presumably will gather increasing momentum.

As a third example imagine that both sides are interested in deterrence as well as attack potential and that therefore each side fixes some low z for its adversary and some high z for itself as its policy goals. As a reflection of this, Figs. 63 and 64 each show four curves:

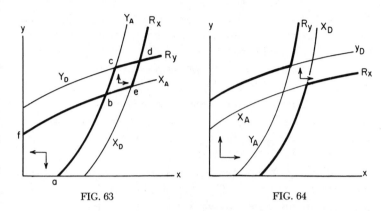

FIG. 63 FIG. 64

Y_A: The numbers, y, which will be chosen by side Y to limit z_x to some value—say, $z_x{}^a$—such that Y can attack, threaten, or intimidate X for any value of x.

X_A: The numbers of x which X will choose so as to limit z_y to—say, $z_y{}^a$.

Y_D: The numbers of y chosen by Y so as to maintain z_y at some level—say, $z_y{}^d$—and thus deter X for all values of x.

X_D: The numbers of x chosen by X so as to maintain z_x at $z_x{}^d$ and thereby deter Y.

It should be noted that in the figures X_A lies below Y_D, and Y_A lies to the left of X_D, which means that the number of missiles the deterring side requires surviving is greater than the attacker can allow to survive if he is to attack; that is,

$$z_x{}^a < z_x{}^d$$

and

$$z_y{}^a < z_y{}^d.$$

Figures 63 and 64 then show two possible policies for each side. Figure 63 shows the case in which each side is satisfied, either to be able to attack, or to deter, but not both. The reaction curves are shown as heavy lines. To repeat, R_x indicates the values of x side X will attempt to achieve for each value of y selected by Y, and similarly for R_y. At low values of x side Y can attack, threaten, or intimidate at no cost up to point a. The number y required to be able to attack then increases rapidly to point c. Up to this point, side Y has been unable to deter an attack upon itself. After reaching point c, further increases in x will allow Y to continue as a potential attacker only at greatly increasing costs, as shown by the extension of curve Y_A beyond c. Instead Y picks the cheaper policy of deterrence only, following the curve Y_D to point d and beyond. If side X has a similar policy, X's reaction curve is as shown by the other heavy line. It can be seen that points of stable equilibrium exist at the origin and at point d, while point b is one of unstable equilibrium.

Figure 64 pictures the situation when both sides insist on both a deterrent and an attack capability. At low values of the opponent's variable, deterrence is more expensive than, and inclusive of, attack. At high values of the opponent's variable, attack potential is more expensive than, and inclusive of deterrence. As shown in Fig. 64 the situation is inherently explosive; no mutually satisfactory solution exists.

Interactions with z Variable: The Economic Model Extended

The models above describe interactions and possible equilibria under the assumption that each side simply fixes the values of z_x and/or z_y which it finds acceptable. Such an account ignores the fact that as the arms race proceeds and increasing magnitudes of resources are diverted from civilian consumption, investment, and research, the loss of such civilian goods tends to brake further expansion of armaments. To allow for the disutility of foregoing other goods, the economic models of Chapter III must be extended for a two-sided account.

Suppose first that both sides are concerned only with deterrence. Figures 65 and 66 show the range of possible situations

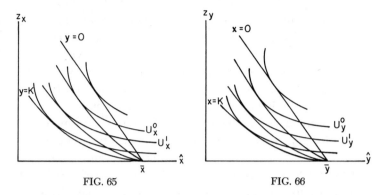

FIG. 65   FIG. 66

for sides X and Y respectively. Each diagram shows a set of cost curves, *one for each value of the opponent's force magnitude*. The reader is referred to Chapter II for a demonstration that with greater numbers in the opposition's missile force, the deterrer's cost curve rotates counterclockwise. The straight, 45° line through the initial resource point represents the case of the adversary's having zero missiles. Even at this value some positive z is preferred, at the cost of some resources, as shown by the coordinates of the point of tangency between those cost and utility functions.

Figures 67 and 68 now show the same information as contained in 65 and 66, only transferred to x and y axes. Remem-

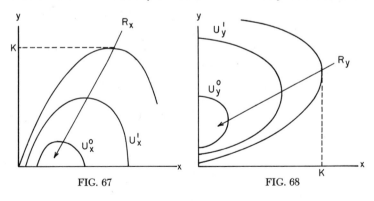

FIG. 67   FIG. 68

149

ber $\bar{y} = y - \hat{y}$; and $x = \bar{x} - \hat{x}$! Traveling along any utility contour such as $U_x{}^o$ in Fig. 65, as x increases, one crosses first low, then higher, then lower values of y. Conversely, traveling along a single cost function for $y = k$, first low, then higher, and finally again lower utility contours are crossed. By repeating this operation (assuming the utility function known) utility contours can be constructed as shown in Fig. 67 with utility increasing in the direction of the arrow. By an identical argument contours such as $U_y{}^o$ shown in Fig. 68 can be derived from Fig. 66. Corresponding to each point of tangency in Figs. 65, 66, is the highest (rightmost) point on a utility contour in Figs. 67, 68. In other words, the highest points of the utility contours in Fig. 67, or the rightmost points in Fig. 68 show the utility-optimizing selections of x by X, and y by Y respectively. The locus of such maxima is a curve. This curve is the reaction function consistent with the assumption that utility is maximized (rather than that $z = K$ as in the previous section). The utility contours for both sides can be placed in the same diagram, the maximum points of each set of contours connected, as shown in Fig. 69, and the two reaction functions, R_x and R_y combined.

We shall delay until a few pages attempting to explain and criticize the notion of a "solution" to an interactive model of the type we have at hand. Our major purpose at this point is simply

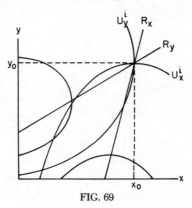

FIG. 69

to demonstrate the two-sided, interactive models of the arms race can be constructed with a straightforward extension of the tools fashioned in previous chapters. Nevertheless, if a reaction function is taken to have the same meaning here as explained in the preceding section, then the reaction functions of Fig. 69 result in a stable equilibrium at (x_o, y_o).

The preceding model has been developed for two sides interested in deterrence only and therefore exclusively interested in their own retaliatory potentials. In a similar fashion an interaction model may be constructed on the assumption that both sides are concerned only with their potential as threateners and attackers. Figures 70 and 71 describe two possible utility-maximizing responses of side Y to a parametric variation on the

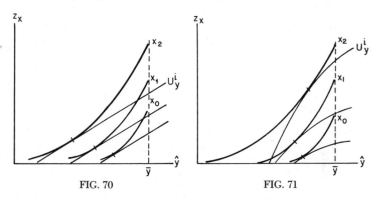

FIG. 70   FIG. 71

decision variable of the opponent. It is demonstrable that the various cost curves which begin at $x_0, x_1, x_2, \ldots$ are such that for parallel straight indifference curves the fewer the opponent's missiles, the fewer of one's own missiles does one choose to build at the utility optimum. Figure 72 shows the straight parallel utility contours for side Y transferred to the x-y plane where utility increases in the direction of the arrow. The line labeled R_y shows side Y's utility-maximizing reaction curve. A similar reaction curve can be derived for side X. If both side's preferences are captured by parallel straight utility contours,

151

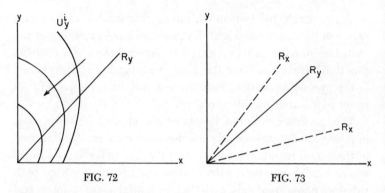

FIG. 72   FIG. 73

then X's reaction curve must lie entirely above Y's or entirely below it. If R_x were to lie above R_y as shown in Fig. 73, the origin is a point of stable equilibrium—if below, the origin is a point of unstable equilibrium.

If the utility contours were not limited by an assumption of linearity, of course the reaction curves of Fig. 73 could intersect and reintersect in various ways. This is just as true for the "pure" deterrence model as for the "pure" attack model. The shape of the reaction function depends upon both the utility and cost curves. In particular, if preferences on both sides are as shown for Y in Fig. 71, then two curved reaction functions will result.

Now, lastly, allow that both sides are both deterrers and potential attackers as well. Introducing such duality in motivations would seem to do no violence to the notion of interaction as applicable to the armaments contest. Indeed, to the contrary, such duality in reasons for accumulating weapons should allow for richer variations in the interactive process. Figure 74 gives a sampling of such possibilities; points of stable and unstable equilibrium are labeled "1," and "2," respectively.[2]

[2] Michael Intriligator, "Economic Models and Deterrence," a paper presented at the American Political Science Association Convention in New York City, September 1963.

152

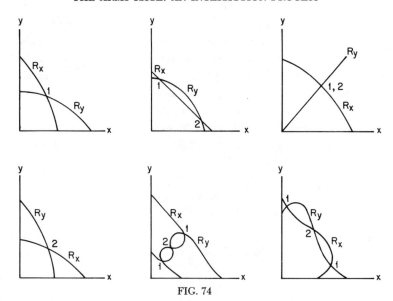

FIG. 74

Interactions with Yield, Accuracy, and Hardness as Variables

To this point in the chapter we have considered interaction models in which only numbers of missiles on either side are allowed to vary, and in which the objective on both sides is to deter or to threaten. The case in which one side wishes to deter and the other to attack or threaten attack can be easily encompassed by the foregoing analysis. The case of an arms competition where the variable is not numbers of missiles, however, is awkward to describe with the tools thus far employed. Yet an obvious feature of the arms race now under way is that competition exists over not only numbers but yields, accuracies, reliability, warning systems, and so on, as well. The competition in armaments is in no small part a qualitative technological contest. Hitherto our analysis has been partial analysis throughout, in the sense that the values of yield, accuracy and hardness have been held constant. Rather than construct an entire new

153

diagrammatic apparatus for the case in which the numbers of missiles are held constant and yield, for example, is the variable, we shall retain the tools now familiar to the reader and discuss the implications of a race for larger yields and greater accuracies in the context of total equilibrium analysis.

To begin with, it can be shown, as in Appendix A that progressive increases in the yield of the attacker's warheads, or increases in accuracy of his missiles (lower C), or decreases in the hardness of the defender's missile sites (higher K) all: (1) shift the cost curve of the defender as shown in Fig. 75 and (2) shift the cost curve of the attacker as shown in Fig. 76.

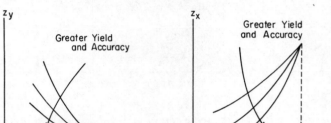

FIG. 75   FIG. 76

Within the confines of the assumption of this book that each side seeks high *numbers* of its own survivors and low *numbers* of enemy survivors,[3] two interesting observations on a race in yields and accuracies seem to the point. The first is that if (1) a side has a fixed and unchanging *number* of missiles and if (2) in the short run it cannot respond to increases in yield and or

---

[3] Other measures of achievement in attack or deterrent potential could be total yields surviving measured by zW, or total square mileage which those z survivors of zW megatons could cover with blast over-pressure. A measure of this latter is $zW^{2/3}$. Glenn A. Kent, *On the Interaction of Opposing Forces under Possible Arms Agreements,* Occasional Paper No. 5 (Cambridge, Mass.: Center for International Affairs, Harvard University, 1963) discusses the pros and cons of a variety of possible indices of success.

accuracy of the adversary's missiles by increasing the hardness of its sites (a reasonable assumption since this is time-consuming and expensive) and if (3) no allowance is made for secrecy, then a race over yield or accuracy has the interesting feature that one side can only compensate for its loss of deterrence—following from the other's increase in yield or accuracy—by increasing its own first-strike potential. In other words with the above three assumptions, an arms race becomes increasingly attack-oriented. Each side compensates for its own loss of deterrent by reducing the enemy's deterrent.[4] Figure 77 shows marginal utility on the

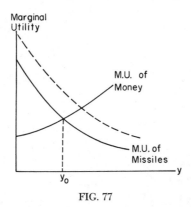

FIG. 77

ordinate and numbers of missiles on the abscissa. In the case assumed earlier in which the utility deriving from one's own surviving missiles and from the opponent's survivors and one's own money are all logarithmic functions, the effect of an increase in an opponent's yields or accuracy is to raise the sum of marginal utilities deriving from missiles as shown by the dotted line. If the number of missiles is fixed at y_o, it will certainly pay to spend money to improve one's own yields and/or accuracies, which is to add to one's attack potential.

[4] Our "theory of war" would suggest that as such a race progressed, the intensity of mutual provocation would recede.

The second observation is that if both numbers, and yields and accuracies, are variable, all mutually interact, such that a race over accuracies may reinforce or nullify the race for superior numbers. Figures 78 and 79 give an example. Suppose our

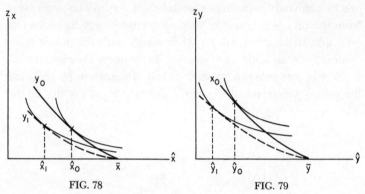

FIG. 78   FIG. 79

attention is restricted to deterrence, and that some initial equilibrium occurs with missile forces x_o and y_o. If now side X increases the yield or accuracy of its missiles, Y's cost curve shifts as shown by the dotted line in Fig. 79. It would be a coincidence if, under the new circumstances, Y should find an optimum in spending enough to buy just y_o missiles as before. Rather, Y should prefer to increase or decrease its missile inventory— this depending on the character of Y's utility function. If Y changes its numbers from y_o to say y_1, this will cause X to be faced by a new cost curve—say, the dotted line in Fig. 78. (Each value of x implies a single cost curve for Y, and each value of y a curve for X.) If X is now confronted by a different cost curve, he will most likely be led to change his numbers from x_o—say, to x_1 (x_1 may be greater or less than x_o). This in turn will cause another change in Y's cost curve (not shown) leading to a new optimum y. This in turn leads X to a new optimum. The process continues indefinitely, or until both sides find an optimum position compatible with the other's optimum. The limitation to

156

two dimensions precludes a graphical analysis of an arms race in which numbers and yields and accuracies all are variable; that is, it precludes a total equilibrium analysis in diagrams. Nevertheless the foregoing account suggests that the inclusion of accuracy and yields as variables can intensify or retard the race to build numbers of missiles; it can substantially affect the relative strengths of adversaries at a mutual optimum, and could be decisive in determining whether a "solution" will be reached in an arms race.

As a simple example let us compare two cases: one in which the yield or accuracy of each side's weapons is fixed and the second in which each side optimizes its allocation between numbers and accuracy[5] for every number of enemy missiles.

Take the case of each side having an interest only in its attack potential. Figure 80 diagrams how, for an enemy missile

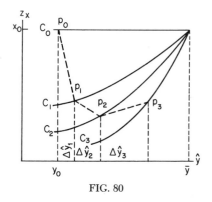

FIG. 80

force of x_o, side Y will allocate between numbers and accuracy. Suppose the budget is limited so that if all money is spent on missiles and none on guidance, y_o missiles can be bought; but

[5] Or yield—since the principle of the effects of yield or accuracy upon such interaction models is identical, only one more variable will be added rather than two or three.

such directionless missiles cannot kill enemy defending missiles at all. The point P_o represents the result. If $\Delta\hat{y}_1$ of resources are diverted from numbers of missiles to guidance systems, the curve C_1 obtains and therefore side Y attains point P_1. In the diagram the best combination between numbers of delivery vehicles and their accuracies is shown as point P_2, when total expenditure is $\bar{y} - \hat{y}_o$. The marginal costs of increasing accuracy are $\Delta y_1, \Delta y_2, \ldots$ The vagaries of cost in improving the accuracy of missiles make it possible, even under the simplifying but severely limiting assumption that the utility contours are straight lines, that increases in the enemy missile force will cause the attacker to *reduce* the number of his missiles while making them more accurate. To verify this assertion the reader should have to construct curves hitherto denoted C_* or C_{**} through all points such as P_2. If this is done for various values of x_o in Fig. 80, the validity of the statements can be demonstrated. Thus, with the inclusion of accuracy as a new variable and with adjustments for optimizing on this variable, reaction curves can intersect and reintersect as in Fig. 74.

THE MISSILE RACE AND DUOPOLY THEORY

To the reader familiar with the economist's explanation of duopolistic markets, the similarity between this theoretical structure and our arms races is striking. The point of this section is to set forth an explicit comparison of the two, and to explore the possibilities for "solutions" in arms races as suggested by duopoly theory.

Essentials of Economic Duopoly

The theory of oligopoly is meant to describe the principles behind and the results of the behavior of a profit-maximizing firm that buys its inputs and/or sells its outputs in markets in which its influence over price is more than negligible. Duopoly refers to a special case in which only two firms sell a single homogeneous good to a large number of buyers. Duopsony refers to the special case in which only two firms buy a single homogeneous input from a large number of sellers. Thus, duopoly (duopsony) theory is taken normally as referring to the firm as the decision unit. Further, the two firms, if duopolists (duopsonists), are limited by a single market-demand (supply) schedule.

Consider the duopoly case. Assume a downward sloping market-demand schedule for the single good produced by both firms; therefore, the greater the total quantity offered for sale by both firms combined, the lower the unit price at which the market is cleared. Both firms receive this price for each unit they have offered for sale. It is characteristic of duopoly that a single market-demand schedule is posited, over which neither firm has control.[6] Figure 81 shows the total cost curve, *TC*, of firm number one, and the total revenue curve, *TR*, indicating gross sales when the second firm produces nothing. Costs are assumed to remain unchanged regardless of the action of the second firm, but the possibilities for revenue decline as the second firm increases its output. The total revenue curves TR', TR'', . . .

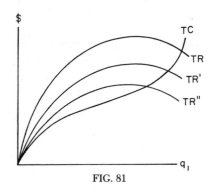

FIG. 81

[6] Advertising by means of which a firm can alter the demand for his product could be introduced here, but for drawing the simple comparison intended, advertising can be left out.

denote the first firm's revenue possibilities as the second firm produces and offers increasing quantities of the good in question.

Profit equals revenue less costs. Figure 82 shows the profit contours derived by making this subtraction in Fig. 81. In Fig. 82 $q_2{}^i$ indicates all combinations of output and profit attainable by the first firm when the second firm's output is fixed at $q_2{}^i$. In the figure $q_2{}^0 < q_2{}^1 < q_2{}^2$; profit $= \pi$. In Fig. 83 the same information is transferred to $q_1 - q_2$ axes, with the profits of the first firm denoted by $\pi_1{}^i$, and $\pi_1{}^0 > \pi_1{}^1 > \pi_1{}^2$. Suppose the first firm maximizes its profit for every value of q_2 which the second, for reasons not yet explained, happens to choose. The

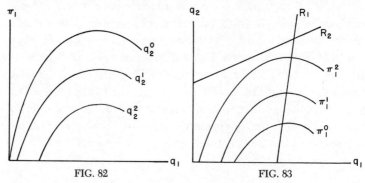

FIG. 82   FIG. 83

locus of such maxima connects the highest points on all the curves $\pi_1{}^i$. This is the first firm's reaction curve, and is denoted by R_1. The reaction curve of firm number two is derived by an analogous procedure. It is labeled R_2 in the figure (isoprofit curves not shown). Such is our account of duopoly presented in this abbreviated fashion to allow for comparisons with the interactive aspect of arms races.

Duopoly and the Arms Race Compared

Compare the figures above with Figs. 67 and 68. Except for the labels they are identical. The major difference between the duopoly model outlined, and the interactive model of the arms race developed beforehand would seem to be the existence and central position of a market-demand schedule in the duopoly case (or supply schedule in the case of duopsony). No such corollary exists in our account of arms races. The reason for this, however, is not difficult to find.

Duopoly theory is a special branch of the theory of the producer, whereas our account of the arms race reduces as an economic theory, to a special case of the theory of the consumer, or of one who exchanges one good (money in this case) for another (security, or intimidating power). Duopoly and oligopoly theory have been very largely occupied with the behavior of the firm, for the simple reason that as a decision unit within the realm of conventional economics the consumer is taken as having an imperceptible and, therefore, negligible effect upon the price or exchange ratio at which he must trade. The consumer of received economic theory has at his disposal an income or wealth denoted by say $\overline{M}$. His preferences, as revealed by a hypothetical experiment, are summarized by a set of indifference contours between money, M and good Q. The consumer must trade along the price line, whose slope, is fixed by the price of the good in question. While the price is determined by the aggregate preferences of all consumers plus the profit-maximizing behavior of all firms, the individual consumer is powerless to affect this price. The idea of monopoly, partial or total does not ordinarily arise within the context of consumer choice. Professor Duesenberry has suggested that the *utilities* to the individual of differing amounts of a good may be inversely related to the relative amounts possessed by others,[7] but in general, economic theory does not dwell on the possibility that one person in the act of trading may influence directly and substantially the *price* at which others may trade.

In a theory of the contest to accumulate missiles as presented here, on the other hand, there are only two "consumers," each wishing to maximize its own utility, and each having

[7] James S. Duesenberry, *Income, Saving, and the Theory of Consumer Behavior* (Cambridge, Mass.: Harvard University Press, 1949).

a direct effect upon the terms on which the other can buy the "good" in question. *In other words, our theory of the arms contest, in particular of the missile duel, reduces to an extension of duopoly theory into the region of consumer behavior,* a region which in general is considered the preserve of "perfect competition." In speaking of the arms race or the missile duel we are speaking of a class of *economic* problems and not of a unique problem foreign to economics. Our "consumer" is indeed limited by an exchange line which determines the price he must pay in exchange for the good he acquires, in this case missiles surviving (of his own or the enemy). But the position and shape of this exchange line is determined by the expenditures of the second party. In economic duopoly the source of interdependence between rivals is a market, exterior to both. In our duopolistic theory of consumption the interdependence is direct; one rival's "consumption" influences his opponent's utility directly, proceeding through no market intermediary. Formally, the decisions as to how much of a good to produce and how much deterrence to buy are identical.[8]

---

[8] The formal identity is illustrated as follows using notation established earlier:

Market Duopoly	*Arms Race*
Firm 1 attempts to:	Side Y attempt to:
Max $\pi_1 = pq_1 - C_1(q_1) = f(p, q_1)$	Max $U_y = f(z, \hat{y})$
subject to: $p = g(q_1, q_2{}^o)$	subject to: $x_o = h(z, \hat{y})$
or $q_2{}^o = h(p, q_1)$	

It may be useful to point out that the model of an arms race developed in this study also compares with a mutually interactive competition in external diseconomies. Suppose firms 1 and 2 are competitive suppliers, from amongst a large number of similar firms. Neither 1 nor 2, therefore, can influence the market price by altering the amount it offers. This is shown in Fig. 84 by drawing the total revenue schedule straight and through the origin. However, firm 1's costs increase with increases in the output of firm 2, the cost increase being due to external diseconomies imposed by 2 on 1. When 2 produces $q_2{}^o$ the first firm's cost curve is shown as $TC_1{}^o$; when 2 produces $q_2{}^1$, $TC_1 = TC_1{}^1$, and so on: $q_2{}^o < q_2{}^1 < q_2{}^2$. If the second firm's cost schedule increases with greater q_1, a diagram similar to Fig. 84, only pertaining to 2, can be constructed. Consequently, iso-profit contours, reaction curves and an entire interaction apparatus similar to that in the body of the text follow.

DUOPOLY SOLUTIONS TO THE ARMS RACE

For years economists have amused one another with proposed solutions to duopoly situations. The purpose of this section is to explore the applicability of such notions to the particular sort of interactive process typified by our arms race, and to develop an idea of the implications of such solutions to arms races, to a country's security and strategic posture. We begin with the definition of solution.

A solution is achieved wherever a pair of decision-variables (x, y) attain certain values—say (x_o, y_o)—from which neither side is inclined to move once achieved. Different combinations of (x, y) will appear to exhibit this characteristic under different assumptions as to the psychology, behavior, intercommunication, and the legal limits of the situation. Whatever these assumptions, the features common to all solutions is that for the values obtaining at the solution, each side is confirmed in its expectations about the behavior of the opponent and, therefore, has no need to change the value of its decision-variable. The values comprising a solution, in other words, are mutually self-confirming. If each side takes the other's decision as given, and adjusts to it, the outcome of the adjustment is the same values each started with. Figure 85 and figures to follow will be used to illustrate a number of such solutions.

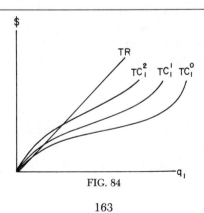

FIG. 84

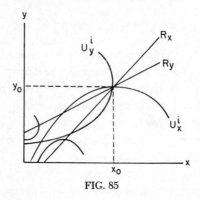

FIG. 85

The Cournot Duopoly Unrelenting-Arms-Race Solution

First, consider the case in which both sides, X and Y derive utility only from the capability to deter. Figure 85 shows two reaction curves R_x and R_y for side X and Y respectively. It will be recalled that the reaction curve is the locus of points denoting the maximum utility available to one side for every value of the decision-variable of the opponent. Thus, the curve R_x connects the peaks of all X's utility contours (which are concave to the x-axis), and R_y connects the peaks of all Y's utility contours (which are concave to the y-axis). The two curves R_x and R_y intersect at the point (x_o, y_o). At this point side X is faced with y_o missiles; X's best position or maximum utility is achieved when he maintains just x_o of his own missiles. In doing this X confronts side Y with x_o missiles. Side Y now maximizes his utility by choosing y_o missiles—just the number which led X to select x_o. Thus, both sides' expectations are confirmed at the value (x_o, y_o).

Now turn to the case in which each side is not interested in deterrence and therefore not in surviving missiles with which to retaliate, but rather is interested in striking first or in making a credible threat of striking first and is occupied, therefore, with the numbers of enemy surviving missiles. Figure 86 shows a set

164

of cost curves for various enemy numbers of missiles, y_0, y_1, y_2, . . . , and a utility function consistent with the properties

$$U_x = U_x(\hat{x}, z_y);$$

$$\frac{\partial U_x}{\partial \hat{x}} > 0, \frac{\partial^2 U_x}{\partial \hat{x}^2} < 0;$$

$$\frac{\partial U_x}{\partial z_y} < 0, \frac{\partial^2 U_x}{\partial z_y{}^2} > 0.$$

Figure 87 then shows these utility contours transformed into x–y space. The contours have all a positive y-intercept, are all

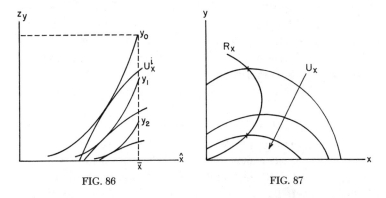

FIG. 86   FIG. 87

concave from below, and reach maxima in y first at increasing, and then at decreasing, values of x.

It was shown previously that linear utility functions result in a trivial equilibrium at the origin, whether stable or unstable.[9] If, in contrast to the linear assumption, the above utility function is assumed, reaction curves are as shown in Fig. 88, where the curvature of R_x at high values of x indicates the increasing pain-cost of giving up money to buy missiles, and the decreasing benefits of *reducing* enemy survivors as the enemy's total force increases. A stable equilibrium exists at (x_0, y_0).

Now imagine that each side in the arms competition is inter-

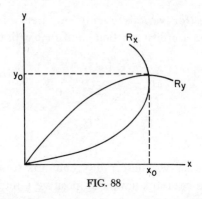

FIG. 88

ested in both deterrent and attack potential. Clearly *the level of armaments obtaining at a Cournot solution will be greater than if either deterrent or attack potential alone figured in a side's preferences.* Since utility derives from two sources it will pay each side to accumulate missiles beyond the point at which marginal utility from one source alone equals marginal utility of money.

The major criticism of the solution at the intersection of the reaction curves in the case of economic duopoly is that it imputes too great a naïvete to the firm. The firm acts on the assumption its rival will hold its output constant, yet this assumption is repeatedly proven false. It would seem plausible to assume the firm learns to anticipate its rival's reaction. This criticism can be leveled at our model of the arms race also, but Cournot's behavior assumption should continue to have appeal. To suppose a country's leaders have explicit knowledge of their own preference function is a step with which many would quarrel; to suppose explicit knowledge of the rival's preferences is perhaps too heroic; yet this is required if one is to anticipate his reactions. Further the simple naïve assumption leading to an equilibrium—if any is to be found at all—at the intersection of either side's reaction functions has appeal in that it describes a

[9] See p. 152.

blind behavior, not strictly irrational, merely shortsighted. It is, of course, true that one major element in deciding how many missiles or bombers to build should be our guess at the number now possessed or to be possessed by the enemy. Postponing considerations of uncertainty, the relevant question within the context of a duopolistic description of the arms race is whether included in our guess of an enemy's missile force are estimates of his reaction to *our* missiles. If we ignore the fact that how many missiles to build depends upon how many the enemy builds, which in turn depends on how many we build and so on, we conform to the behavior of the naïve duopolist.

The Pareto Optimal Mutual-Disarmament Solution

If both X and Y were concerned solely with deterrence and if both were able to observe the rival's as well as their own utility functions, then the classic Pareto optimal solution shown in Fig. 89 would appear to be attainable.[10] In this figure the broken curve joins all points in the x-y plane from which

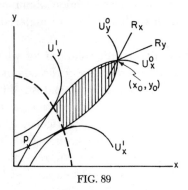

FIG. 89

[10] There may also be something to recommend the point P in Fig. 89 as a point to seek in a disarmament negotiations. At P arms are greatly reduced from (x_o, y_o) with *no loss* in utility on either side. At P both X and Y have greatly reduced deterrence and therefore may be less likely to be provocative. But as discussed later in this section at P both X and Y are very vulnerable to attack.

167

no movements can be made without damaging the position or reducing the utility of at least one of the two sides. The reader should recall that utility contours closer to the x-axis represent greater utilities for X, and contours closer to the y-axis greater utilities for Y. Starting from the Cournot solution (x_o, y_o), for example, by moving along curve $U_y{}^o$ side X could improve its own position to $U_x{}'$ while Y suffers no loss, or by moving along curve $U_x{}^o$ side Y could improve its position to $U_y{}'$ while side X suffers no loss. Within the cigar-shaped, shaded area it will be seen that both X and Y can improve over $U_x{}^o$ and $U_y{}^o$ respectively, simultaneously.

Of the possible types of behavior and the ensuing "solutions," that of Cournot duopoly seems best as a description of the arms-build-up process early in the contest. The complexity involved in maximizing under the assumption the enemy remains unchanged is in itself a formidable task. To do better than the Cournot duopolist, requires reflection on the nature of the two-sided process, a grasp of the opponent's position and motivation, and no little introspection about one's own ends and means. All of this is least likely to materialize early in an arms race.

The possibility of duopolistic solutions for which one or both sides must anticipate the reaction of the adversary does, however, seem genuine later in an arms contest. With a substantial accumulation of weapons, and lapse of time, a learning process should be expected to occur. In particular, if an equilibrium point such as (x_o, y_o) in Fig. 89 were reached, it is plausible to suppose a lapse of time would result in reflection on both sides over the benefits of cooperation. The appeal of Fig. 89 as a diagram of the gain possible with limited disarmament is strong. The most preferred, or Pareto optimal, section of the cigar-shaped area of improvement for both sides is the Von Neumann Morgensten solution to the duopoly problem, and it is toward that contract curve we should hope disarmament negotiators might strive.

In so far as our model of the arms race reflects reality, certain features of the Pareto optimal solution are worthy of mention. The first is that complete and total disarmament is not likely to be the best solution. Only if the utility curves are of the shape shown in Fig. 90 is the *origin* the best position, from which

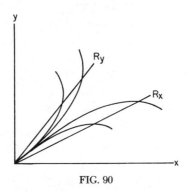

FIG. 90

neither side can move without damaging the other. In other words, *to the extent that the arms race is conceived to be a deterrent race, the belief that total disarmament is the best solution implies belief that there is no equilibrium short of the unstable equilibrium of the origin.* This is shown by the necessarily diverging (or converging only beyond attainable bounds) reaction curves of Fig. 90. The second point to remark is that to reach the contract curve solution both sides must restrain their accumulation of arms below what the intersection of reaction curves would dictate. In other words disarmament must result in less money being spent on strategic weapons by each side. A third point is that in such an arms-limitation scheme as that diagrammed in Fig. 89 at least one side would have to accept a lower level of security via deterrence, that is, a lower own-z, than obtains at the naïve duopolist solution. This loss of utility via less deterrence would be more than compensated for by an increase in utility deriving from resources retained for other uses.

169

The fact that for mutual partial disarmament at least one side must forego some security arising from its retaliation potential can be proven most easily by plotting equal z_y and z_x contours as was done in Figs. 59 and 60. Figure 91 shows many such contours for z_x and for z_y, with the arrow in each case indicating the direction of increase in the z. Suppose some point in the x-y plane was the naïve equilibrium at the intersection of X's and Y's reaction curves. Remember, both X and Y are deterrers only. The shape of the utility contours through that point determines the cigar-shaped area in which simultaneous improvements (increases in utility) for both sides are possible. This is shown again in Fig. 92. A movement toward the contract line

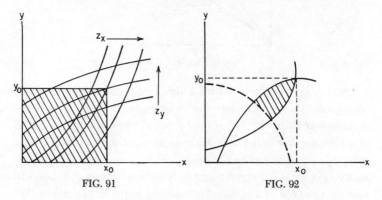

FIG. 91   FIG. 92

within the shaded area of Fig. 92 and starting from (x_o, y_o) must be a southwest movement. (The utility contours determine the limits of the direction of movement, and the cigar-shaped area must lie in a NE-SW direction, as dictated by the construction that at the intersection of reaction curves each utility contour reaches a maximum.) Therefore, returning to Fig. 91 the southeast direction of movement requires that at least one of the two values, z_x or z_y must decline. Therefore, at least one side must lose potential for deterrence by having its own z decline.

Now consider the situation when both X and Y seek only an

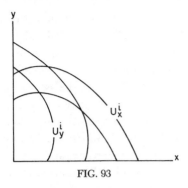

FIG. 93

attack potential. Figure 93 shows X's and Y's utility maps for this case. Observe that no contract curve exists; the origin itself is the only point from which no movements can be made to make one side better off without diminishing the utility of the other side. From every other point in x–y space both sides can be improved simultaneously. We suggested aforegoing that a Pareto-optimal contract curve implies that partial disarmament is preferable to total disarmament. That conclusion, however, depends upon the shapes of the utility contours, which in turn depend on the assumption that both sides are retaliators only. This inference is absent from an account of a two-sided contest to acquire first-strike potential. If each side operated solely from this aggressive motive, then indeed the best (joint-utility-maximizing) solution would be complete and total disarmament.

We can now approach the case in which each side derives utility both from an ability to deter and from an ability to attack. A Cournot equilibrium solution obtains at some combination of missiles on either side (x_o, y_o). Corresponding to (x_o, y_o) is a combination (z_x^o, z_y^o) and two indices of utility U_x^o and U_y^o. Imagine now that both sides begin to disarm. As demonstrated by Figs. 91 and 92 at least one side must suffer a decline in its own z. It seems plausible to suppose in the interests of equity of symmetry that each of the two rivals will allow its own z to

171

decline. Suppose for the sake of argument that this is so. Then as disarmament progresses both sides will suffer a decline in their own z, but will be more than compensated by the resource savings allowed. Imagine the two rivals stopped somewhere on a contract curve as in Fig. 92 (where the assumption of deterrence only is made). At such a point money savings would no longer justify further reductions in z_x and z_y, if X derived utility only from z_x and Y only from z_y. But in the case being considered here, X also gains utility from lower z_y and Y from lower z_x. Therefore, both X and Y can beneficially disarm further—until the possible savings in resources plus the decrease in the opponent's z are just balanced by the utility lost from the reduction in one's own z. In other words, not only does the introduction of a desire to threaten attack tend to increase arms on both sides at a Cournot solution; it also tends to decrease armaments at a Pareto optimal, partial disarmament solution over and above the reductions allowed when both sides wish only to deter.

It should be noted that subject to the assumptions maintained thus far, partial mutual *disarmament reduces deterrence potential* of at least one and probably of both sides, while it *increases attack potential* of at least one probably both sides.

Once the restriction of a duopoly solution wherein numbers only are variable is relaxed, it is possible that a disarmament arrangement whereby both sides improve their retaliatory capacity and decrease their first-strike potential may be reached. If both sides agree to reduce the accuracies or the yields of their missiles, this has the effect of making each a less potent attacker, and therefore, each a more potent defender.[11] Numbers could then be reduced on both sides without reducing the deterrent power of either side from the initial number-yield-accuracy combination. There is, however, a disadvantage to disarming via reducing the accuracy or yield of one's weapons, but

---

[11] If the war is a sequence of pure counterforce blows, lower yields and accuracies would diminish deterrent capability as well.

the disadvantage cannot be explained within the structure of our model. The disadvantage is that with very inaccurate missiles, if one is attacked first and wishes to retaliate, one can only retaliate against cities, or one is pushed in that direction. Our model is limited by the assumption that what deters a potential attacker is the fixed probability that a retaliatory strike is not counterforce, but rather counter-city. The point remains, however, that insofar as disarmament is restricted to limitations in numbers of missiles, the gain to either side is not in "security" via retaliatory capability, but in a money savings, utility-wise, greater than the loss in this potential for retaliation.

The Leader-Follower: Unilateral Disarmament Solution

If one of the two adversaries in our arms race can anticipate the preferences and, therefore, the reactions of the second, while the second can or does not do the same, then a leader-follower[12] type of solution can be found. Figure 94 shows such a solution at (x_1, y_1). Side X is the leader; by choosing the value x_1, rather than x_0, X can induce Y to choose y_1. At (x_1, y_1) both X and Y are better off than at (x_0, y_0) since $U_y{}^1 > U_y{}^0$ and

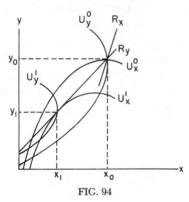

FIG. 94

12 Heinrich von Stackelberg, *The Theory of the Market Economy* (New York: Oxford University Press, 1952).

173

$U_x{}^1 > U_x{}^0$. The point (x_1, y_1) is on side Y's reaction curve. Both sides improve their positions because of X's ability to anticipate Y's reaction to his decision.

The rationale for suggesting such a solution for duopolistic, market-oriented, profit-maximizing firms centers about the idea of a disparity in size between the two firms. There is a large firm and a small one; the small one conforms to the policies of the large one, allowing the larger firm to determine price or quantity. The large firm foresees this and in effect controls output of the two-firm industry.

The argument from a disparity in sizes would not seem to apply to arms races as imagined here. The leader-follower argument does nevertheless seem to find a reflection in the position of the "unilateralist" for disarmament, of those who argue for disarmament by the West with no agreement with the Soviets. The assumption here is surely that the Soviets would react to our one-sided disarmament by reducing their own weapons inventory. It is interesting that the much simplified assumptions about the nature of war used to generate the arms race in Chapter II seem reasonably close to the "unilateralist's" preoccupation with the all-out-attack-all-out-retaliation form which war with missiles could take. To the extent that those assumptions are true, the analysis of this book lends some support to a partial unilateral disarmament (by X in Fig. 94 from x_o to x_1). The argument lends none, however, to the case for *total* unilateral disarmament. This analysis provides some rationale for the idea that one should begin negotiations for an arms-control agreement by voluntarily and unilaterally *partially disarming*. Figure 95 illustrates this.

Suppose our current position were (x_o, y_o). If disarmament negotiations are undertaken from (x_o, y_o) with a view toward reaching the contract curve a–a, the range of possible solutions is b–b. Within the range b–b both sides can improve over $U_x{}^0$ and $U_y{}^0$, and the exact division of utility is assumed to depend

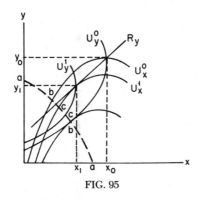

FIG. 95

upon cunning at negotiation, bargaining strength, chance, and so forth. If now side X is considering an initial unilateral reduction in arms, as a gesture (perhaps to get negotiations moving), he, X, can only move along Y's reaction curve, since Y is not yet playing the game. Suppose X disarms to x_1. Side Y follows, disarming to y_1. Side X is now on $U_x{}^1$ and Y is on $U_y{}^1$. From the point (x_1, y_1) negotiations over further, mutual, disarmament can lead to the contract curve in the range c–c. As between beginning negotiations from (x_o, y_o) and (x_1, y_1) two things have happened to the range of possible outcomes: (1) the range has narrowed, and (2) in a sense, the range c–c is more favorable to Y than to X. It may be, however, that the move is useful to X if X wishes to raise the lower limit of his negotiating position, for example, or if a narrow bargaining range is deemed necessary for any ultimate agreement at all.

Maximin Threat: Survival-Extinction Solutions

There is another analogy between arms races and duopoly worth making, in which each side considers the possibilities for threatening its rival or for punishing him.[13] It will be seen that the threat is in the nature of a blackmailer's threat, for if

[13] Martin Shubik, *Strategy and Market Structure* (New York: John Wiley, 1959).

175

the threatener must carry out his threat, he too will suffer. Figure 96 shows the situation with which we propose to deal. Point (x_o, y_o) denotes the point of equilibrium if each side were to maximize its own utility for every choice made by the

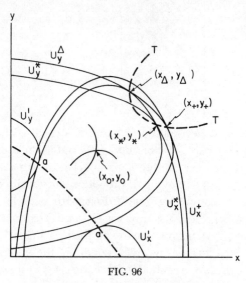

FIG. 96

opponent and were to assume that the opponent does not change his choice variable in response to one's own decision—that is (x_o, y_o) is the naïve duopoly solution. Suppose now, for reasons soon to be discussed, that side X wishes to punish Y by reducing Y's utility. Side X can do so by increasing his armaments, that is, by increasing x. In doing so he, X, must decrease his own utility as well. This follows from the fact that the point (x_o, y_o) is a utility maximum for both sides. The same is true of side Y, which can punish X by increasing y but in doing so must harm itself as well. If X is doing the threatening and Y is assumed to respond by maximizing its own utility, and if X is determined not to allow its utility to drop below $U_x{}^*$, but *is* prepared to *maintain* that lower utility, then X can reduce Y

176

to $U_y{}^*$, which is the maximum U_y side Y can attain if X maintains $U_x{}^*$. At (x_*, y_*) both sides achieve their objectives, X to punish Y while keeping $U_x = U_x{}^*$, and Y to minimize this punishment at $U_y{}^*$.

If instead Y wished to punish X, and X maximized utility, and if Y insisted on maintaining $U_y{}^\Delta$, then equilibrium could be attained at (x_Δ, y_Δ) where X attains $U_x{}^*$. Again if X threatened a minimum utility of $U_x{}^+$ and Y's utility maximizing response were $U_y{}^\Delta$ then the point (x_+, y_+) would be a solution. In fact an entire set of such points exists and is described by the curve TT in Fig. 96. In the parlance of economics this is known as a threat curve. There is, of course, no logical reason for supposing, if both sides X and Y can fulfill threats, that the minimum utility one side will deliberately choose is the same as the maximum utility it can attain in response to the threat from its rival to choose its own minimum. For example, X may deliberately choose $U_x{}^+$ forcing Y to $U_y{}^\Delta$, while Y as a threatener would only choose $U_y{}^*$ allowing X a utility greater than $U_x{}^*$.

To carry this analysis a step further suppose sides X and Y are at (x_o, y_o) as a start, that bargaining over disarmament is under way and that each side can threaten to punish the other, but would do so only to improve his own prospects for a favorable outcome. If side X can threaten Y with $U_y{}^\Delta$ by choosing $U_x{}^+$, then side Y should be pleased with any level of utility greater than $U_y{}^\Delta$. Similarly if Y can threaten X with $U_x{}^*$, then X should gain if a bargain is struck giving him anything greater than $U_x{}^*$. In short, the possibilities of making threats by one side or by both, expand the range of possible outcomes—the assumption remaining that the final outcome will be on the contract curve. In Fig. 96, if X can threaten Y with $U_y{}^\Delta$ and Y can X with $U_x{}^*$, then the range of final outcomes is over a–a on the contract curve, as shown.

Implicitly we have assumed each side is a deterrer only. Now imagine both sides are potential attackers. A first-strike two-sided model, while it alters the contract curve, does not seem to alter the characteristics of the threat curve; and the analysis of the foregoing sections on a two-sided deterrence model would seem to apply with one peculiarity—the threat curve passes through the origin. Figure 97 shows the two branches of the

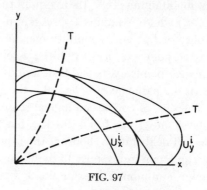

FIG. 97

threat curve. The left-hand branch shows the locus of points at which side Y will elect to maintain a certain U_y and X will react so as to maximize U_x subject to the constraint imposed by Y. The right-hand branch of the threat curve shows the locus on which Y maximizes utility subject to the fixed utility constraint established by X—the opposite of the left-hand branch.

Viability Analysis of the Arms Race

There is a considerable body of literature on the subject of how, given the maximin threats of either side, the division of utility should proceed in arriving at a solution. Such proposed solutions as may be found in the literature on duopoly should have some application to the problem of arms negotiation. Suppose the arms race is viewed as a long struggle of attrition. If one side is considerably more wealthy than the other, it may try to bludgeon the other into ultimate submission simply by outspending the other. If Y is less able to withstand a low level of satisfac-

178

tion X may count on being able to strike a favorable bargain at a later date. It may be that side Y is indeed richer than is X, but politically less capable of laying out money with little visible security in return. For any reason whatever one or both sides in the arms race may have its "breaking point." One measure of such a "breaking point" might be some absolute limit on the amount of resources which a side can devote to defense. Another could be an absolute lower limit to the number of survivors from a first strike by an enemy which one side can allow. There may be an upper limit on the numbers of enemy missiles to survive one's own first attack. Some limitation may exist as to the ratio of attacking to defending forces. Or there may be some minimum utility which a side is prepared to accept.

Figure 98 shows the last of the above possibilities. Each side

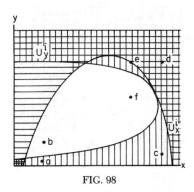

FIG. 98

is supposed to have some level of utility below which it cannot survive. Its government may fall, its people may revolt, its army defect, or in general, the country forced to such a low level of utility, may accommodate and adjust to the role of being dominated. In Fig. 98 the area with vertical shading is the area in which Y cannot survive; the area of horizontal shading is the region in which X cannot survive; the unshaded region is one joint survival, and the crosshatched area one of joint extinction.

179

This leads us to concentrate upon the survival-extinction dichotomy posed in Figs. 98 through 102 as distinct from the optimum decision, utility-maximizing sequence, characteristic of previously considered solutions to arms race models. If the curves of minimum utility for survival are as drawn in Fig. 98 then both sides can indeed survive under all conditions.[14] That is, side X cannot choose x so as to preclude (1) Y's choosing a y which will place both in the region of mutual survival or (2) Y's choosing a y which will force X to change, returning Y to a region of survival. If an initial point is a, for example, by increasing y, Y can reach say b. If the initial point is c, Y can increase y to d whence X will decrease x to at least e and Y in turn can reach f. Figure 99 now shows a case in which one side

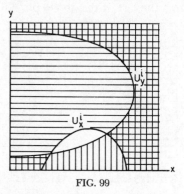

FIG. 99

can preclude the survival of the other. In Fig. 99 side Y can keep X in X's extinction region and survive, while X cannot do the same to Y. But to force non-viability on Y, X must accept non-viability for itself.

Thus far we have considered a low utility accruing to one side as a limitation on "survival," over the long run. We now wish to introduce into the analytical apparatus constraints on

---

[14] This treatment follows Kenneth Boulding, "The Theory of Viability," in *Conflict and Defense* (New York: Harper, 1962), chap. iv, pp. 58–79.

the region of survival in addition to minimum utility. The introduction of constraints other than a minimum-utility constraint
is not strictly rational. The utility or preference function is supposed to compare all combinations of security and wealth with
all others so as to rank every position conceivable against every
other. It makes sense to introduce a *minimum* utility acceptable
because utility may be conceived as short-run. Deliberately
choosing a low present utility may be worthwhile if it forces the
enemy to change, to concede, and in the long run to raise our
own utility. The justification for introducing other constraints
independent of utility can only be that, as a matter of fact,
within the decision-making machinery disagreements over the
value of security vs. money result in other arbitrary limits being
established.

As an example of such an additional constraint, let us assume
that some minimum number of one's own missiles surviving an
enemy first-strike is "required." Figure 100 then shows that the

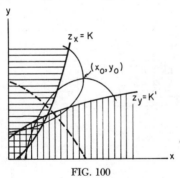

FIG. 100

possibilities for reaching the contract curve may be narrowed
by the additional constraint. Other values on z_y and z_x could eliminate the contract curve solution. In the figure the area to the left
of $z_x = K$ is non-viable for X, and the area below $z_y = K'$
is non-viable for Y. It can be seen that this additional constraint
could in principle (1) eliminate all solutions at arms levels below

(x_o, y_o), (2) limit the range on the contract curve at which a solution is possible, or (3) have no effect upon equilibria points or on the possibilities for negotiated solutions.

Suppose, as a different example, that some maximum defense budget exists, regardless of the opponent's position. Such a limitation is most likely to affect the possibilities for making threats. If the limits on defense expenditure are as indicated by B_x and B_y, in Fig. 101 the entire maximin threat curve is eliminated, and with this the applicability of the utility contours through threat points to possibilities for negotiated agreement.[15]

A third and last type of outside constraint to be considered here is the minimum ratio of one's own forces to the enemy's and vice versa. Suppose side X refuses under all conceivable circumstances to be outnumbered by more than 4 to 3 (shown by line $\overline{X}$). Suppose the enemy has the same absolute constraint (shown by Y). The Fig. 102 shows us the unshaded area the region

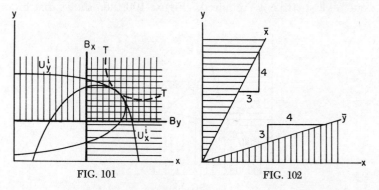

FIG. 101   FIG. 102

of mutual viability. It is quite obvious that this type of constraint can drastically change the possibilities for solutions within a utility-maximizing context.

---

[15] This has interesting implications for a unilateral policy of budget limitation. While $50 billion may be a perfectly adequate defense budget, a gratuitous announcement that it is not to be exceeded removes incentive for the adversary to negotiate arms reductions, on acceptable terms.

VI · SECRECY AND INTERACTION
IN THE ARMS RACE

Thus far, in our theoretical descriptions, secrecy, shortage of information, or uncertainty have played no role in the interactive character—the two-sided aspect—of the arms race. Chapter IV dealt with the effects of secrecy upon one side alone. The intent of this chapter is to introduce imperfections in information into the duopolistic-interactive constructions of our analysis, just as in Chapter IV we added uncertainty to the models of Chapter III. In doing so, we seek a theoretically unified understanding of the effects of secrecy and the value of information in the arms race, in general, and in today's specific competition to build missiles with hydrogen warheads, in particular.

The reader who has followed the discussion to this point will realize that, while the principles involved in describing the race to build missiles are conceptually simple, the number of variables and the mathematical relations involved makes our descriptive and cataloguing effort complex. Our approach to the effects of incomplete information upon the interactive models of the preceding chapter and their "solutions" will be taxonomic. We wish to survey the effects of the various types of uncertainty outlined in Chapter IV under the varying assumptions (1) that uncertainty exists for both sides, (2) that it exists for one side only, (3) that it is fixed in its extent and magnitude such that less imperfect information cannot be purchased at any price, and (4) that improvements can be made in the state of the information available at a cost. In the first part of this chapter we shall deal with the case of a fixed uncertainty being imposed;

in the second part the theory is developed to include trade-offs between hardware and information. Since an exhaustive account of the effects of secrecy is impossible, we shall seek a representative range of cases in selecting examples.

UNCERTAINTY AS A PARAMETER
IN THE INTERACTION MODELS

It has been established that the effects of uncertainty can be represented by a shift or rotation of the cost curve, whether for the defender or the attacker. Figures 103 and 104 show sche-

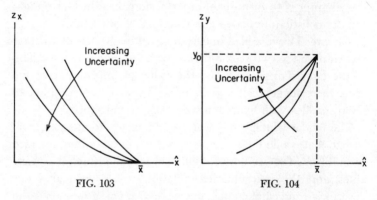

FIG. 103   FIG. 104

matically the nature of such shifts. For a detailed exposition the reader is referred to Appendix A. This chapter first undertakes an analysis of the effects upon interaction models of the introduction of a fixed level of uncertainty.[1]

It is known that for the defending side, the side concerned with deterrence and therefore with retaliatory potential, the effect of uncertainty whether over (1) number of enemy mis-

---

[1] Conforming to earlier definitions uncertainty is constant if the *probability distribution* on the uncertain parameter is constant.

siles (2) yield and accuracy of enemy missiles or (3) hardness of own missile sites can be equally well represented as in Fig. 103 by shifts in the cost curves. Let us begin with the assumptions that uncertainty takes one of the above three forms, that in the arms race each of the two sides is only interested in deterrence and let us explore the effects of uncertainty when it is introduced as a parameter in the interactive model.

We denote by σ, the "degree" or state of uncertainty existing for the defender. Figure 105 then shows the cost curve to side

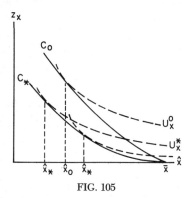

FIG. 105

X of obtaining retaliatory power under the assumptions that the enemy has a fixed strength, $y = y_o$, and first, that perfect information exists $\sigma = \sigma_o = 0$ (illustrated by C_o) and second, that some fixed uncertainty exists $\sigma = \sigma_* > 0$ (illustrated by C_*). Evidently if, as we assume, side X has no recourse but to accept uncertainty as it is introduced, then X's reaction to misinformation as shown in Fig. 105 is a utility-maximizing response, just as in the perfect-information case. (Side X simply maximizes utility in either case.) It is clear that the utility-maximizing-resource input to defense may be more, or less in the uncertain than in the certain situation or may be unchanged. Depending upon the configurations of C_o, C_*, U_x^o, and U_x, $\hat{x}_*$ may fall to the left or right of or may coincide with $\hat{x}_o$.

185

The Minimal Role of Uncertainty

Consider the simple case when resources devoted to defense are unchanged by the introduction of uncertainty, the case for which in Fig. 105, $\hat{x}_o = \hat{x}_*$. As a further simplification assume that the cost curve for the uncertain case with $y = y_o$ is the same as the cost curve for the certain case with $y = y_1$. (Uncertainty is identical in its effects to an increase in the true number of enemy missiles.) This is shown in Fig. 106 by: $(y = y_o | \sigma = \sigma_*) = (y = y_1 | \sigma = \sigma_o)$. Under these restrictions the introduction of uncertainty simply causes all the curves of Fig. 106 to shift down one, such that the only difference between the perfect and imperfect information cases is the *numbering* of the cost curves. If this is true, then as in Fig. 107 the only effect

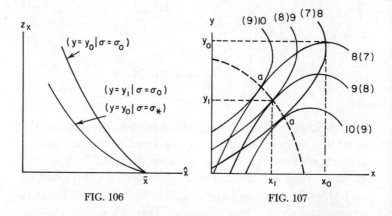

FIG. 106   FIG. 107

of such uncertainty upon the equal utility contours in the x-y plane is to renumber all such contours, assigning to each a lower number than in the certain situation.[2] As a result, the reaction curves of each side are unchanged.

These assumptions, it would seem, restrict the influence of

[2] The numbers in Fig. 107 are purely illustrative.

secrecy, misinformation, and uncertainty to a minimal role. Let us proceed to examine the effects of imperfect information under these extremely restricting assumptions. Since neither the shape of the utility contours nor of the reaction curves is affected by uncertainty as imagined here, the naïve duopolist solution is unchanged by its introduction. Figure 107 shows the utility contours for both sides X and Y. Each contour is numbered twice; the numbers in parentheses denote the utilities which obtain when the side in question, as a defender or retaliator, is uncertain of the opponent's, the attacker's, missile force. The numbers out-of-parentheses denote the utilities obtaining along the same locus when no uncertainty exists. Within the limits imposed by our initial assumptions the model seems to point in the direction of two possible effects of withholding, or conversely of releasing, information. It seems clear that obtaining information can serve as a substitute for increasing arms for the defender, or that a mutual surrender of secrets can serve the same purpose as mutual limited disarmament. In the case of secrecy, or imperfect, or incomplete information, the utility available to side X is 7 and to side Y is 7 if each follows the naïve duopolist pattern and both end up at the intersection of the reaction curves.[3] If sides X and Y cooperate in partial disarmament but refuse to release information to one another, they may reach the contract curve of Fig. 107 in the range a–a. At one point in this range, X and Y each has a utility of 8. Figure 107 shows that with no disarmament a complete exchange of information from the initial position (x_0, y_0), could, make $U_y = 8$ and $U_x = 8$ attainable for Y and X respectively. An exchange of secrets makes $U_y = U_x = 9$ attainable, if, in addition, partial disarmament to $x = x_1$ and $y = y_1$ were accomplished. The process can work in reverse, of course. Therefore, it seems clear in principle that the good effects of disarmament can at least in part be reversed or neu-

[3] Again the numbers used are purely illustrative.

tralized by an increase in secrecy. The effects of secrecy and disarmament interfere with or cancel one another.[4]

Another example is indicated in Fig. 108. Suppose side Y can

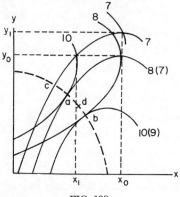

FIG. 108

release or withhold information but X cannot; therefore, there are two alternative numbers for each of X's utility contours since Y's secrecy affects only X, and one number only for each of Y's contours, since X has no choices about withholding information. If Y keeps its secrets from X, the naïve duopoly solution results in $U_x = 7$ and $U_y = 8$ (reaction curves not shown). If now side Y offers to tell X its secrets but announces that it, Y, expects a consideration in return, then X might justifiably consider two possibilities: (1) disarm unilaterally just short of x_1, since at this level (x_1, y_0) his own utility is the same as it was at (x_0, y_0) when Y was secretive (this increases Y's utility to 10); or (2) allow Y to increase y to y_1, by the same reasoning. Since in the case of this second alternative Y's utility declines, the solution at (x_0, y_1) may presumably be ignored. If now the release

[4] Recall Secretary Gilpatric's remarks: "... at heart there is no getting away from the fact that disarmament and secrecy are inconsistent goals ..." "Remarks by Deputy Secretary of Defense Roswell L. Gilpatric at the Aerospace Symposium, Air Force Academy, Colorado," *Department of Defense News Release No. 1308-62*, August 13, 1962, p. 18.

of information by side Y is to be linked to a mutual-disarmament agreement, then Y's offer to give up his secrets should have the effect of changing the possible limits of the disarmament-negotiation outcome. If the process were viewed as consisting of two steps, first a movement from (x_0, y_0) to (x_1, y_0) and then a movement to the contract curve, a–c would seem to be the relevant range on the contract curve whereas a–b had been the range before a release of information had been considered. An argument could be made that the new range should be c–b, c being reached when all the advantage of information release and disarmament goes to Y and b when it all goes to X. It is clear in any case that if the outcome of negotiations is actually a point such as d when no secrets are released, then the actual point of solution must be to the northwest of d once information is released, since Y must be presumed to profit somehow in giving up its secrets unilaterally.

The second major effect of the introduction of secrecy into our interaction models, in this overly simplified form, is the effect on the possibilities for making threats, conducting cold wars of attrition, and so forth, as in the final section of Chapter V. Figures 109 and 110 diagram this second category of effect of imperfect information. The numbers in parentheses indicate utility levels once incomplete information is introduced. In Fig. 109 the primary effect of the introduction of uncertainty is a concomitant reduction in arms at the maximum threat. It would seem that, if the assumptions of this study are close to the truth, and, if also one side is attempting to outspend the other or deliberately force the other to a politically untenable position, *then the introduction of incomplete information may result in a lower level of armaments on both sides.* In Fig. 109 suppose X is attempting to punish, outspend, and outlast Y. Assume side X can withstand a $U_x = 10$; Y then maximizes U_y subject to that constraint. As Fig. 109 shows, Y can achieve $U_y = 10$ when perfect information obtains on both sides. Now sup-

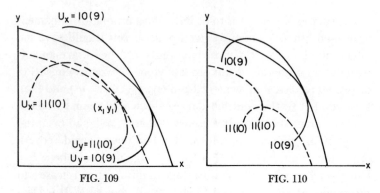

FIG. 109   FIG. 110

pose both X and Y withhold secrets from each other. This is shown by the dotted lines in the figure. As a result of Y's introduction of secrecy over its missile characteristics (such as yield or accuracy) the utility attached to each of X's contours falls by a constant amount (that being the assumption of this section). Therefore if X still can withstand $U_x = 10$, X must change to the dotted contour of Fig. 109 if he is to keep that same utility once uncertainty about Y enters. In response Y will maximize U_y subject to $U_x = (10)$, and a threat point (x_1, y_1) will be reached.

Suppose now that only Y and not both X and Y introduce secrecy. In this case the numbers in parentheses apply only to X. If X is attempting to wage a war of attrition on Y but Y can cause uncertainties to occur in X's calculations, then by withholding information from X as to its own, Y's, missile parameters Y can improve its best response to X's threat. If secrecy is introduced by Y, X must reduce his arms to x_1 in Fig. 109, and at (x_1, y_1) Y maximizes U_y at a value of 11. Next, allow that both sides introduce uncertainty but to differing degrees. Then it remains possible that Y (who is being threatened by X) is better or worse off with $U_y(x_1, y_1)$ than he was originally. The number in parentheses at $U_y(x_1, y_1)$ may be greater or lesser than or equal to the number outside of parentheses at $U_y(x_o, y_o)$

when no secrecy obtains. Whether this is so depends upon the relative magnitudes of misinformation between X and Y—that is, upon the relative magnitudes of the shifts in cost curves due to uncertainty on either side.

It could be, as in Fig. 110, that mutual withholding of secrets entirely eliminates the maximin-threat strategy. If uncertainty causes such major shifts in cost curves as suggested there, then a maximin-threat strategy under uncertainty is not attainable because an entire region of mutual tangencies between U_x and U_y has been precluded as having too low a utility for X or Y to sustain.

Another interesting permutation can result equally when one or both sides withhold information from the adversary. We shall illustrate the case with Fig. 111, by supposing for simplicity

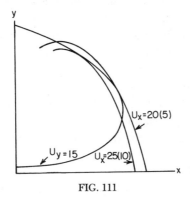

FIG. 111

that only one side, side Y, has the option of keeping its missile characteristics concealed. Originally, when both sides had perfect knowledge of the numbers and kinds of missiles available to the other, suppose X's "breaking point" was $U_x = 15$; and let $U_y = 15$ be Y's breaking point. Figure 111 shows that under perfect information X can at will move to a U_x lower than $U_x = 20$ and in doing so, eliminate or exhaust side Y, since for

$U_x < 20$, Y cannot reach $U_y = 15$. Therefore Y must perish. But suppose now Y were able to conceal information from X. Now the numbers in parentheses apply to X's utility contours, and it is Y who can eliminate X. If Y limits U_y to say $U_y = 15$, side X can no longer survive, for it cannot reach $U_x = 15$. Side X can at best reach $U_x = 10$. Side Y's ability to keep secrets has in this case completely reversed the roles of X and Y; X is vulnerable where Y was vulnerable before. For this result to obtain, it is not necessary that one side alone have the ability to withhold information; both sides can withhold information so long as one of them can withhold more than the other, or one side is more sensitive to information withheld than the other.

The Effects of Uncertainty Extended

We have thus far developed and illustrated the results of imperfect or incomplete information in interactive models of the missile duel under the most simplified assumption possible. As new complications are introduced in an effort to explore the complexity of the arms race, of secrecy and of the inter-dependencies between the two, it will not be economical to repeat the effects illustrated in the previous section. It should not be supposed on that account, that the features already discussed are not also present after misinformation becomes more complicated.

Now we shall admit two further complications to our considerations of the effects of imperfect information, but shall keep to the case in which each side is concerned only with deterrence and therefore with retaliation. The first is illustrated by Figs. 112 and 113. There it is supposed that effects of uncertainty are similar to those pictured earlier in this chapter, in that uncertainty causes the cost curve constraining X to rotate counterclockwise about the point $(\bar{y}, o)$. But instead of assuming, as was done earlier, that the optimum x chosen by X when $[(y = y_0) \mid \{(\sigma = \sigma_*) > (\sigma_o = 0)\}]$ is the same as the

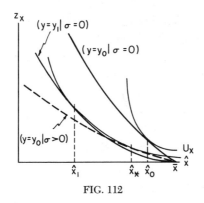

FIG. 112

optimum when $[(y = y_1)|(\sigma = \sigma_o)]$, that is, that $\hat{x}_1 = \hat{x}_*$, we shall now allow $\hat{x}_* > \hat{x}_1$ as in Fig. 112 or $\hat{x}_* < \hat{x}_1$ as in Fig. 113. While the effects of uncertainty in the first section of the present chapter were only to *renumber* the indifference curves of either side as they appear in x-y space, in the case now before us uncertainty will effect changes both in the numbering and *shape* of the indifference contours. For the present, confine your attention to one particular aspect of the change due to the introduction of uncertainty; namely, the change in the maximum of each constant utility curve. In other words attend to the shift in reaction curves brought about by uncertainty. (It

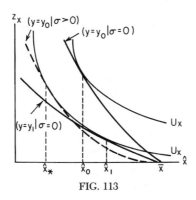

FIG. 113

193

will be remembered that in the previous sections the reaction curves were unchanged; only the utilities at various solutions were changed.) Figures 114 and 115 illustrate two simple varieties of adjustment in reaction functions.

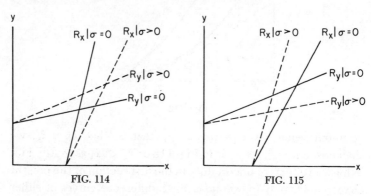

FIG. 114   FIG. 115

If the effect of uncertainty over the numbers of enemy missiles or their yield or accuracies is to alter the optimum points as shown in Fig. 112 then the resulting shift in the reaction curve may be as in Figs. 114 or 115. If in Fig. 112 at the maximum in utility for each y, X builds more x than for the same y with no uncertainty, but less x than for the same utility with no uncertainty, that is, if

$$(\bar{x} - \hat{x}_o) < (\bar{x} - \hat{x}_*) < (\bar{x} - \hat{x}_1),$$

or

$$x_o < x_* < x_1,$$

or

$$\hat{x}_o > \hat{x}_* > \hat{x}_1,$$

then, as Fig. 114 shows, the new reaction curves intersect at greater values of x and y than did the curves intersect under no uncertainty. If in Fig. 112, the optimum utility for each y results in a lower value of x than the same y would call forth if known with certainty, that is, if,

194

$$(\bar{x} - \hat{x}_*) < (\bar{x} - \hat{x}_o) < (\bar{x} - \hat{x}_1),$$

or

$$x_* < x_o < x_1,$$

or

$$\hat{x}_* > \hat{x}_o > \hat{x}_1,$$

then, as Fig. 115 shows, the reaction curves intersect at lower values of x and y when uncertainty exists than when complete information is available. Finally Fig. 116 shows old and new

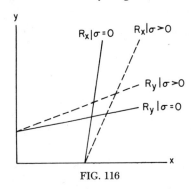

FIG. 116

reaction curves derived from Fig. 113. In this case, each y calls forth greater x under uncertainty than under perfect information when the optimum in utility is chosen, and for a given utility optimum more x is built when uncertainty exists, that is,

$$(\bar{x} - \hat{x}_1) < (\bar{x} - \hat{x}_o) < (\bar{x} - \hat{x}_*),$$

or

$$x_1 < x_o < x_*,$$

or

$$\hat{x}_1 > \hat{x}_o > \hat{x}_*.$$

If this is true, the reaction curve under certainty always implies greater values of x and y at the naïve duopolist's solution.

The point to be made here is that uncertainty (1) *can cause a step-up in the arms race toward an equilibrium where each*

195

side is more heavily armed, or (2) *can cause a retardation in arms* as in Fig. 115. As a theoretical abstraction this can be seen to be true from the preceding figures and argument; the question of whether it is in fact plausible depends upon the utility function assumed, and upon the exact effect of uncertainty upon the position and slope of the cost curve.

To summarize: *in principle, uncertainty of the type envisaged can in fact make a fundamental qualitative difference in the character of an arms race and the sort of solution possible.* The shape of the reaction curve may be changed entirely by the existence of uncertainty. As an example, Fig. 117 shows two

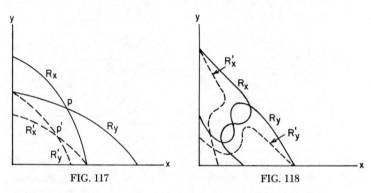

FIG. 117   FIG. 118

reaction curves, R_x and R_y, intersecting to bring about a *stable* point of equilibrium at p. R_x' and R_y' denote feasible reaction curves once uncertainty is introduced, with an equilibrium at p'. The point p' with the curves R_x' and R_y' is an *unstable* equilibrium point. Figure 118 is an example in which *uncertainty eliminates two points of equilibrium altogether.*[5] These two examples are founded upon the assumption that uncertainty causes each side to *reduce* the size of its utility-optimizing

[5] Michael D. Intriligator, "Economic Models and Deterrence," an unpublished paper presented at the American Political Science Association Convention in New York City, September 1963.

missile force from what it would be if complete knowledge obtained.

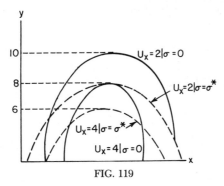

FIG. 119

Further Extensions of Uncertainty

It now remains to consider two other aspects of uncertainty in the situation in which both sides are concerned exclusively with deterrence or retaliatory potential. The first is the change in the *shape* of the equal utility contours in the x-y plane. In Figs. 119 and 120 the results of uncertainty in the x-y plane and x-z plane are shown respectively. The dotted lines designate utility contours under less-than-perfect information after uncertainty causes alterations in cost schedules as explained in the

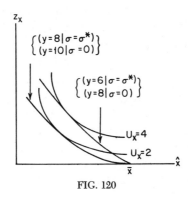

FIG. 120

197

preceding section. It can be seen that as far as the form of the utility contours is concerned, the effect is to make them less U-shaped. Figure 121 shows this result for sides X and Y simultaneously.

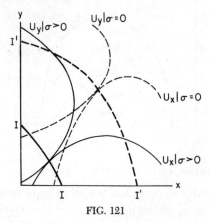

FIG. 121

When both side's utility curves display less curvature, the locus of points of tangency between U_x and U_y shifts toward the origin as shown by the solid curve II. Contrast this with the dashed curve $I'I'$, the contract curve before uncertainty is introduced. The first contract curve is below the second. It should be observed that this result is independent of the question of the change in the maximum point on the utility curves, or the question of change in shape of the reaction curve. Whether the new equilibrium of the naïve duopolist is at greater or lesser values of x and y, the contract curve, which is the locus of points of common tangency between X's and Y's utility curves, shifts in toward the origin. Thus, the *opportunities for reaching a partial-disarmament agreement are restricted to settlements at higher levels of armaments on each side, when perfect information is maintained.* It is quite possible in addition, that the total of utilities along the contract curve is less in the perfect-information case than in the imperfect-information case, such that a paternalistic observer would always choose II over $I'I'$, and therefore by this criterion incomplete over complete information.

The last aspect of uncertainty to be covered in this section concerns the relations between the effects of uncertainty and the size of the missile force in question. The question is whether the differences between cost curves with uncertainty and cost curves under certainty increase, decline, or remain constant, as the numbers (yield, accuracy) of attacking missiles increase. Figure 122 with the solid curves showing costs under

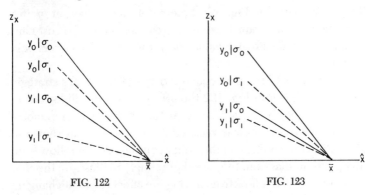

FIG. 122   FIG. 123

certainty and the broken curves the costs under uncertainty (for given numbers, yields, or accuracies) *defines* what is meant by saying "the differences between certain and uncertain cost curves 'increase.'" In Fig. 122 the two curves labeled y_1 *diverge* more than the two labeled y_o, while the "degree of uncertainty," σ_1, is the same. In Fig. 123 the differences in cost curves as between perfect and imperfect information are defined as insensitive to the true numbers of enemy missiles; the introduction of uncertainty results in shifts in cost curves which do not vary with the value of y. Lastly, the difference made by incomplete information may decline as true numbers increase.

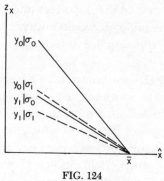

FIG. 124

This is defined by Fig. 124 where for low values of y (for example, y_0) uncertainty causes a great change in the cost constraint, while for greater values of y, the cost curve alters only slightly.

If the effect of the true characteristics of the rival's strategic force is as shown in Fig. 122 the utility contours will look as in Fig. 125, while if Fig. 124 is a true picture of the effect of numbers on the uncertainty cost curves, utility contours are as shown in Fig. 126. The numbers on the utility contours do not follow from any previous diagram; they are there simply to illustrate the consequences which follow from having the effects of an unchanging degree of uncertainty in the cost constraint (1) increase and

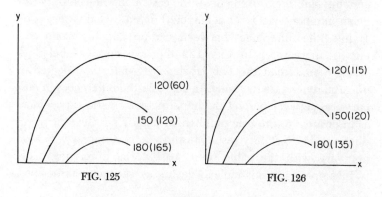

FIG. 125   FIG. 126

(2) decrease, with true numbers (or yield or accuracy). The utilities in parentheses indicate preference levels under uncertainty. The numbers outside parentheses denote pre-uncertainty utilities. Note that possible changes in the shapes or maximum points of the indifference contours are ignored.

Figure 127 next gives an example of what can result from

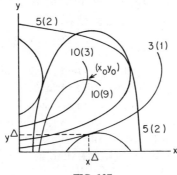

FIG. 127

the different effects of the two previous diagrams. In this figure side X is affected as in 125 and side Y is affected as in 126. Again the numbers in parentheses show utilities once imperfections in information have been included, while the other numbers denote the original pre-uncertainty utility contours. No allowance has been made in Fig. 127 for changes in the shapes in general, or in the coordinates of the maximin point in particular, due to uncertainty. Suppose side X, alone, could threaten to withhold information from Y; that is, suppose X could threaten the numbers in parentheses on the curves U_y. If this is part of the process of bargaining over disarmament, X may make the threat in order to drive the solution on the contract curve close to the point (x^Δ, y^Δ) where $U_y = 3$, the same value as Y should attain at (x_o, y_o) if X carries out his threat to keep secrets and Y cannot do the same. If both X and Y can make this threat and carry it out by tightening up on security measures, still Y would appear to be more vulnerable to X's threat than X is to Y's, since Y loses more than does X if both sides carry out their threats. On the other hand, the numbers in parentheses may represent levels of utility below the threshold of long-term survival for one side or both. It might be, for example, that side Y can allow $U_y = 3$ indefinitely while side X will collapse when $U_x < 9$. In that case Y's threat to withhold information will dominate X's similar threat.

Uncertainty by the Attacker

The effects of uncertainty when both sides are oriented toward striking first follow quite straightforwardly from the apparatus already constructed. Suppose side X wishes to threaten attack; the effect of uncertainty is to raise the cost curve as shown in Fig. 128.[6] If the same iso-utility contours are represented in x–y space by Fig. 129, then it is easily seen that the

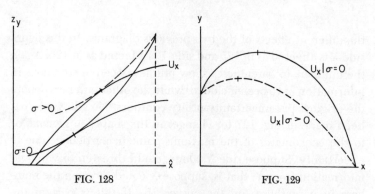

FIG. 128   FIG. 129

effect of uncertainty is to shift all utility curves down, and to lower the value of x at the maximum value of y on every U_x curve. This results in a shift in X's reaction curve to the left. *Therefore, if the reaction curves of both X and Y are placed on*

[6] The case illustrated is for uncertainty over locations or vulnerabilities of the defender's missiles, or over yields or accuracies of the attacker's missiles.

the same diagram, it can be seen that uncertainty would bring about a reduction in the arms race equilibrium point. Lastly, Fig. 130 shows how the introduction of uncertainty (1) lowers the maximin threat solution, and (2) leaves the contract curve unchanged as a point at the origin.

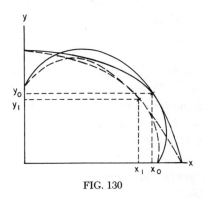

FIG. 130

UNCERTAINTY AS A VARIABLE IN INTERACTION MODELS

So far we have discussed the implications of uncertainty for interactive or duopolistic models of arms races under the assumption that no trade-offs exist between intelligence acquisition and hardware. Now we explore the consequences of relaxing that assumption. No effort will be made to deal with every combination of uncertainty as to numbers, yields, locations accuracies and so on, nor with every combination of attacker-defender, attacker-attacker, and so on, nor with every asymmetry possible between the two adversaries such as disparities in wealth or ability to keep secrets. Instead we shall rest with a few cases, content to point out some of the implications for a duopolistic interpretation of the arms competition of allowing a side to reduce its uncertainty by allocating resources to intelligence. It should be emphasized that while the analyses of previous chapters serve as way stations *en route* to a unified theory, they are of descriptive merit themselves. In many cases no change over previous analyses results from the introduction of this new trade-off possibility. When this is so, it is unnecessary to develop the new mutation of the model at length. In short, this section cannot pretend to offer a truly comprehensive, unified theory following from Chapters II through V. We offer the beginnings of certain central elements of such a theory. In order to do this for a two-sided model we must extend the analysis of Chapter IV on the intelligence-hardware optimization for one single side, proceeding upon the assumption that the reader is familiar with the basic theoretical apparatus to the point that he prefers the omission of great detail.

Optimal Intelligence-Hardware Allocation and Interaction Models: Two Defenders

The intent of this section is to explore the effects upon a two-sided deterrence model of the complications addressed in the second section of Chapter IV. Two varieties of interaction have already been compared: the first, in which no uncertainty exists and each deterrence-oriented retaliator chooses a number of missiles so as to maximize utility in response to his opponent's choice of numbers, yield, accuracy, and so forth; and the second, in which each side does the same thing except under some fixed uncertainty imposed by its opponent. Figure 131 shows three cost curves for side X, now presumed to be the defender. C_x^o shows the cost curve for some value of $y = y_o$ under complete information and perfect certainty conditions. Curve C_x^1 shows the cost curve for the same y_o, for a maximum fixed uncertainty for side X. Curve C_x^* shows the cost curve when X is allowed to optimize the intelligence-hardware trade-off.[7]

[7] See p. 132 for the derivation of C_x^*.

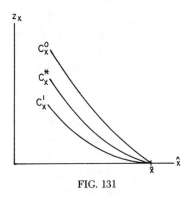

FIG. 131

Figure 132 then shows three utility contours on x–y axes, U_x^0, U_x^1 and U_x^* each corresponding to the cost curve sets, of which one of each is given in Fig. 131. If x and y were interpreted as total *budgets*, then for the case of curve C_x^* the contour (U_x^*) would be appropriate. But x and y stand for numbers of *missiles*, and for C_x^*, a part of the total cost is always allocated

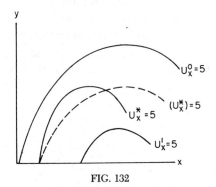

FIG. 132

to intelligence (that is, not spent on missiles). Therefore the broken utility contour (U_x^*) overstates the numbers of *missiles*, x, which side X chooses to counter the number y. In the cases of (C_x^0, U_x^0), and (C_x^1, U_x^1), no such overstatement exists since the entire budget goes for missiles and none for intelligence.

205

Before proceeding it should be noted (1) that $U_x{}^o$, $U_x{}^1$, and $(U_x{}^*)$ all refer to the same utility level (shown as 5 for illustration); (2) that the curve $(U_x{}^*)$ is more U-shaped than $U_x{}^o$, but less so than $U_x{}^1$; and (3) that the highest point on $(U_x{}^*)$ is between the highest on $U_x{}^o$ and $U_x{}^1$. The curve $U_x{}^*$ now shows $(U_x{}^*)$ *less the amount spent on intelligence*—that is, it shows the number of *weapons* actually acquired along a utility contour of constant magnitude under the assumption that some of the budget can be profitably allocated to information acquisition in response to various values of y. At low values of x very little is spent on intelligence; therefore the curves $U_x{}^*$ and $(U_x{}^*)$ are close together at the left x-intercept. At greater values of x more is allocated to reducing uncertainty, and the curves $U_x{}^*$ and $(U_x{}^*)$ are correspondingly far apart at the right x-intercept.

The question now arises of what happens to the contours if the opponent increases security precautions that cause X's marginal-cost schedule for improving information to rise. Figure 133 illustrates the result. *For the same value of utility* it can be seen (1) that X's utility—maximizing response will occur at a lower value of the opponent's missiles, y (that is, $y_* > y_+$), and at a higher total budget (that is, $(x_*) < (x_+)$). Figure 133 shows

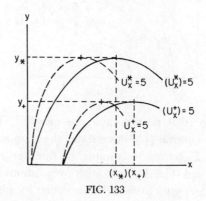

FIG. 133

$(U_x{}^*)$ from Fig. 130 and $(U_x{}^+)$, where Y has raised security precautions. The highest point of $(U_x{}^+)$ is to the southeast of the
highest point on $(U_x{}^*)$. The two curves $U_x{}^*$ and U_x, showing
numbers of missiles rather than total budgets, are drawn in as
well. It would seem to be indeterminate whether the peak of
$U_x{}^+$ is to the left or right of $U_x{}^*$. This is relevant if the effects
of uncertainty (as here considered) upon side X's reaction function are to be decided. Geometrical analysis alone cannot prove
whether or not the increase in security measures taken by Y
induces X to increase the fraction of his increased budget
going to intelligence enough to result in a reduction in numbers
of *missiles*. Both cases can be constructed with equal ease.

These constructions, nevertheless, allow us to discuss some
of the effects of secrecy-which-can-be-reduced-at-a-cost-in-
intelligence-effort upon the duopolistic solutions to the arms
race. These effects will be due to changes in the shapes and
positions of the utility contours and in particular to the reaction
functions of each side. Figure 134 shows two sets of utility con-

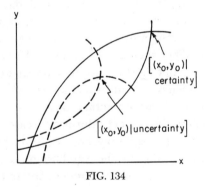

FIG. 134

tours each for X and Y. The broken set of curves describes the
indifference maps when uncertainty exists. The figure suggests
first that the naïve duopoly solution occurs at a lower level of
armaments, since the reaction curves of each side rotate toward

the axis of the opponent. While the introduction of secrecy, which can be overcome in part and at a cost, increases the total *budgets* of both sides at the naïve duopoly solution, it would seem to follow from Fig. 133 that uncertainty introduced as a variable can cause the reaction curves of sides X and Y to change position as illustrated by Fig. 135 (where the solid lines

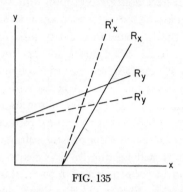

FIG. 135

portray reaction under full information and the broken lines under variable uncertainty). It is indeed true as argued in Chapter IV that by consciously adjusting its own security precautions X can effect such an alteration in Y's reaction function, and Y in X's. But short of this the most that can be said is that there is a tendency, if X and Y maintain unchanging security precautions, for the Cournot solution to occur at levels of armament lower than in the perfect information case.

In summary it is probable but not necessary that the numbers of weapons existing at the equilibrium (x_o, y_o) are less when intelligence effort can overcome uncertainty than when perfect information exists, and it is probable but not necessary that the Cournot duopoly values of (x_o, y_o) are less when uncertainty can be overcome at a cost, than when it cannot be overcome. It is not necessary because allowing information to be reduced at a cost may increase the budget enough to increase numbers of missiles even after allowing for expenditure on intelligence.[8]

Although Fig. 134 does not demonstrate the fact, it suggests that at the equilibrium with partially overcome uncertainty, a lower level of utility obtains for both sides—since both require a larger total budget than under either the complete secrecy or no secrecy cases. The figure further suggests that the possibilities for either side's making minimum-utility, or cold-war-of-attrition threats, are limited to lower values of x and y, because of the shift toward the origin of the entire indifference maps of both X and Y. Without a mathematical analysis which postulates the specific utility functions for both X and Y as well as the marginal-cost function for the reduction of uncertainty, nothing unequivocal can be said about the change in the position of the contract curve due to the introduction of partially overcome uncertainty and therefore nothing about the effect of such uncertainty upon the possibilities for mutual, partial, joint-utility maximizing disarmament.

Optimal Intelligence-Hardware Allocation and Interaction Models: Two Attackers

It remains to discuss the effects of optimizing the allocation between effort to build missiles and to discover locations of unknown enemy-missile-sites upon our duopoly-type models of the arms race. Each side is taken as an attacker. The essential effects are diagramed in Figs. 136 and 137. Figure 136 shows three cost curves tangent to the same utility contour (linear for simplicity of illustration); the curves are labeled C_1, C_2, C_3. Curve C_1 is the cost curve for $y = y_1$ under a maximum uncertainty assumption. Curve C_3 is the cost curve for $y = y_3$ under a complete information assumption. Curve C_2 is the cost curve for $y = y_2$ given an optimum allocation between hardware and

---

[8] The possible implications of these facts for the unilateralist-partial-disarmament solution will be left as an exercise for the reader.

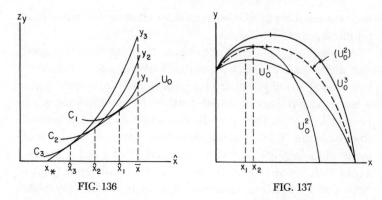

FIG. 136   FIG. 137

intelligence. Observe that $y_1 < y_2 < y_3$. The value $\bar{x} - \hat{x}$ in the case of C_2 does not indicate numbers of missiles built; rather it indicates total funds devoted to missiles plus intelligence by side X. Figure 137 then shows the same utility curve in x–y space. The value $U_o{}^1$ indicates the combination of x and y which yield U_o when maximum uncertainty exists, $U_o{}^2$ the combination yielding U_o when optimized allocation exists, and $U_o{}^3$ when complete certainty is assumed. It will be noted that $U_o{}^2$ in Fig. 137 is derived from $(U_o{}^2)$, a utility curve in broken lines which denotes total X budgets and not X missiles. The curve $U_2{}^o$ is derived from $(U_2{}^o)$ by subtracting amounts allocated to intelligence as one proceeds along C_2 in Fig. 136 from $\hat{x} = \bar{x}$ to $\hat{x} = \hat{x}_*$. These amounts increase with $\bar{x} - \hat{x}$. It cannot be determined through geometric analysis alone whether the maximum y on $U_o{}^2$ obtains at a higher or lower value of x than the value of x obtaining when $U_o{}^1$ reaches a maximum. That is, in Fig. 137 x_1 may be greater or less than $\dot{x}_2$. Consequently, while it is known that, as shown[9] in Fig. 138 $R_x{}^1$ and $R_y{}^1$ intersect at (x_1, y_1) to the southwest of the intersection of $R_x{}^3$ and $R_y{}^3$ (at (x_3, y_3)), it is indeterminate whether $R_x{}^2$ and $R_y{}^2$ (not shown)

[9]Revert to the assumption of a curve-linear utility map to avoid the trivial equilibrium (stable or unstable) at the origin entailed by linear indifference curves.

210

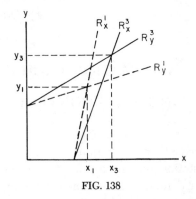

FIG. 138

intersect southwest or northeast of (x_1, y_1)—$R_x{}^1$ being X's reaction curve under maximum uncertainty, $R_x{}^3$ X's reaction curve under complete certainty, and $R_x{}^2$ X's reaction curve under optimized uncertainty, and similarly for $R_y{}^i$. In short, while we can show the general effect of optimized uncertainty in comparison with perfect information, no generally valid comparison can be made between optimized uncertainty and maximum uncertainty.

Another effect of uncertainty on an attack-oriented arms race can be seen in the shift in the utility curves inward, toward the origin. This reduces the possibilities for playing a game of attrition, or for making threats to outspend an enemy. In particular, it would seem that the specific shift shown from $U_o{}^3$ to $U_o{}^2$ in Fig. 137 makes it more difficult to threaten and relatively less difficult to respond to a threat since that branch of X's utility curve which X would use in making threats against Y shifts more than the part which X uses to respond to Y's threats.

VII · INFORMATION EXCHANGE
AND ARMS CONTROL

It is commonplace that negotiations for an agreement on arms control, on limitations on testing or fabricating nuclear weapons, or on partial or complete disarmament have been plagued by disputes over inspection and verification of compliance. The purpose of this chapter is to carry our analysis of the role of information in arms races a step further—to investigate possibilities for the conscious manipulation of information as an element in arms negotiations.

In a way, such an analysis, as seen by the policy maker or planner, can scarcely be more than facile. For years, a vast array of scholars, analysts, and bureaucrats have sought avenues of retreat from ever-mounting stockpiles and risks of nuclear cataclysm. Men, politics, and economics—in their complexities and inertia—all constitute monumental obstacles to progress in this direction, however, and the essence of the difficulty cannot be encompassed by a few diagrams. Hence, again, this chapter is not to be considered as normative.

At bottom, the role of secrecy, or conversely of information in arms agreements can be characterized in either of two ways. On the one hand secrecy may be regarded essentially as an objectively valuable military weapon. In this case, secrets are good in principle, to be retained and, to be surrendered, if at all only at a high price. On the other hand, a plausible contrasting view is that the secrecy barrier to arms agreement is very largely a procedural obstacle. This derives from the notion that once some substantial disarmament materializes, tensions will relax and hostilities subside, as well as the obsession with secrecy and espionage—that is, that between brothers secrecy will vanish because it serves no useful purpose. If disarmament, partial or total, led to a relaxation of tensions such that the existence of remaining arms were not regarded as a threat, then *a fortiori* concealment of that existence would be pointless. If an arms-limitation agreement were to result in a Soviet-American entente then indeed misinformation would bear little penalty and secrecy would be of small value. From this point of view it seems to follow that persuading the Soviets to relax security barriers and to permit inspection is essentially a problem of altering protocol, and that Soviet disarmament initiatives to the extent that they are circumscribed by denial of verification and inspection, are essentially bogus. Possibly there is some truth in both these approaches to secrecy in the arms race. Reconciliation of the two views, however, should require a theory of alliances and the role of information therein. That would be a treatise in itself.

The tools developed to this point for describing the arms race and the role of information therein have all proceeded from the supposition that underlying hostilities, suspicions, and rivalries are fixed and given. Technically this amounts to saying we have made no allowance for changes in a side's preference function or indifference curves due to relaxation in tensions or reduction in hostilities. In short the analysis of this book is based on the assumption that disarmament or no, adversaries remain adversaries. This may be a pessimistic assumption. As above some would argue the exact opposite. Even so, the analysis developed aforegoing suggests that if it is true that fundamental enmity, fear, and suspicion are unalterably given, still a degree of conscious mutual cooperation can improve the position of both sides simultaneously. To revert to technical terminology, the arms race is indeed a variable-sum game, exhibiting elements of both competition and cooperation, such that it is not true that whatever one side gains the other must lose. Alternatives exist that allow both sides to gain simultaneously—or both sides to lose. One good area for conscious mutual cooperation is information exchange.

Within an assumed context of unrelenting fear, mistrust, and hostility, military secrets do indeed, in many cases, have an objective military value—a value measurable in the quantities of weapons and men (or of resources in general) saved for other purposes by the existence or imposition of secrecy. This value, however, may be positive *or negative*. While it is mistaken to think that an advantage in secrecy is not really worth something, it is important to remark that in some cases it may be absolutely detrimental.

The Direct Effects of Information Exchange: A Simple Example

A simple and straightforward application of these principles can be constructed first on the assumption that one of the two rivals in the arms race enjoys complete certainty and perfect knowledge about the strategic capabilities of his enemy, while the other is ignorant and uncertain about the capabilities of the first. Let the adversary who keeps his own secrets but knows all about the other be called X. Side Y has no secrets of its own but is uncertain about X's capabilities. Suppose Y is uncertain only of the accuracy of X's missiles. Might it be worthwhile for Y in these circumstances to make a lump-sum payment in cash to X if X were to give up his secrets? If for reasons of international prestige or etiquette it were thought to be unseemly for a great power to sell its secrets for gold straight out, can Y find another means of buying off X? Figures 139 and 140 illustrate the problem for the case in which both sides are interested only in deterrence. In the diagram $C_x{}^0$ illustrates X's cost curve when $y = y_0$. Curve $C_y{}^0$ illustrates Y's cost schedule when $x = x_0$ and Y is uncertain about the true accuracy of x_0, $C_y{}^1$ the cost schedule if $x = x_0$ and Y is certain of that true value. An equi-

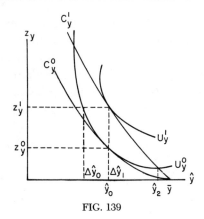

FIG. 139

librium has been reached in the arms race as shown at $(x_0, z_x{}^0,$ $U_x{}^0)$, and $(y_0, z_y{}^0, U_y{}^0)$. The figure illustrates quite clearly, that with a cash payment, from these initial conditions Y can profitably bribe X to release its secrets.[1] Side Y may pay X with cash up to a maximum of $\Delta\hat{y}_0$. Alternatively Y may pay by disarming

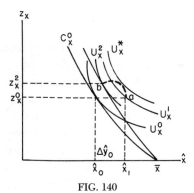

FIG. 140

---

[1] Detailed, step by step, explanations of diagrams are relegated to footnotes in this chapter. In Fig. 139 if X releases its secrets and Y remains fully armed at y_0, Y enjoys $U_y{}^1 > U_y{}^0$, and $z_y{}^1 > z_y{}^0$. Y can afford to pay anything up to $\Delta\hat{y}_0$ to X. From the point $(\hat{y}_0, z_x{}^1)$ a sacrifice of $\Delta\hat{y}_0$ will place Y back on $U_y{}^0$, his original equilibrium indifference contour. Alternatively, Y may disarm by absorbing $\Delta\hat{y}_1$, out of its military budget. This returns Y to $U_y{}^0$. If Y disarms by this amount he cannot make any cash side payment to X.

215

up to a maximum of $\Delta \hat{y}_1$. Between these two extremes, Y can both disarm and bribe X with cash and still end up better off than he was at $U_y{}^o$. One interesting feature of Fig. 139 is that if Y disarms from y_o slightly, he may be able to make an even greater side payment to X without falling below $U_y{}^o$, than if he did not disarm. Figure 141 gives an exaggerated example. If Y

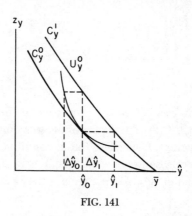

FIG. 141

does not disarm he can pay X, $\Delta \hat{y}_o$, whereas by disarming to $\hat{y}_1$, Y can pay $\Delta \hat{y}_1$ out as a cash bribe. $\Delta \hat{y}_1 > \Delta \hat{y}_o$.

Now consider the effects of these various measures on X. Figure 140 shows that if Y combines disarmament and cash bribery, an entire set of points such as a and b are available to X.[2] The broken curve a---b of Fig. 140 touches $U_x{}^*$ as the highest utility contour. Therefore insofar as the direct effects of the information exchange are governing, one should expect side Y to be limited by $U_y{}^o$ and $U_y{}^1$, in its range of bargaining outcomes, while U_x is limited to the range $(U_x{}^o, U_x{}^*)$. What ex-

[2] If Y simply makes a direct payment to X without disarming, the value $z_x{}^o$ remains unchanged, while the bribe allows X to reach $U_x{}^1$ (point a). If this means of payment is followed, z_x is unchanged but $U_x{}^1 > U_x{}^o$. For side Y, $z_y{}^1 > z_y{}^o$, and U_y is unchanged. If on the other hand Y simply disarms to $\hat{y}_2$, X will enjoy $U_x{}^2$ and $z_x{}^2$ (point b).

act pair (U_x, U_y) is to occur is determined in the processes of bargaining. What more can be said about the outcome of such bargaining? If deterrence is truly the only motive for accumulating arms, then X does not profit directly from concealing the (say) accuracy of his missiles from Y. This secrecy on X's part only reduces the value of z_y, and X is unconcerned with that value. Subject to the restrictions of this section, therefore, there is no minimum positive payment below which X would not profit by releasing its secrets.

If it is supposed that monetary bribery is unlikely, one obvious, clearly identifiable "solution" stands out. The side receiving information may disarm until the side releasing the information has gained as many potential surviving missiles as the side receiving it has gained, so that both profit equally from the transaction in terms of increase in deterrent potential. This can be easily diagramed as in Fig. 142.[3]

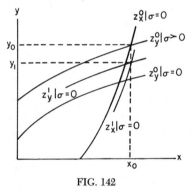

FIG. 142

Another possibility exists for making the payment from Y to X. Side Y might transfer some of its missiles to X. This however is equivalent to paying X off with money and allowing X to use

---

[3] Before the release of information, for expenditures x_0 and y_0, $z_x = z_x{}^0$ and $z_y = z_y{}^0$. If X were to release his secrets freely, Y could attain $z_y{}^0$ for lower expenditure of y. The easily identifiable solution proposed above occurs at $(z_x{}^1, z_y{}^1)$ when $x = x_0$, $y = y_1$, such that $(z_x{}^1 - z_x{}^0) = (z_y{}^1 - z_y{}^0)$.

the money to build more missiles—a process to be described later by means of interactive, total-equilibrium analysis.

The above illustration establishes that in principle it can make sense to concede something to a rival who excels at keeping secrets, in return for the information he withholds. Within the context of the arms race it can pay one side to bribe secrets out of a rival. If direct money pay-off is deemed undignified, a variety of other means of accomplishing the bribery is possible. Among this variety some combinations may seem more "natural" than others, so that the problem of how to share the joint benefit of the negotiation is reduced. One natural solution is "equal benefit" as measured by a deterrence index.

Our analysis preceding has been based on the assumption that one side only has secrets. It is quite clear that these principles are equally applicable if instead of one, both sides keep secrets and wish to trade. The model can be generalized to account for this possibility in a quite straightforward fashion.

Further Implications of Information Transfer

No one would wish to minimize the practical difficulties of paying a premium to the side which excels at secrecy. Theoretically speaking, however, the first and most obvious footnote to the foregoing argument is that it is only valid if some means is available whereby the side receiving the information can verify it as true, and the side releasing the information can verify that the other has indeed partially disarmed. In short, an arrangement for trading secrets for money, or secrets for arms reduction or, for that matter, secrets for secrets, itself requires inspection and verification, no less than a scheme to trade arms reduction for arms reduction.

How then might a side which had kept it a closely guarded secret, just what, for example, the accuracy of its missiles was, now *prove* that its vehicles are so accurate and no more. Assuming that technology is available to verify or falsify a claim of accuracy the problem of proof still exists. This is obviously so because there exists incentive for deceit. Side X, in releasing "information," would wish to persuade Y that his missiles are less accurate than in fact they are. If successful, X would thereby trick Y into conceding a greater measure of disarmament. This is true whether X wants deterrence, or intimidation potential, or both. Excessive deceit by X may be discovered by Y, however, and lead him to cancel the arrangement. As a result some incentive exists to limit one's dishonesty.

From an abstract point of view neither of the foregoing factors presents an insurmountable obstacle. One way to solve the problem of cheating is for the uncertain side to prepare a schedule showing how his own uncertainty diminishes with greater freedom of inspection. The more freedom he is allowed to inspect the closer does he approach complete certainty and the more, in consequence, would he willingly disarm to obtain the information. Having prepared this schedule Y allows X to choose the inspection procedures he, X, prefers. Side X then knows he will receive a greater bribe, in money or arms reduction, the greater freedom of inspection he allows Y. It may, of course, now be argued that Y, in preparing the schedule, has an incentive to be systematically dishonest, an incentive to overstate his own uncertainty for any combination of inspection procedures. This is true; here again unlimited dishonesty will be self-defeating. The inspection vs. uncertainty schedule may itself (implicitly perhaps) become an issue at dispute in bargaining. The point is that at some stage bargaining must occur— which is to say a determinate answer to the problem cannot be stated outright.

The above argument reinforces the point made early in this chapter—namely, that the reciprocal advantage deriving from conscious, mutual manipulation of the arms race does not depend on relaxation of hostilities or increases in friendship between the two adversaries. Even after allowance for cheating, deceit, suspicion, and so forth it can pay both sides to undertake an exchange of information. The two rivals need not come to trust each other as brothers for an information exchange to prove beneficial to both. This conclusion is based on an analysis in which both sides *use* the agreements to the maximum of their own selfish advantage, to include cheating of all descriptions, and in which each side recognizes that the other will do the same.

Indeed, suppose an arms-limitation agreement is reached with provision for inspection. The Soviets expect us to exploit our limited access during inspection tours, by increasing our espionage effort. Therefore they would have agreed to the arms scheme only if they saw a net advantage to themselves given that we would increase our subversion. We then would be foolish[4] to forego exploiting the new access for subversion, since we would already have paid something—in terms of disarmament concessions—to obtain the opportunity. Here, a theoretically plausible, if in fact fanciful, possibility comes to mind. In receiving information on missile characteristics a side may demand extensive verification concessions, and in return subsidize the foreign counterespionage service. Whether such an alternative is feasible is open to question. Yet it emphasizes the central element in our approach to secrecy and arms negotiation—namely that if secrecy is recognized as being objectively valuable and as a substitute for arms, and if the range of negotiable features in a side's military posture is expanded to include exchanging information for information, information for money, and information for disarmament, as well as disarmament for disarmament, then buying information from an adversary is in principle no different from agreeing to disarm. In both cases a *quid pro quo*, mutually beneficial, transaction results. It is interesting that a scheme which recognizes information, its con-

---

[4] To the extent there are moral objections against espionage, we would not be "foolish." Ethics may oblige us foreswear some avenues toward arms agreement.

cealment and uncovery, as economic variables, removes some of the burden of seeking certainty from the side in the uncertain position and makes the other side share in *proving* that the information it releases is in fact true. The problem of how to convince an enemy that one's missiles are of accuracy not greater than C thousand feet, or carry warheads of yields not greater than W megatons, or are of reliability not greater than r percent is by no means trivial. Similarly, how to persuade an enemy that one's missile-carrying submarines are actually at such and such locations, or indeed that one has just so many missiles or bombers and no more is not a problem with an obvious and direct answer. To carry it a step further, how does one lie persuasively, when the enemy is suspicious, when he recognizes one's interest in lying?

A parallel here between the uncertainty to which a side may be subject over an enemy's military posture and the uncertainty over features of his own force structure ought to be drawn, lest the entire notion of disarming "just" to get a rival's secrets appear too bizarre. For the fact is that a country suffers the same inconvenience whether it is (1) uncertain of the vulnerability of its *own* missile sites, the susceptibility of its command and control network to annihilation, the reliability of its own missiles, the psychological capacities of man in an attack environment . . . ; or (2) uncertain of *enemy* numbers, yields, locations, and so forth. Uncertainty raises the *costs* of "security" in both cases. Weapons are substitutes for sure knowledge. Uncertainty over any or all of these factors is characterized by shifts in the cost curves as discussed in Chapter IV. Equally in both situations, the question arises whether more should be spent to increase reliability, test men and machines further, or improve foreign intelligence on the one hand, or simply double up the partly unreliable system on the other. *The prospect of diverting funds from quantities of arms to improvements in information can be just as promising as a means of improving security and/or lowering total costs whether the information sought is about one's self or about one's enemy.*

Nor is the foregoing argument essentially altered if the effort and costs of intelligence activity are introduced as explicit variables into the preceding analysis (as in Chapters IV and VI). The rival's secrets are worth a price whether one or both sides maintain costly intelligence gathering and espionage thwarting activities or not. Figure 143 gives an example of this. Suppose

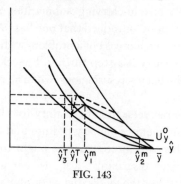

FIG. 143

the equilibrium budget is $\bar{y} - \hat{y}_1{}^T$, with $\bar{y} - \hat{y}_1{}^m$, spent on the weapons themselves, and the remainder on intelligence effort. In the process $U_y{}^o$ is reached (see pp. 130–132 for a complete explanation). If now X, the side withholding the information, offers to dismantle its own counter-intelligence apparatus and turn over its secrets to Y, Y would willingly pay as much as $\hat{y}_2{}^m - \hat{y}_1{}^T$, by disarming to a level, $\hat{y}_2{}^m$, and dismantling a branch of its intelligence service. If side X were willing only to *relax*—not completely abolish—its security measures, Y would, as a maximum price, pay less. For example if the cost of intelligence were reduced as shown by the heavy broken lines of Fig. 143, Y would pay as much as $\hat{y}_1{}^T - \hat{y}_3{}^T$. Further ramifications of such analysis are left as an exercise to the reader. Releasing secrets entirely is simply a limiting case among a wide range of alternative relaxations of security policy. In theory the magnitude of the concession by the side releasing information is continuously variable.

Further Complications: The Motive to Attack Included

The above discussion concentrates upon the mutual deterrence case. What if one side or both derive utility from a capacity to intimidate the adversary with a first-strike threat? It will be useful to develop our theory in this direction somewhat and to handle a few of the complexities posed in possible exchanges of information.

Suppose Y is uncertain of how many missile sites X has got, and is ignorant of the locations of those sites as well. Side Y has a fraction of X's missiles located, knows that some remain unlocated but is uncertain of that number. This is shown in Fig. 144. Side X, as drawn in Fig. 145, has complete knowledge of both Y's numbers and locations.[5]

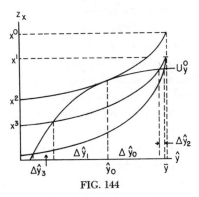

FIG. 144

[5] Number x_o indicates Y's conservative estimate of X's true total number of missiles, x_1 the true total. Number x_2 is the number Y thinks remain to be located; x_3 is that true number. Before a transfer of information Y spends $\bar{y} - \hat{y}_o$, and X, $\bar{x} - x_o$. If then X releases information on numbers only, Y can disarm by $\Delta\hat{y}_o$. Alternatively, Y can make X a cash payment in the amount $\Delta\hat{y}_1$. As argued previously various combinations of money bribery and disarmament are possible; one "natural" bargaining outcome might be one which allows X and Y equal reductions in z_y and z_x respectively.

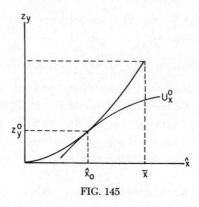

FIG. 145

Let us now inject a new element of complexity into the analysis. In any possible agreement to transfer information, the question arises, of whether it is possible to release information about only one single characteristic of one's force posture without making public other features as well. Two reasons come to mind why this may be impossible. First, it may be *physically* impossible to release information piecemeal. If one side agrees to allow the other some limited access for determining true accuracies of the first's missiles, for example, it may be impossible to conceal information on reliabilities. In demonstrating accuracy, demonstration of reliability may be inescapable. (Suppose a test series is required to establish accuracy. Some data on reliability will unavoidably be generated.) Or if the object is to verify and confirm numbers, locational information may inevitably arise just by virtue of the physical inspection procedure. It may be difficult to prove how many missiles one has got while concealing their locations.) The second reason for which piecemeal release of information may be unattainable is that it may be physically possible, but technologically impossible to separate the information released. If we release to the Soviets the payload of our Polaris missiles, we may provide them with

224

figures, which when combined with what they know already, allow them to calculate range, accuracy, angle of attack, warning time and so on. As a result it may be impossible really to control which secrets are released, and to what degree. Therefore in practice the variety of feasible information transfer schemes may be quite restricted, such that information can be released only in discrete and relatively large "quantities."

Now the question evidently arises if in releasing some kinds if information one must unavoidably release other kinds as well, whether the two or more varieties reinforce of interfere with each other. To answer this let us return to the discussion centering on Figs. 144 and 145. There, suppose that in releasing information on numbers, X has no choice but to tell Y the theretofore hidden locations of the x_3 missiles. In that case Y should willingly disarm by $\Delta\hat{y}_2 + \Delta\hat{y}_o$, or make a cash payment in the amount $\Delta\hat{y}_3 + \Delta\hat{y}_1$, or some combination between these two extremes. Study of Fig. 144 indicates that both information about numbers and about locations have a positive value to Y. In that sense the two elements of information reinforce each other. It is to be emphasized that this conclusion is based on the assumption that both sides share a common aggressive motive —that is, that both are attack oriented. In fact so long as the context is restricted by the assumption that both sides have only one motive, to deter or to intimidate, and that it is the same for both sides, the direct effects of information release reinforce each other as above. We shall reserve discussion of the indirect, interactive, total-equilibrium effects until later. Confining our remarks to direct effects it is clear that once motives become mixed on one side or differ between two sides, interference can arise. As an example, if one side is deterrence-oriented and the other attack-oriented and if the deterrent-directed side contemplates giving up information on locations it might lose more than its opponent could gain and therefore be insusceptible to bribery.

Before proceeding to a consideration of the consequences of duopolistic interaction certain other possible direct effects of an information transfer deserve examination. For one, it appears possible that an alteration in the information content of the arms race may reorder the desirability of various alternative deterrent or attack systems. Figure 146 is one illustration.

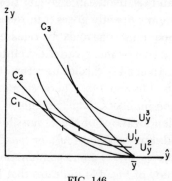

FIG. 146

Curve C_1 is Y's cost curve for building concealed and therefore completely secure missiles. (For a full explanation the reader is referred to Fig. 36 and the argument supporting it on pp. 114–117.) Curve C_2 indicates Y's costs if he should choose an unconcealed force configuration while uncertain of the true value of x, the number of opposing missiles. Clearly Y prefers the U_y^1 attainable when he builds expensive concealed missiles over the U_y^2 attainable if he built cheap unconcealed ones. Now imagine X informs Y of the value of x_1. Curve C_3 indicates Y's cost constraint under conditions of perfect knowledge. This newly acquired knowledge causes Y to prefer devoting his entire budget to missiles—along curve C_3—rather than to divert some funds to hiding the missiles; that is, $U_y^3 > U_y^1$. Thus the introduction of the new information causes Y to alter his force structure preferences. Further, since C_1 is fixed without regard to the information obtaining, Y will not benefit in the least

226

from X's assurances as to the true value of x, unless he, Y, does in fact change from hidden and expensive, to open but cheap weapons systems. Unless Y is willing to change, X's lapse in secrecy is worthless to him. It makes intuitive sense that if one side designs its weapons specifically to be insensitive to his enemy's security precautions, then relaxation of those precautions profits him nothing, unless he changes to a weapons system that *is* sensitive to enemy secrecy. In making such a change, of course, he becomes vulnerable to subsequent alterations in the security policy of the rival. This may in fact be a consideration of the very first importance in appraising the merit of an information exchange scheme. In the case just described, an interesting thing occurs. For Y to take advantage of the curve C_3, he must *give up* his own secrets; he must change to a system allowing X to know where his own missiles are. Side Y's secrecy over location becomes less than worthless to Y; it attains a negative value. This reversal can occur whether X's secrets are about yields, accuracies, or reliabilities as well as numbers.

Still another important feature of a transfer of information could be its effect upon one side's estimate of the rivals *intentions*. Certain features of the opponents's strategic posture will reflect his views on the course he expects war to take, should it occur. If, for example, one discovers great emphasis on yield and very little accuracy in an opponent's weapon inventory, one should be inclined toward the conclusions: (1) that the enemy will not launch a first strike since his missiles are ill-suited to attacking and destroying one's own missiles; and (2) that in retaliation for one's attack against his missiles, he will strike back (or threaten to) with cities as targets—that the counterforce phase of the war will be one sided and very shortlived in other words. If such knowledge of an enemy's intentions and preferences materializes following his agreement to release some secrets, a number of results may follow. First, such knowledge of intentions may provide an incentive for the side gaining it to switch to other weapons. If an enemy has only inaccurate vehicles capable of delivering high-yield weapons such that our missiles sites are not feasible targets then our missiles will not draw his fire in an attack. In this case an anti-missile population defense increases in value relative to a missile-site-protection program, once the relevant knowledge of the enemy missile characteristics is obtained. Secondly, this derivative knowledge of an enemy's preferences and intentions reduces the possibilities for bluffing in the cold war—not that with perfect and complete information no bluffing could occur, but uncertainty about preferences, intentions, and capabilities does enhance the possibilities for bluff.

Indirect Effects of Information Transfer

We can now extend the analysis to account for interaction and total-equilibrium effects, when both partners are motivated by considerations of deterrence and intimidation potential simultaneously. We have not yet in this chapter spoken of indirect effects—those deriving from the interaction at the center of the arms-race phenomenon. Quite possibly such indirect effects might dominate both in degree and direction, the direct negotiated effects of an arms agreement scheme. This constitutes a warning to regard our discussion to this point with some reservation. Enough has been said in Chapter VI about interaction effects to comment without detailed illustration that the degree of information available to one side influences that side's optimum in numbers, accuracy, yield, hardness, reliability, and secrecy (as to these and other features of its strategic force) such that a change in information obtaining may cause changes to be made in all such relevant variables. Equally, all these choice-variables are influenced by the numbers yields, accuracies, and so on, of one's adversary. By virtue of this fact that all the variables on both sides are mutually interdependent a change in the information obtaining in the system will alter every other variable in the course of reaching a new optimum.[6] The practical consequences of this fact are two. First, an arms control or a disarmament agreement which fails to recognize it as a fact and to include the ultimate direct and indirect consequences of an information exchange (or hardware limitation) in its calculations is headed for trouble. Otherwise a compelling incentive would exist to cheat, or to alter force structures in a way not foreseen during the negotiations. As much as possible the governing principle of arms-limitation negotiations must be to trade concessions, such that *after both sides have reacted to those changes and to the other's reactions . . .*, there is a greater degree of security and a lower risk of war. A corollary to this is that both sides should strive to understand the position and preferences of the other (not in the sense of "sympathize with"). Each side must have some grasp of the mechanism that leads its enemy to select one weapon over another, one number over the other and so on. This is essential to an agreement which is in the interests of both sides to respect. In brief, the essential technical problem in an arms-control scheme derives from the cross derivatives in an interacting system; attempting to adjust without accounting for the entire system may be futile, and lead to disappointment.

Figure 147 is a simple illustration of this principle. R_x and R_y indicate reaction curves under perfect information; $R_x{}^1$ and $R_y{}^1$ under uncertainty conditions. Before an agreement to exchange information the arms race has settled at (x_1, y_1). Both X and Y perceive that both can improve their positions *at* (x_1, y_1) by exchanging secrets. Suppose an exchange takes place with no restrictions on subsequent behavior other than to maintain information flow. Both X and Y now have incentives to move

[6] This is a general statement covering such well known cases as the advantages of cheating at low arms levels and consequent sensitivity of the role of information in arms control agreements to the level of armaments.

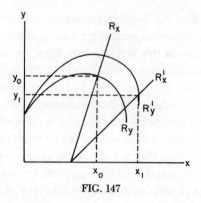

FIG. 147

toward (x_o, y_o). But at that point, side X may be worse off than he was at (x_1, y_1) before the information exchange.

As a contrasting case, failure to encompass interaction effects may cause a side to *underestimate* the merit of an information exchange. In Fig. 148 a stable equilibrium with secrets withheld occurs at (x_1, y_1). Under perfect certainty, equilibrium is reached at (x_o, y_o).[7] If either side in this example should fail to take into

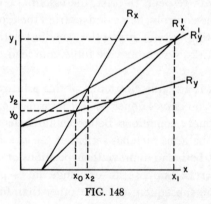

FIG. 148

[7] The total savings to X from a mutual information exchange is $x_1 - x_o$ of which $x_2 - x_o$ is due to his own release of secrets and $x_1 - x_2$ is due to Y's release of secrets. Similarly for Y, the total saving is $y_1 - y_o$; that due to his own secrecy is $y_2 - y_o$, and due to X's secrecy $y_1 - y_2$.

230

account the effects of its own release of information upon the utility-optimizing arms procurements of the enemy, it would underestimate the benefit it would inherit from an information exchange agreement.

This argument that each side should strive to understand the position and preferences of the other is subject to two serious qualifications. The first is that an adversary's preferences—not to say one's own preferences—are subject to very considerable uncertainty. Anything like certain knowledge of the opponent's reaction curve will not be realized in practice, and discovering even wide limits on the shape and character of that function may in fact be a monumental task. Moreover—and this is the second qualification—one or both side's preferences may change in the course of time. That is, indifference maps may alter from one period to another. Both of these variations could be handled with a diagramatic or mathematical analysis. But the exposition would be complex in the extreme. The qualitative significance of these two possibilities, therefore, will be left to the reader's reflection.

Another important way for an arms-control scheme to lead to disappointment is for one or both parties to the agreement to ignore the duality in motivation, toward deterrence and attack, in the real world. Each side should recognize the opponent's motives to be both deterrence- and intimidation-oriented. Without anticipation of and recognition of reactions stemming from an arms agreement, the balance between the two motives could change in an undesirable manner. One specific danger would seem to be that the arms race become oriented more toward attack. This could happen, if as a result of arms negotiations the number of potential survivors were reduced on both sides. It is possible, that the utility of both sides could be improved by arms agreements while both lose in deterrence potential; a decrease in the enemy's potentially surviving strategic missile force may more than compensate for the decrease in one's own number of potential survivors, and this may happen simultaneously on both sides.

One way it could happen is through an exchange of information. Suppose two rivals conceal from each other both the locations and true numbers of their missiles. Imagine that an agreement is undertaken to limit the numbers on each side. Each of the two adversaries demands inspection rights. Assume it turns out that by inspecting for numbers, locations are necessarily discovered as well. It is possible that this would result in both sides having a less secure, lower order deterrent potential—that both sides find they can attack better and deter less well. It is also possible that *both sides prefer* this latter situation. Unless such possibilities are anticipated, an arms control and information exchange agreement could raise the risk of war by making both sides trigger happy. If such effects are anticipated they can be compensated for, by lowering yields (in this example), or otherwise diminishing the attack potential of the missile force on either side.

These are a handful of examples of the role information can play in the variable-sum game of arms negotiation. As highly stylized as is the model in this chapter it nonetheless suggests a point of departure for reflection on the implications of the theoretical structure devised earlier for secrecy and the disarmament impasse. But the model is stylized and can be used only with caution. In particular it gives scant attention to irrationality in the arms race—let alone the rationally calculable advantages of appearing irrational. A positive theory of the arms race must leave a place for nonrational behavior, which is to say theory and verification along the lines undertaken by Lewis Richardson.

APPENDICES

A SIMULATION MODEL:
UNCERTAINTY IN DETERRENCE AND ATTACK

This appendix has two purposes. The first is to substantiate certain claims made throughout Chapter IV and in particular in the section on secrecy as a parameter in the basic economic model. There it was alleged that uncertainty shifts or rotates the cost curves, or technological constraints, facing attackers and deterrers. It would be desirable to prove this analytically, but we have had to resort to numerical approximation.

The second purpose of the appendix is to offer an idea of the quantitative implications of uncertainty in the missile duel. One plausible objection to the main body of the study could be that it deals with a mere theoretical curiosity, that in reality the quantitative effects of uncertainty are small—small enough to be ignored. This appendix answers that objection by summarizing a simulation study of the quantitative effects of uncertainty.

ANALYTIC FORMULATION

Let us formulate the problem for side Y. It will be remembered from Chapter II that the probability that less than some number of side Y's defenders survive an attack by X (where that number is z_y) is given by the expression:

$$P(v_y \leq z_y) \doteq \frac{1}{\sqrt{2\pi}} \int_{-\infty}^{t_\alpha} e^{-t^2/2} \, dt, \qquad (42)$$

where $t_\alpha \equiv (z_y - yr)/[yr(1 - r)]^{1/2}$. In this expression r may be a single parameter, or may be representative of the more complex expressions

$$r = s^{ax/y}, \tag{43}$$
$$r = 0.5^{axW^{2/3}K^2/C^2 y}.$$

The effects of uncertainty over r, or s and x, or x, W, K, and C will now be introduced by assuming their values to be given as probability distributions in which they are variates, rather than being fixed parametrically. In the case in which r is directly estimated for example, the *a posteriori* probability, $P(v_y \leq z_y)$ is the weighted average of all conditional probabilities, $P(v_y \leq z_y | r)$; where r takes on the values in a probability distribution, call it $f(r)$. Formally:

$$P(v_y \leq z_y) \doteq \frac{1}{\sqrt{2\pi}} \int_{-\infty}^{+\infty} f(r) \int_{-\infty}^{t_\alpha} e^{-t^2/2} \, dt. \tag{44}$$

If r itself is a function of several further variables (as in Eq. 43) then so is $f(r)$, and the integral may be triple or of a higher multiple. In short the introduction of uncertainty into the missile-duel equations demands that we interpret costs as deriving from probability distributions of probability distributions.

We wish to inquire into the changes in $P(v_y \leq z_y)$ consequent upon the introduction of uncertainty over r, x, s, K, ... This is equivalent to asking how uncertainty effects z_y for given $P = \alpha$; or how y must be altered (or some other cost such as vulnerability altered) to retain z_y and $P = \alpha$ once uncertainty enters. We wish to do this for various degrees of misinformation. In order to do so, it must be decided how to specify uncertainty. We know it is to be represented as a probability distribution; the question is what type of distribution. The essence of the matter can be captured by assuming very simply that the distribution is rectangular. To facilitate the analysis that will be our assumption: a high and low value is postulated for the uncertain parameter; within this range every value is equally likely; outside the range the probability of occurrence is zero. It turns out that analytically the unconditional $P(v_y \leq z_y)$ involves incomplete beta-function ratios. The practical difficulty is that for realistic ranges of y (say from $y = 50$ to 2000 missiles) and of z_y (say $z_y = 10$ to $z_y = 500$ survivors) the incomplete beta-function ratio has not been tabulated. Therefore no direct means of determining the effects of uncertainties is available, and we have had to turn to numerical approximation.

Numerical Approximations[1]

The cumulative normal probability integral was approximated[2] thus:

$$\text{If } t_\alpha < 0, \alpha \ = \ \left\{ \frac{0.5}{a|t_\alpha|^4 + b|t_\alpha|^3 + c|t_\alpha|^2 + d|t_\alpha| + 1.0} \right\}$$
$$\text{If } t_\alpha > 0, 1 - \alpha =$$

$$(45)$$

where
$$a = 0.0195270,$$
$$b = 0.0003437,$$
$$c = 0.1151945,$$
$$d = 0.1968536,$$
$$t_\alpha = (z_y - yr)/[yr(1 - r)]^{1/2},$$
$$r = s^{x/y},$$
$$s = 0.5^{W^{2/3}K^2/C^2}.$$

Equation 45 was solved a large number of times for the three cases each corresponding to one of the three approximations of Chapter II. This stepwise approach investigated the effects of uncertainty in first the less and then the more complex version of the model. In addition to any intrinsic value deriving from a knowledge of how the values $z_y|\alpha$ or $\alpha|z_y$ respond to uncertainties over the less complex representations of r, this approach allows one to limit the number of combinations analyzed in the more complicated models without loss of information. To find the effects of various uncertainties over W, C, and x at a variety

[1] The program is due to Mr. John E. Perry, Institute of Naval Studies, Cambridge, Mass.

[2] Cecil Hastings, Jr., *Approximations for Digital Computers*, RAND Research Study, 1955. Note that for illustration we assume the attacker fires *all* his missiles, $a = 1$.

of values of y, K, $\overline{W}$, $\overline{C}$, $\bar{x}$ ("$\bar{x}$" meaning the mean value of x in the probability distribution $f(x)$) would be an immense undertaking. Therefore, a fairly exhaustive set of combinations was examined only for the first approximation, where that set is reasonably small.

First Approximation. For values of z_y ranging from 50 to 500 and of y from 100 to 1000, the probability was computed first for the following values of r (known with certainty): $r = .3, .5, .7$. Next, about each of these three values taken as a mean, r was assumed to take a symmetric, uniform probability distributions. The assumption that the mean of the distribution on r corresponds to the actual true value is simply a matter of convenience.

In figuring the values of z_y associated with a range on r, that is, in the case of uncertainty, first y and z_y were held constant; next, the conditional probability of occurrence of z_y, that is, the value of α, was simply computed for a large number of equally spaced points in the interval $[r_{min}, r_{max}]$ and averaged. This gives the unconditional probability for the value of z_y selected, that is gives $\alpha \,|\, z_y$. If this is done for one value of y and a wide range of values of z_y one unconditional, cumulative-probability curve can be plotted. From a set of such curves one for each y, values of $z_y \,|\, \alpha$ can be read off for various values of y. The effects of uncertainty on the function:

$$P(v_y \leq z_y) = \int_{r_{min}}^{r_{max}} f(r) \int_0^{z_y} P(v_y \,|\, r) \, dv_y \, dr$$

are shown schematically in Fig. 149. The computation outlined above was repeated a large number of times generating a surface in the variables, α, y, z_y, $f(r)$.

In taking cross sections of this surface it develops uncertainty increases both total and marginal costs of deterrence. Since no unassailable definition of an "equal increment" in uncertainty exists, pronouncements on marginal costs of uncertainty are suspect. It can be deduced, however, that in order to keep z_y constant in the face of equal absolute increases in $(r_{max} - r_{min})$ side Y should have to increase its number of missiles more than in proportion.

238

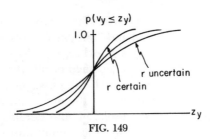

FIG. 149

Second Approximation. The second step in the numerical analysis was to allow for uncertainties over the value of x alone, the value of s being known, and alternately to figure the effects of uncertainty over s when x is known and fixed. The procedure for computing these effects is analogous to that for the first case. First for given parameters (s, x), the unconditional probability was computed for the relevant values of z_y. Such a computation was made over a realistic range for y, s and x. Next, x was assumed to be known only with uncertainty—uncertainty taking the form of a uniform distribution. Lastly, uncertainty was assumed over s, with x known. In effect we started at the point $(x = 500, s = 0.5)$ and investigated first the effects of uncertainty over x at that point and then the effects of uncertainty over s at the same point. This was done for values of y from 100 to 1000. As in the first approximation it turns out that the greater the uncertainty the greater are both "marginal" and total costs. This effect is more pronounced at larger values of $\bar{s}$ and at lower values of $\bar{x}$.

Third Approximation. The third step in the numerical analysis was to allow for uncertainty over the parameters yield and accuracy. Uncertainty over hardness of one's own sites is easily derived from uncertainty over accuracy. As before, in figuring the unconditional values of α and z_y associated with uncertainty over W or C, the conditional value of α was computed for a large number of equally spaced points in the interval $[W_{max}, W_{min}]$ or $[C_{max}, C_{min}]$, and averaged.

For the case of perfect information, cross sections of the multidimensional surface show that changes in accuracy have much greater effects upon the number of potential survivors than do changes in yield of attacking weapons. In the case of imperfect information total and "marginal" costs increase as in the previous approximations. Further, it is demonstrable that the effect of uncertainty over the yield of the attacking missiles is small. If the true yield is small the effect of uncertainty is negligible. Also by comparison with uncertainty over yield, uncertainty over accuracy results in considerable shifts in the cost curves. The more accurate the enemy missiles, the more important is knowledge of this accuracy.

Cost of z_x: Costs of Intimidation Potential

For computational economy it proved desirable to calculate the costs of z_x, that is, the costs of reducing an enemy's retaliatory capacity, directly, according to the formula

$$y = \frac{x}{\log(s)} \, \log \frac{2xz_x + t_\alpha x + [(2xz_x + t_\alpha^2 x)^2 - 4z_x^2(x + t_\alpha^2 x)]^{1/2}}{2(x^2 + t_\alpha^2 x)},$$

$$(46)$$

which is equation 19 (p. 93) solved for y where the attacker is assumed to fire *all* his inventory. For the case of perfect information it is demonstrable that increasing marginal costs of lowering z_x obtain everywhere and that marginal costs become very high quicker with a low number of defenders, x, than with a high number. This conforms to the cost curves drawn in Chapter II. The effects of uncertainty, formulated as a uniform probability distribution about the true value of s, are to raise total costs and "marginal" costs of achieving any given reduction in the opponent's missile force.

COSTS OF UNCERTAINTY: QUANTITATIVE EXAMPLES

A significant relation between uncertainty and costs of deterrence or of threatening a first-strike was established by the mathematical simulation reported on in this appendix. We can now approach the question: Are the effects of uncertainty quantitatively significant? It would appear that in some cases at least the answer is definitely "yes."

In the second numerical approximation, for example, for $s = 0.5$, and $x = 500$, if s is known with certainty, 460 defending missiles are required to assure the defender with 90-percent confidence that 200 will survive a surprise all-out attack. Uncertainty over the value of s, if the range is $s = 0.3$ to $s = 0.7$, raises the required number of defenders to 545. Uncertainty over the value of x from $x_{min} = 250$ to $x_{max} = 750$ raises costs to 500, if again 200 survivors are to be maintained.

In the third numerical approximation for $x = 500$, $K = 2200$, $W = 5.0$ and $\overline{C} = 2500$, uncertainty over the value of C from $C = 1250$ to $C = 3750$ raises the costs of keepnig 200 survivors with 90-percent assurance from $y = 680$ to $y = 1200$, or of keeping 100 survivors from $y = 500$ to $y = 990$. *In this example uncertainty doubles the costs of securing a deterrence force.* On the other hand, uncertainty over the value of W when $\overline{W} = 1$ only raises costs of assuring 200 survivors from 240 to 250. Uncertainty can make a major difference or very little. Uncertainty may also be quantitatively of considerable cost to a potential attacker. Suppose an enemy has 1000 missiles each with a probability of survival $s = 0.5$. If one wished to make the threat of destroying 500 of his 1000, with only a 10-percent chance of failure, and if one knows $s = 0.5$ with certainty, then to back up this threat about 1060 missiles are required (plus some number held in reserve). If, however, the potential attacker is uncertain of the value s, and can only place it in a range of $[0.3 - 0.7]$ his costs of making the same threat rise to about 2000 missiles (plus his reserve).

In short, for the cases reported here, uncertainty can cost a side hundreds of missiles, or billions of dollars. And it should not be thought that this outcome hinges solely upon the particular variety of uncertainty treated in this simulation—namely uniform probability distributions. Other sorts of distributions will give rise to the same phenomenon.

UNCERTAINTY IN RICHARDSONIAN MODELS

Suppose a two player arms race is represented by the equations

$$\dot{x} = f(x, y) = \alpha y - ax + A,$$
$$\dot{y} = \phi(x, y) = \beta y - by + B,$$

as formulated by Richardson, where x and y measure the level of arms on either side, and equilibrium obtains only where $\dot{x} = y = 0$. The model assumes perfect and complete information on both sides. Side X knows with certainty the exact values of x_t and y_t at time t, as does side Y. The parameters or functions α, β show the direct effects of changes in armaments by one side, on the rate of change by the other.

Suppose now we introduce the assumption that side X can only *estimate* y_t at time t, and side Y can only estimate x_t at time t. Suppose that y's estimate, E_y, involves μ_x and σ_x and similarly for side X:

$$E_y = E_y(\mu_x, \sigma_x),$$
$$E_x = E_x(\mu_y, \sigma_y).$$

If it is these *estimates* now which explain the direct effects of one side's arms level upon the other's rate of change, then the equations

$$\dot{x} = \alpha[E_x(\mu_y, \sigma_y)] - ax + A,$$
$$\dot{y} = \beta[E_y(\mu_x, \sigma_x)] - by + B$$

describe the arms race with allowance for ignorance and uncertainty. First, let us ask what changes can occur in the state of knowledge on either side without affecting the equations. Imagine that each side opts for a "safety first" policy and will act on the assumption that the level of the other's arms is the level beyond which there is only a low statistical chance the adversary's true inventory lies. That is,

$$E(\mu, \sigma) = \mu + k\sigma,$$

where k is such that (in the case of Y)

$$P(y > y^*) = P\left[\left|\frac{y^* - \mu}{\sigma}\right| > k\right] \leq \frac{1}{k^2}$$

by Tchebychieff's inequality. Thus

$$\dot{x} = \alpha[\mu_y + k\sigma_y] - ax + A,$$
$$\dot{y} = \beta[\mu_x + k^1\sigma_x] - bx + B$$

describes the arms-race-with-uncertainty explicitly, which in the case of complete information reduces to the original, since

$$\mu_x = x; \sigma_x = 0; \mu_y = y; \sigma_y = 0$$

under those conditions.

The implications of this modification of Richardson's model as to points of stability, and costs and values of secrecy, depend upon assumptions of two sorts. First, a rule must be specified as to what control side X has over μ_x and σ_x as they appear to Y. A similar rule must be specified for Y, μ_y and σ_y. Secondly, assumptions must be made as to how, if at all, Y adjusts his actions to allow for the fact that X does not react to y but rather to (μ_y, σ_y). For simplicity of illustration we assume (1) side X can only influence μ_x by changing x, (2) μ_x will, in fact, always be identical with x, and (3) σ_x is determined by the secrecy precautions taken by X and the intelligence effort by Y (with symmetric assumptions for side Y, μ_y and σ_y). Then the effects of introducing uncertainty into the Richardson model are the following:

Side X may pick any combination of (μ_x, σ_x) as shown in Fig.

150. Y will act on a (say) 95-percent confidence interpretation as shown by the μ_x intercept of the line (with slope k) through the (μ_x, σ_x) selected. Side X might have a policy of keeping σ_x constant or of increasing it more, or less, or in equal proportion to μ_x, as shown in lines *I, II, III, IV* respectively. Imagine that an analogous behavior pattern is predicted of Y. Figure 151

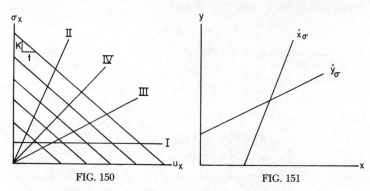

FIG. 150   FIG. 151

now shows two reaction lines (straight lines for simplicity) along which $dx/dt = 0$ (labeled x_σ) and, $dy/dt = 0$ (labeled $\dot{y}_\sigma$). The stable equilibrium case is shown. The lines have the same significance as in the Richardson model except that for any x, y as read from line $\dot{y}_\sigma$ now includes an allowance for uncertainty arising from σ_x and similarly for line $\dot{x}_\sigma$. Figure 152 shows $\dot{y}_\sigma$ derived from Richardson's model. The line y shows the re-action curves for the case of perfect certainty, a stable equilibrium case again. The lines IV_x and III_y correspond to the respective cases of equal and less-than-equal proportionate increases in σ with μ. Curve $\dot{y}_\sigma$ is derived from $\dot{y}$ as follows: take any point, a, on y. The value of x calling forth this $\dot{y}$ under perfect certainty is shown at point b. Under our assumptions in the case of uncertainty the value of x (remember, $x = \mu_x$) at b is associated with a σ_x at point c. The 95-percent (say) confidence equivalent is found by moving along a line of slope $1/k$ to point d. For the value of x at d the corresponding y is read from point e. This value of y obtains then if $x = b$ in the uncertain case and

244

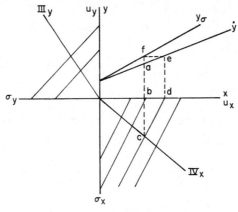

FIG. 152

the relevant point on y_σ is f. For every point on $\dot{y}$, a point on $\dot{y}_\sigma$ is constructed. An identical construction using $\dot{x}$, and σ_y, results in curve $\dot{x}_\sigma$. The curves $\dot{x}_\sigma$ and $\dot{y}_\sigma$ will diverge more from x and $\dot{y}$, respectively, (1) the more IV_x and III_y turn toward σ_x, and σ_y, i.e., the greater the effort to keep secrets, and (2) the greater the value of k, or the higher the confidence level demanded.

INDEX

Armaments, *see* Missiles; Weapons
Arms control negotiations, 27–33 passim, 46, 212–213, 229–232 passim. *See also* Arms race; Disarmament
Arms race: compared with duopoly, 160–163; economic theory as aid to analysis of, 2–4, 11; interaction models of, 143–158; as variable-sum game, 213–214; theories of, 33–46 passim; solutions to, 20–25 passim, 164–182; uncertainty as parameter in (economic basic model), 112–128, (in duopolistic model), 184–203; uncertainty as variable in (economic basic model), 128–141, (in duopolistic model), 203–211
Attack, *see* First-strike

Ballistic missile early warning system, 108
Bargaining problem, 22–23
Bluff, possibilities for, 228
Boulding, Kenneth E., 41, 44; *Conflict and Defense,* 180n, 36n, 41; *A Reconstruction of Economics,* 23n
Bower, Robert D., 86n
"Breaking point," 179
Bribery, 214–218
Budget limitation, unilateral policy of, 182n
Burns, Arthur Lee, 42–44 passim

Capabilities, 6–9, 25–26
Confidence, danger of reducing opponent's, 81n
Constraints, non-economic, 23
Cost-benefit considerations, 8–9
Cost schedules, 9–10, 89

Costs, marginal, 55, 86
Cournot, 22, 23n, 24–25, 164–168 passim

Deceit, 218–221 passim, 229
Deterrence, 1–2, 8–9, 14–15, 32; choice of forces and numbers for, 97–100, 103–106 passim
Disarmament, 5, 26, 46, 187–188; mutual, 25; partial, 198; unilateral partial, 25. *See also* Arms control negotiation; Inspection
Duesenberry, James S., 161
Duopoly, 20, 158–162; duopolistic solutions, 20–25 passim, 164–182, 184–211
Duopsony, 159

Economic theory, aid to analysis of arms race, 2–4, 11
Enemy, need for knowledge of, 46
Equilibria, time paths to, 23, 25

First-strike, 8, 28–30 passim, 49–53 passim, 58–62, 100–106 passim, 112

Gilpatric, Roswell L., 5–6, 7, 188n

Hastings, Cecil Jr., 237n
Hoag, Malcolm W., 42–44 passim
Hooke's law, 37, 39
Huntington, Samuel P., 38–41, 44; "Arms Races: Perequisites and Results," 38, 39, 40

247

INDEX

Indifference curve, 58. *See also* Preference functions

Information: amount of and quality as variables, 26; exchange of, 214–232; manipulation of, 28, 187, 224–225; value and relevance of, 5–11 passim, 29, 108–110, 120, 221–222; technological, 6n; *see also* Uncertainties, with imperfect information

Inspection, 10, 212, 218–220 passim

Intelligence. *See* Information; Secrecy; Uncertainties, with imperfect information

Intentions, 6–7, 29, 227–228

Interaction models, of arms race, 143–158

Interdependence, 143n

Intriligator, Michael, 152n, 196n

Kahn, Herman, 48n

Kent, Glenn A., 84n, 154n

King, James E. Jr., 31

Leader-follower solution. *See* Stackelberg, Heinrich von

Marginal utility, 12–14 passim

Maximin curve (optimal threat), 22, 25; Survival-Extinction solutions, 175–182 passim

Minuteman, 8, 55, 115

Misinformation. *See* Uncertainties, with imperfect information

Missile duel, 70–71, 86–89, 107–108

Missile race. *See* Arms race

Missiles: cost schedules of, 15–16; less than all out exchange of, 49–50; improvements in, 31–32; model restricted to, 4; value of possessing, 14–15, 78–79; importance of surviving, 12–14

Model, 4, 11–16, 44–46, 80–84, 100n; "comparative static," 95n; *see also* Arms race, solutions to; Arms race, theories of

Morgenstern and Von Neumann solution, 22, 167–173

Motivation, duality in, 231–232

Oligopoly, 158

Optimal threat. *See* Maximin curve

Pareto, 22, 25, 167–173

Perry, John E., 237n

Phelps, John B., 46

Polaris, 2n, 9, 48, 115

Post-strike strengths, determination of, 53–58

Preference functions, 58–62, 68

Provocation, 13–14 passim, 19, 30, 78–79, 155n

Rapoport, Anatol, 37; *Fights, Games and Debates*, 36n, 37n

"Reaction curves," 21–22, 24

Recklessness, value of giving appearance of, 82–83

Retaliation, 8, 13, 30, 108, 112–113, 197–199; degree of, 58–62; limited, 47–48; potential war as probable, 76–80 passim

Richardson, Lewis F., 33–42 passim, 44, 232, 242–245; *Arms and Insecurity*, 34n, 37n

Schelling, Thomas C., 41–44 passim; *The Strategy of Conflict*, 1, 20, 32, 42, 43

Scherer, F. M., 14n

Second-strike. *See* Retaliation

Secrecy, 5–6, 19–20, 25, 26, 212–213, 214; *see also* Information; Uncertainties, with imperfect information

Security, fruitlessness of absolute, 45

Shubik, Martin, 22, 175n

Snyder, Glenn H., 50n

Spending, massive as threat, 32–33; *see also* Maximin curve

Stackelberg, Heinrich von, 22, 41n, 173–175

Strikes. *See* First-strike; Retaliation

Survival-Extinction solutions. *See* Maximin curve

Technology, importance to national objectives, 42–44 passim, 49

Threats. *See* Provocation

Uncertainties: with imperfect information, 17–20, 23–26, 110–112, 221; in Richardsonian models, 242–245; in deterrent and attack (simulation model), 235–241; as parameter or variable in arms race solutions, *see* Arms race, solutions to

Unilateral disarmament solution (leader-follower). *See* Stackelberg, Heinrich von

U.S.S.R., 5–6, 7n, 55, 115, 213, 220

United States, 5–6, 32–33, 55, 112

Utility, levels of, 24–25; *see also* Breaking point; Marginal utility

Von Neumann and Morgenstern solution, 22, 167–173

War, 27–32, 39–40, 47–51, 76–80 passim

Weapons, 45–46, 55, 108; information and choice of, 8–9, 11, 16–25 passim, 94–97 passim; *see also* Missiles; Technology